Typically Gillian

Gillian Firth

SWEETSPIRE LITERATURE
——— MANAGEMENT ———

Acknowledgements

Dedicated in memory to my dad, then to my long suffering mum and of course Bro my little brother. xxx
I couldn't live without them.

To those of you that have made a happy difference to my life, wherever you may be, thank you. These are my thoughts: in my skin.

Table of Contents

Catch Up With Me.

Where do I start?

Sitting here in front of a blank screen again, without my wheelchair or any walking aids propped up and waiting for me the background now, eager and raring to go. This is a good place to begin after the initial four years of frustrating rehabilitation.

I have been here before and for those of you that haven't, this is my second book, (ooer listen to me lovey, darling, sweetie). 'Gillian Mk 2' being my debut, which you really should have read; but never mind, I will give you a quick run down to get you up to date.

So, in 1994, I had a serious traffic accident.
A Traumatic Brain Injury (TBI) is the diagnostic description of my injury, I was in a coma for six weeks. Then in and out of various medical institutions—I was pretty messed up and confused for a number of years afterwards.
The car wasn't so lucky, apparently, it did not survive and was no more.
I, on the other hand, did.

My husband failed me, well Pathetic (nick name awarded in Gillian Mk 2) "I've found somebody else ..." and he buggered off (bloody men). He didn't witness the progress I made and never saw the new flat I ended up in. So both emotionally and physically crushed, I killed the lonely and sad times writing a book. I was psychologically lost and didn't know anybody in this small town.

I was fed up of playing the computer games Minesweeper and Solitaire on my own—it was an old second hand machine that would do little else. Well, I couldn't do anything else with it.

Oddly, the book just began by chance—as I experimented with the word processor.

So we have Pathetic to thank for that. It's weird how things work out, eh?

When the writing began I was reading bits of it aloud, at every given opportunity, to the dismay of my mum and Spruce Girl (the poor support worker with years of me under her belt). Well they were an accommodating audience. People laughed with me, rather than at me, in the right bits and this encouraged me to keep going until the final full stop.

A disabled artist friend designed the book's cover and I had a few relevant photos to include; I was fired up and ready to be discovered, but didn't know what to do next. I had approximately two hundred pages of thoughts and memories, an ego trip in script really. I did know that something had to be done with it. I sought out a local proof-reader, that's what writers do. She loved it and I was buzzing with anticipation.

Well I was convinced that a publisher would literally tear it from my artistic little hands, then happily pay me lots of money for the privilege of printing my words, so the manuscript was sent to four publishing houses and I waited for the response.

The standard rejection slips came from them all, which is disheartening when you look at some of the rubbish that is in print and on the bookshelves. I spoke to one chap on the phone and asked him why.

He said, "To be honest Gillian, unless you are a well known name, you've got no chance".

Well, that's just marvellous.

My mum rang and yelled the instruction "Turn the television on"; but by the time I had reacted and found the right channel I had missed the advert. It was for a local self-publishing surgery. My imagination had started to do somersaults again and I found out about it.
Uncannily, it was all going right, the surgery was running on the same day that Spruce Girl and her car were with me. We went along and I was armed and ready for this challenge.
There were six other writers present, a roomful of would be Darlinks with precious notions of discovery. This is when I smugly noticed that only one person held the complete package as it were.
Me.
I was clutching an all-inclusive, singing and dancing autobiography that was juicy and ripe for development. Everything seemed to be screaming at me to do this, my mum and dad were encouraging. "Publish it yourself? Yeah, why not?".
Sounds easy-peasy doesn't it? Mm, that's what I thought.
Wrong!

I had to go through the text like a million times, no seriously I did, when it was being converted from A4 (computer print-outs) to the book format. I kept noticing silly mistakes in the text, gaffes galore, which was just bloody annoying when I had paid good money for the 'proof-reader' to do this for me.

With modern technology being unpredictable, you often have mysterious gremlins appearing unannounced. When a specimen book was printed whole lines of writing had jumped about, these chunks of text had to be moved back to their original positions.

I was messing about with this performance for ages—it could only be done in Spruce Girl's time too—then the photographs had to be positioned and copied. The process took up as much time as writing the bloody book! The back cover had to be designed, then the blurb written (hadn't thought about that part) and the chapters were given titles then had to be slotted in.

On the back there is another picture of me, it was done by a street artist in York. I loved it, so sat for another artist. But he had drawn every wrinkle and I looked like a used T-bag. (binned it)

But I persevered with the task and just had to keep going.

The very first book put in my itchy hands had a green tinted cover, the printed face had a sickly hue. Which I replicated, when I was told how much this coloured and arty sleeve would cost me. The prints from here on were monochrome and, I felt, more poignant. Well they were much cheaper and this made a whole lot of sense to me, otherwise I predicted being stuck with a pile of colourful and expensive self-published work.

Writing the book was often an arduous task, getting it into print was a thankless pain in the arse. But holding the neat collection of bound words, with my name clearly on the front, was one mean buzz.

Oh yeah … I got a new love, a man who just got into the credits of the self-published work (hopefully he's been removed by my publisher). Scoutman, who has been renamed, who eventually appears in 'Typically Gillian' as Pathetic Two. One and the same, just letting you know.

The plot grows thicker and you have to read on now.

Incidentally, there are three green copies of Gillian Mk 2 floating about. I have a sickening feeling that Pathetic Two has lifted one of them …

I feel pretty poisonous right now—my reasons will be disclosed later on. Anyway Gillian Mk 2 was becoming a planned reality.

CHAPTER I

A Novel Life 1999

The hard work on Gillian Mk 2 had nearly been done, but the fiddling about and finishing off was time consuming. Did you know that self-publishing is also known as vanity publishing?

Which I understood when the man helping me positioned my name on the cover design. At first it was small and insignificant in a corner at bottom. "I want it bigger than that!" I moaned, and made him change it.

At first the clever ass responded by enlarging my name so it covered most of the sleeve; I looked at him and raised my eyebrows, "Yes. But no. That just looks silly". So the front of the book looks good and you can see 'Gillian Firth' clearly, but couldn't they put anything on the spine?

I believed them because I had no idea and so the first prints are not complete: they have a blank white space where my name and the book's title should be.

But I didn't really care—the cover looked brilliant and at last a real book was happening.

A really strange thing happened about this time. I was more engrossed than ever with the book when a girlfriend called and distracted me with some welcome news.

She had been a member of the Lunch Club, formed by a group of us involved with one of those new made up educational courses (that teach you how to say no). My friend now worked for a company that watches and monitors CCTV footage. Her news was that one of her male colleagues had noticed me on the streets wobbling about town precariously, with a pocketful of forgotten lists probably. He thought I was drunk and so he followed me on camera, to make sure I was alright. On the verge of calling for medical assistance he had decided that I wasn't pissed and from here on continued to seek me out for observation. On this particular day he zoomed in on me and told his colleague/my lunch club friend, "I've seen her before and I've been watching out for her. She's totally gorgeous!". Apparently he was very animated and verbal.

My friend looked at him sideways and told him, "I know her", then eventually agreed to call and inform me that I had an admirer.

I was given his telephone number, call me sad or desperate—whatever. I called him immediately, being needy, for attention, but for some healthy male adoration.

This man became Fruitcake, a nick-name given to him by me months later when he was in plain clothes at a fancy-dress party. I told him, "Put a cherry on your head and then you could be a fruitcake?", I laughed, loads.

Anyway he came to the phone and I gushed, "Do you want to meet up for a drink?". He offered nothing but said, "It's up to you".

Alright, I thought of my nearest local pub and asked him if he wanted to join me there? "It's up to you", he answered calmly.

So again I made an executive decision and carried on, "OK, erm, what time would you like to meet?". I was a little irritated when he responded "It's up to you".

Now I sighed quietly and arranged the blind date, but I was a bit miffed with his reaction and surprised that he didn't sound more enthusiastic.

The night came and I was dressed up appropriately, well casually as it's a jeans type of venue, even messing about and doing the make-up.

So I was sitting alone and waiting for the mystery man, all excited, super-keen and early, when this chap walked up to me and asked "Are you Gillian?".
He had seen, or rather admired, me before? I looked him up and then down, before I replied "No".

Visualise a bewildered face falling and a confused brow furrowing, I explained myself: "You're late, I thought you'd stood me up, you bastard".
I smiled briefly and then laughed, I honestly thought he was going to run away, he looked so genuinely scared but I didn't give him time to think about it and had already changed the subject.

He came to the flat on another day and drank coffee whilst we chatted. I had an enormous amount of time for him and he was good for me. I was quite happy to be his friend, even though there were times his conversations were alien to me. He still made me chuckle though and he wasn't full of himself or really boring, but I didn't think for one moment that he wanted any more from me.

I am slow, mentally and physically, and although I do catch up sometimes the chances are that I missed the boat.
Blimey, again.
That's an impediment of brain damage. It's a real pain being so dense and unaware (ok stupid), especially when you are convinced that you are alright and that it wasn't you.

One evening Fruitcake came to the flat and I opened a bottle of vodka, which I wholeheartedly encouraged him to consume in copious amounts—well he is over eighteen and I didn't force him to drink it. Needless to say the innocent night got very silly, he literally couldn't walk home safely or quietly and he still lived with his parents, so it made sense that he crashed at the flat with me.

No, I know what you are thinking, nothing happened because we were incapable and that's not what I wanted from him at all. May have been on his mind? I dunno. He is a bloke after all, so it was definitely on his brain at some point in the proceedings, but he was trashed and had no control over anything.

He was a nice kisser though and I enjoyed that attention; the hugs were needed too. He was also the first man that had sought me out and had actually followed through.

Alright I might have assisted, he did need a little encouragement and the alcohol helped, but hey if that's what it takes …
Told you I was desperate for lurve. (or any attention … basically)

I still love going to bingo with my mum and had arranged to meet Fruitcake, after a session, for a drink, "There's someone I want you to meet", he had insisted.
Fabulous another excuse to practice with mascara and stuff, this is what I wanted and needed, a slice of adult normality.
I am actually quite nice, sometimes, but with obvious and off-putting mobility difficulties.

So I walked into the pub and was called over by Fruitcake, who was looking out for me again, the smiling man with him had nice eyes and subsequently laughed at all my jokes. I became a comedian, with an appreciative audience, as I recounted most of the gags from Gillian Mk 2.

I had just been going through it in great detail (so remembered quite a few) and was unashamedly telling jokes to impress. They were both laughing so I went on and on, well the floor space had been opened up for me, what else is a girl to do?

Until about um? Closing time.

But I had secured a second date, this time with the smiling man.

So Tuesday evening came and I was ready and waiting, which in itself is a rarity. Think I managed to look at my watch and sigh impatiently every three to five minutes. My patience has since improved, though not by much, and my trustworthy adage is still 'you wait long enough, then you die'.

I am quite good in that he had an hour to show himself, only then did I convince myself that he wasn't coming.

I eventually called Fruitcake and asked for Scoutman's telephone number, then when I called him at home his mother answered. Oh my God—all the men in this town are indecisive mommie's boys. "I'm sorry, I forgot", he said and I heard the unruffled indifference. I laughed too but with disbelief.

Although I was disappointed and annoyed with him, obviously, my keenness to meet this man another time meant that I persevered.

He wanted to see me again and arranged a time for the next day, I grinned because it worked for me, I was extremely happy with this result.

I told Spruce Girl when she arrived the following morning, "I've got a daate! To-oo-night!", I sang the words and did the dance—a smug and confident wobble.

Spruce Girl had her serious support worker head on: "Does your mum know? You be careful!", I laughed but she was glaring at me, "Gillian, I'm not kidding, you don't know who he is!"

I shook my head at her and sighed, "I will be on my own forever if I take any notice of you and my mum". Then I put the kettle on indicating that the conversation was over.

She got on with the ironing and was quite happy, I lit a cigarette and thought about what she'd said,

"What are you going to do with him?"

So I was waiting again: with the computer on I had something to occupy my mind. I wasn't clockwatching this time, but getting myself ready and keyed up for another anti-climax.

He won't turn up, he'll forget again, he'll find something better to do—self-doubt niggled at my flagging confidence.

I jumped when the intercom sounded. There he stood and he smiled. "Sorry about yesterday", he beamed apologetically then I led him into my bedroom.

He nodded and grinned, then sniggered. His smirk soon faded when he was guided past the bed to the warm computer chair. "I've written a book!", I said this with a smile and was nodding at him.

When seated he looked at me sideways like I had lost the plot. "Really!", I carried on, "This is what's going to be in print soon". Whilst pointing at the screen I laughed, then shrugged at the bewildered visitor, "I hope".

Pages of Gillian Mk 2 were glowing, intriguingly, on the screen and he had no choice really. Bless him. It was impossible to avoid the inevitable, no matter how quick you are, so read it he did.

Now, sadly, he had a better idea of what he might be letting himself in for.

A few hours later he knew exactly what had happened to me and also had a snapshot of Gillian Mk 1, a glimpse of the previous life I had enjoyed. Scoutman shook his head and glanced at me, then he sighed "It's brilliant, but very sad and upsetting".
I felt like a hero, fighting for the cause, bouncing with the power of the enlightening written word.
By literally spelling out how devastating a TBI can be, I had just watched a virtual stranger laugh then cry and growl at the world with me.

Being the diva, Darlink, that I am, I was totally loving this unadulterated admiration. Just loving it.
With no shame, everything that I'd written was true, there is nothing to hide and I also had nothing better to do with my time. It didn't worry me that Scoutman knew so much, whereas I only knew his name and that he was Fruitcake's friend: the written word had a lot to say and had saved me the bother.
I offered to give Scoutman a massage and told him to lie on the bed, "I'll get rid of the tension and distress that I've caused". I am good at backs and the muscles on his front got attention too.
'It started with a kiss' is warbling softly and romantically in my head, he was like a little boy indulged with a big bag of toys and sweets, he'd never had a real relationship apparently and I had just blown his mind.
There was no going back, an understanding had been forged and he asked when he could see me again. The next date was arranged for the following day, Scoutman was smiling a lot like a smug cat with too much cream.

Fruitcake went ballistic when I happily told him the good news, that Scoutman was my partner now. The new boyfriend wouldn't, and couldn't, say anything to his mate and so left the chore to me. Yipee. I felt awful, with surprise, when Fruitcake started crying.

But was vexed then bristled with irritation when he sobbed, "So, let me get this straight. You're dumping me, for my mate?".

So he is clever and I couldn't have put it better myself. Well actually I could and did, "I'm not 'dumping' you anywhere, silly boy. You will still be my good friend".

A simple misunderstanding, he was reacting to what he wanted to believe was happening, I was putting him back into the picture. He was feigning anger to mask his disappointment. I understood that and felt for him, yet at the same time I was bored with the melodramatics.

When at a loss sarcasm is always a good choice I feel, "You've escaped a life of Gillian? Just think how lucky you are". But the laughter wasn't mutual and I diffused the situation by buggering off and making coffee.

I still drink a lot of coffee, on someone's advice decaffeinated was tried. Mmm, I still drink a lot of fat coffee …

Two weeks after I met my new man it was his birthday, he was almost christened Valentino apparently—should have been Pathetic Too as it happens, but it was to be a sad day with timing as his grandmother had died.

He told me that she had played a very large role in his childhood, he acted out the devoted middle offspring and was devastated. Being Typically Gillian, more than ever now, I launched myself into action. Well actions do speak louder than words and I wanted him to know that I cared, so I had a huge and manly bouquet of classy flowers made up.

When standing outside the shop, clutching this cumbersome display of affection, I decided to walk to his home and deliver them in person.

Then, with my jerky walking, I set off. In the right direction, as far as I knew, but I kept knocking the delicate flowers with monotonous regularity.

The thought of handing over a bunch of battered stalks had me cursing my spontaneity, a rational fear that intensified as the journey got longer, I wasn't even sure if I was going the right way and I didn't really remember the house number. I thought I remembered, but my short term memory is totally unreliable, so doubts were niggling at my impulsiveness.

It was a long walk, it was further away than I had imagined, and I was starting to chunter crossly at myself for being so bloody stupid.

Then I smiled when I saw, and thankfully recognised, his big car.

I grinned as I knocked on the door because I had remembered correctly and the hike hadn't been for nothing. But the flowers were given with a straight-face, the card in the greenery simply said 'Thoughts. Gillian', I was invited inside but declined. I didn't really want to sit in a room full of crying and sad people, "It's a family time, I'm a virtual stranger".

So I went home.

One day Scoutman took me to his brother's house, his sister-in-law and two nieces were also there, this was the day I realised for the first time that I loved him.

As I walked down the garden path, to the back door, he was clearing the walkway in front of me. Kicking all the loose debris under foot out of my way, I loved him because he didn't turn back to me for recognition but just did it as a matter of course.

Inside there was an awkward patch when the younger girl said, "Shut up", I of literal interpretation glared at her and responded, "I hope you are not talking to me".

She is a smart cookie and this never happened again.

She's also a 'veggie', which I don't understand especially when it's part-time or selective that is; they only eat fish or chicken. I do recall attending an antivivisection meeting as a student, curiosity spurred this action and I quickly sat on my sheepskin coat. My interest disappeared as I listened to a scrawny man in glasses. He was proudly and smugly telling, a collection of would-be impressionable followers, that him and his gang had illegally entered a laboratory then smashed it up to rescue a guinea-fowl. Yes you have read this correctly, ONE bird. I left in disgust.

When I was a student my landlady had told me we were going to have another undergraduate living with us, the new boy was an Irish Buddhist who was vegetarian. Yippee, can't wait, I thought. When he arrived my landlady was brilliant.

I was enjoying the home-cooked offerings of vegetarian lasagne and the like, the landlady went a bit mad with vegetable dishes. But one day I found myself at the till with an empty packet.

On the way to lectures I had called into a supermarket and had eaten the cooked sausage, without thinking, before it had been paid for. So don't think I could be a veggie.

But I do like the niece, she's bright and funny.

Anyway, I was banished outside with the rabbit for a smoke, the bunny kept burning its whiskers so had to stop, whilst his brother printed out information about a place we planned to visit. This gave all the details we needed about Beamish. I was amazed with the abilities of 'tinternet' (Peter Kay) and impressed with the coloured print. My old computer took ages to print one page of one colour and wouldn't do anything else.

Scoutman had recently been made redundant, just before meeting me. He had been working in the same factory since he had left school. This was brilliant because we had a lot of spare time to kill and we got to know each other very well.

With his redundancy money he bought a Vectra. Fruitcake commented with malice, "You after his big car?".

Mate, again I couldn't have put it better myself but, that's none of your business!

At the beginning of relationships you do have the happy, happy, boingy, boingy stage. You do!

When he starting staying over for the entire night, my neighbours didn't comment but smiled slyly and nudged me in secrecy. Well he lived in a noisy street and had a skinny single bed at his mum's so of course the better choice was to stay in a quiet double with me.

My little friend Teeny—an old neighbour who appears in Gillian Mk 2—paid me a visit and looked over her mug of coffee to question me, "Has he got a toothbrush and razor here?".

I thought about this, "Erm … yeah?".

She sniggered and then nodded with her old head (she's younger than me but is much too sensible) "Bet he'd love to live here".

Nah, I explained the situation. He pays his mother rent and goes home to sleep still, but he does stay here with me sometimes.

Remember I told you he was a scout leader? Well when I first went along to the meeting there were two assistants, they were alright kinda. One was easier to manage than the other. I tried to get along with both of them, mainly because of Scoutman. One of them was so odd, as in he was not my cup of tea, I found him boring and it was virtually impossible to hold a normal conversation with him.

A nice enough bloke, but …

We had nothing in common and he would change the topic mid dialogue.

Unbeknown to me.

So we'd be talking, or trying to, then I'd simply have no idea what about.

Scoutman was his friend but would sometimes fib, unashamedly, to avoid meeting him.

The other guy was dedicated and simple. He was accused of dodgy dealings with and by some equally dubious boys, I can say no more except his mum was lovely but he had to leave.

He was nice and he worked hard for the movement—we missed him. I eventually became an assistant scout leader myself, getting my own woggle—ooer, that's what you get when you are seeing and involved with a scout leader. If you can't beat them join them, which meant going on training courses.

Scoutman had managed, in twenty years service, to avoid going on any of these educational camps.

I on the other hand was excited and ready for the challenge, being a new experience junky, because it was different and involved a change of scenery.

It wasn't too long before my first camping experience was arranged, for and with our troop of youngsters. I was actually quite looking forward to it, being escorted by my new man.

I was still at school, a child myself, the last time that I slept outside under canvas and it was a laugh.

Take note I was young, when sleeping anywhere away from your parents is brilliant.

Therefore quilts with pillows and central heating aren't so important. (Essential)

So I was very excited and looking forward to our scout camp, getting involved with the planning, as much as I could. Everything was done and organised, all the food and equipment was taken to the campsite with the boys—by a convoy of driving parents.

On site the scout leader ordered all of us about, until we had a coherent and functioning unit, putting up tents and marking the different areas that were designated to various tasks. Stepping back I was impressed with the layout of the camp. We all knew where the food was and where to cook it, then where we were sleeping.

At the end of the day we were all happily drinking cocoa, and singing rubbish songs, around the campfire.

I was even happy at bed time, with the romantic prospect of sleeping 'under the stars', with my hero.

That was until I actually did it. I had a 'good' sleeping bag, apparently, and a floor mat (a skinny and pointless sheet of foam). So I simply snuggled down, to get comfortable and turn off.

Remember that I was still nice and warm, positively glowing, from the big and clever fire.

But this is when I realised what a thin waste of time the stupid mat was! I was fidgeting madly on the hard (grr still?) ground, to desperately soften and crush the numerous boulders and rocks.

But whilst moving about you are still thinking 'I will find a comfortable spot', 'It'll be alright in a minute', 'I'll fall asleep soon, no problem', 'I'll be fine'

Oh my gawd—curses and grumbles—not.

There must be a knack to getting comfortable and going to sleep. Scoutman was snoring now and quite content, I tried not to growl or think about how miserable this was.

Then, Oh yes it gets worse, my feet started to get icy cold.
Like a rampant disease this feeling spreads, gradually and slowly, until the entire body is consumed and aching with shivers. It was spring and too cold to sleep outside, on the goddamn floor, who's stupid idea was this?
The snoring bloody scout leader, that's who. But look, he's quite alright thank you.
Needless to say but I was not, not cosy or snug anymore and most definitely not relaxed, there is nowhere to go and nothing you can do. Then I needed a bathroom, what a nightmare.
No!

I tossed then turned and tried to ignore the calling; believing it would go away if I didn't think about it. Because to relent meant getting out of the zipped bag and climbing into the cold—then crawling over discarded clothing and struggling with the fastened tent.

Scoutman was still asleep apparently, he wasn't woken up by and didn't react to my clumsy fumbling, as I fussed to get outside. Lurching out into the pitch black and freezing night, I stood up straight. Then in dismay I looked into the distance at the toilet block. It was a sightless walk over rough and potholed ground, for ten minutes, to get to the toilets.
Then with a frown I glanced around, at the still and silent campsite. It was an easy decision to make and nobody would see me, nobody would know, I wobbled and shivered around to the back of our tent out of immediate sight.

In position I pulled my pants down quickly in desperation, then stumbled backwards on the uneven footing. But I couldn't stop the flow; so I ended up urinating all over the canvas of the tent and also my lower garments. When I had finished the big wee, a huge sigh of relief escaped, everything was tugged back up.

Ugh. Oh, my, God.

Bloody hell, I growled at myself. Then looked up quickly when I heard the scouts giggling.

They were still inside their tents, but they weren't all asleep either, so I crawled back into my deluxe bedroom.

On my hands and knees I paused to look at Scoutman; in no real rush to mess about with the sleeping bag but eager for some sympathy and understanding. My gaze lingered and he came across as smug—he was still kicking out zeds in his warm and comfortable sleep.

I was suddenly really annoyed, that this understanding stuff wasn't happening, so I hit him.

Now he was confused and wide awake, then I could tell him about my nightmare and wet pyjamas. Neither of us really went back to dream land, later he complained that he couldn't go back to sleep because he was too cold

Nahh.

But was I bothered? Go on ask me, was I bovered though?

In the morning we had a cooked breakfast that took a lot of preparation, fires had to be made then the food had to be rationed and collected from the storage tent. But eventually the boys did a good job and we had a well cooked brekkie scout style. There's nothing wrong with rubber eggs, crunchy bacon and black sausages; less risk of salmonella and things I say.

Toast, that was another story, it was a pain that took forever but the boys were quite happy with their toasting forks in the roaring flames. They had no worries, as they were waiting for water to boil—for all the greasy washing up. Now I was happy—sitting with a coffee and a cigarette watching them –

I didn't have to help at all because I have a big woggle. So I don't do washing up.

Anyway Scoutman and I were organising the relevant activities, with educational scouting themes, to kill time before lunch.
The only regret I had, other than not bringing my bed and a hot water bottle (which I vowed to bring IF there was a next time), was not being able to join in with the games and physical activities.
I couldn't run or jump, to complete the teams, so was neither use nor ornament.

Scoutman got a new job, factory work in the food industry, he was pleased to be working again.
Like the dutiful girlfriend I asked how it had gone, at the end of his working day.

On the Monday he told me, "We made rice crispies and put them into boxes".
I smiled with interest and asked how this was done? He explained, in detail.

I questioned him on Tuesday and he told me, "We made rice crispies", then he looked at me and rushed to disclose that the boxes were bigger!

Wednesday, wait for it, he made some more rice crispies. But the cereals were bigger to add interest.

On Thursday I didn't ask but he told me, yep he made the crispies of rice.

Friday he whooped, "We did something different today", I laughed with him and was happy that he looked so animated. "We made cocoa pops!", he disclosed with a grin and was obviously pleased with himself. I smirked as I shrugged, "Brown rice crispies", then felt stupid when his face fell and he wasn't smiling anymore.

"Well that's different?". I tried to be light hearted, "People eat rice crispies … and they make cakes?"
When you're in a grave—stop digging!?
But no, I went on, "Somebody's got to do it?".
I really wasn't trying to piss him off, so I just shut up.

Meanwhile I had started doing a catering course, at the local college, this had involved an interview to assess my needs and difficulties before it started. Mainly for whilst I was working in the hazardous big kitchen, with hot ovens and sharp knives, the supervision was a constant so everybody was covered.
The tutors on this course were absolutely brilliant, this description is not is not big enough and does them no justice, I tried very hard and loved it.

Love trying new things, it often crosses my mind how fortunate and lucky I am. That this can and does still happen, although I often need assistance and cannot do some things alone.
Still.

There are times that I try on my own and when I have broken or ruined something, generally shrugging with a heartfelt and genuine oops sorry, that's when defeat is admitted and I ask for help.

Onlookers will scowl at my obstinacy and comment, "I knew that was going to happen, why didn't you ask me to do it for you?", at which point I growl with crabbiness and explain, "Because I thought I could do it for myself?".

The work required on Gillian Mk 2 was finally done, it was over at last and I was impatiently happy but now I had to decide, how many copies did I wanted for the first print run?
Dunno. How many is enough?
Darlink.

Spruce Girl was very enthusiastic, "Just get ten to start with, or you'll be stuck with them and you don't want that".
I was disappointed and stunned by her attitude, so grimaced with my answer, "Erm … no".
Then shook my head and explained, "Ten's bloody rubbish, it's a good book. It will sell".

But my confidence was rattled, maybe she had just laughed at the numerous readings to humour me.
Scoutman helped me out with this dilemma, when he commented out of his bum, "Get fifteen or twenty then", he grinned at me and then shrugged.
Now I was just cross, "NO! You said it was good too!". Without thinking the words of world domination blurted out, "If it's going to be done, I'm not messing about and playing with TEN!", defiant and petulant are better descriptions of my manner.

They looked at each other, with mutually raised eyebrows, then shrugged at a loss and asked me, "How many you going to have done then?".

In the weighted pause I looked at Joey, who was attacking his bell with vigour, "I'm going to get … a hundred".

I nodded with certainty. Spruce Girl guffawed with encouragement, "You go girl". Dad nodded later, "I'll lend you the money don't worry".

So we picked up the two boxes of paperbacks, with blank spines. I was chuffed to bits and held a finished book to my chest, "I wrote this".

It was, and basically still is, a thrill. When you hear the old wise words "Everyone has a book in them!", I can smirk and say done it.

Now I can go one better with a SECOND book, a number of readers have requested this saying that they want to know what Gillian does next. How good is that?

'Gillian Mk 2' apparently leaves my followers mid life and curious for more.

Nice one.

People were asking who is pictured on the cover?

Erm … me. Here's me thinking how clever it was, even though the artist responsible lost the original picture.

I was told it looks like the actress Gillian Anderson. I know, how weird is that? (same name …).

All of the staff teaching on my catering course have got the book now, I did wait until they knew me a little. A female tutor was one of the first 'real' readers to give me an opinion.

She was inspirational and couldn't have said better things, by all accounts Gillian Mk 2 had been a compulsive and hilarious read tinged with genuine tears.

I think she was the first person to speak, who wasn't really obliged to say anything at all.

This may have been when I officially became a Darlink, for real with reason I believe. She mentioned the book a few times and had opened my eyes to the fact that my work struck a chord.

The book was a rambling sequence of events, the writing of which had simply quashed lonely time, that had already made a difference to more people than I could have imagined.

I was surprised by the eloquent and obviously heartfelt disclosures, my story was spelling out a complete nightmare of an alternative life. The written account was really getting to people and they were telling me with vocal smiles.

I told you that I was being approached, it still happens today, women would come up to me and grin with humour as they nudge me to say, "I've got a Pathetic at home!".

The mere mention of or even the word 'book' and I would go into one, always ready to be a sales pitch, well I had to because it was self-published and so I, effectively, was the shop.

My families' eyes would roll and they would shake their heads, when I was trying to sell my book to somebody I'd just met, but I would not be deterred.

'I don't read', that was an easy one to dispel and I would persevere, 'It's got pictures'.

'I've got no money', I did bite my tongue if they were smoking in a pub or something similar, you can save up or pay me in instalments? (worth a try)

Ask Santa for it, that was another good one, Xmas is always around the corner.

My determination worked most of the time; I think some people bought it to simply shut me up, my embarrassed family would laugh and mutter 'sand to the Arabs'.

Spruce Girl and Scoutman had to take me quite a few times, to where it was printed, to pick up more copies. Each time the pile of new books was daunting, but they weren't there long. My shop was open all the time—I also had agents, my mum, Bro, Spruce Girl and Scoutman got rid of a few copies for me.

The local newspaper had run my story, mainly because I had marched into the reception and paraded the book announcing, "I wrote this!". Thereby demanding coverage.
A few of the local papers printed the article and I collected all the cuttings, 'Gillian's car crash fight back told in new book'. There's no stopping me now and Scoutman was there—to support my enlarged head.

I loved the fact that Gillian Mk 2 was reaching a selection of readers. The mother of a disabled woman called me to order a book, also a lot of the older women at bingo invested in my time.
Another mother of a head injured friend, I had met her son at the rehabilitation unit but he wasn't a residential client, sent me a card after she had read the book. She too had brilliant things to say, "You made me laugh then cry then laugh again". Now she had a "better understanding", apparently, of what her son was going through.

Thankfully I was keeping all these things, I was still shocked and surprised that my words were having such an effect, many people were talking to me about the book and I was collecting all the fan mail.

My biased opinion of Gillian Mk 2, I can and do still read it, was widespread.

Ooer, how fabulous.

A small and local book shop took some off me, on a sale or return basis, they sold quite a few and were restocked regularly.

But he closed down, so it was up to me again.

Back in the real world I now had the chef's whites for my catering course, with some brilliant black and white checked trousers, then had my own set of knives as a Xmas present. Did a strange and paranoid thing with my knives, so everybody knew they were mine from my set. They were all clumsily marked with liquid paper, then a black 'G' was drawn.

Not so weird, as it happens, all the other students had done the same with theirs.

Met and got along with one student in particular, he gave me a lift to college.

He was about my age and he was already a working cook, at an old people's home, his girlfriend was fab too.

We were on the dough part of the syllabus and I remember this well. To begin making the bread, all of the dry ingredients were placed onto your work surface in a hollow 'O' shape.

Then the warm water, containing the yeast, is poured into the middle. With your finger you gradually incorporate the flour from the centre outwards, using a circular motion, eventually you reach the outer edge then have dough ready for kneading.

The two of us were opposite each other and sharing the same workspace, EVERY time we did this—honestly EVERY time! I was concentrating on rotating my ingredients and I would hear a snigger—followed by, "Oh no!".

Signifying that he had got carried away and broken his 'O'—again! So there would be a mad panic, as a river of yeasty water ran all over the place, then I would screech and try to shield my mixture! Whilst he tried to gather all of his.

My assistance would be sniggering in the background, shaking her head with wonder.

But eventually the dough was gathered and left to rise, as we cleaned HIS mess up.

Amazing, his bread was always alright, we were doing different presentations and it all looked very clever like we knew what we were doing.

So I was taking home a variety of cobblers and plaits, then batches of pastries and a selection of home-made soups, it all looked and tasted very professional.

Scoutman was bringing home bags of different coloured rice crispies. I generally don't bother with breakfast—yes I know you should, so the many bags of coloured examples eventually went soft and got thrown away.

Spruce Girl, who likes her food, preferred my offerings and had nothing but praise for my endeavours.

A folder of associated course-work was handed in, complete with fussy arty bits cut from food magazines, I was having a great time and it got a good grade, it was educational fun.

I met a variety of really nice people on this course, from the college staff—tutors and assistants to the other students. None of them made any derogatory comments about or to me, that I heard anyway, I thoroughly enjoyed myself here and had a lot of fun learning new things.

The writing class didn't fit into my plans at the moment, but I went occasionally to say hello to the regulars, I wasn't really writing anymore anyway. I didn't really have the urge to, Gillian Mk 2 was in print now, other things were occupying my time.

I did go to show them the finished article: to gather the expected praise, it was mainly because they had all laughed with me in class that I was more determined to go further.

Alright I was secretly hoping to get shut of a few too.

Which I did, knew they wouldn't let me down, unnecessarily going into sales mode as I'd got loads to get rid of. The thought of Spruce Girl and Scoutman sporting 'I told you so' T shirts, with a pile of books collecting birdseed, was a sickening spur.

Only my mum has the qualifications and is allowed, nay expected, to do that.

But, of course, she doesn't NEED a T shirt.

Summer holidays and no college so it was time for jollydays, my written work was nearly up to date … well there wasn't much and it wouldn't take me long to do, Scoutman got his times sorted at work so we're set to go away. Yipee!

Handbrake, stop. Expel all notions of Sangria and brown bodies, he didn't own a passport!?

I couldn't believe it, but a holiday TOGETHER is what counts, that's getting sorted when we get back I promised him. It WILL happen, being his age without this document is pants, I would make him apply and pay for a ten-year passport on our return.

But first things first, I needed a new bikini anyway.

With our new love a caravan was booked on a site in Devon, we didn't know anything about it and were eagerly open-minded. Well a few mobile homes in a field … albeit a nice field.

Thankfully we had arrived in daylight hours, so we had time to stock-up our bar, initial investigation had revealed that the nearest pub was half an hours drive away. Mm …

Actually this was ideal, it was a cheap night with no arduous walking and you knew where the toilet was … near, everything was immediately to hand.

We took in a lot of the sights and filled the week cleverly, potteries with cream teas and country walks, then at night we drank loads of cheap booze in our local and convenient pub.

Nomad a friend of mine, that I met when living with the man who was to be my husband, had come back into my life. When I was living abroad he was working and bumming around/exploring the States, we kept in touch via the postal service that was able to track Nomad down, well at this time he happened to be in Devon so we arranged to meet.

He took the original photograph that was used on the cover of Gillian Mk 2, which the artist lost, I have a feeling he will be in and out of my space forever … not literally he's now settled with a woman, but he's still Nomad to me.

Anyway he took us into the countryside, to explore the magnificence of Dartmouth, we could see the imposing prison in the picturesque background. A wild pony came up to us and started to chew on Scoutman's big car, there were teeth marks on the boot.

Hungry pony in Dartmouth

We visited an aquarium and I bought him a pottery sea-horse (ah).
We also got two soup cups for coffee in the caravan because it was
only supplied with thimbles, which are no good to anybody.
I've still got the said mugs, they could have vented my disappointed
rage on a tiled kitchen floor! But they're still used, always on reserve
for when all the other vassals in the flat are used and dirty.
So …

My Aunt and Uncle live in Devon and we had to go and see them,
I was with them when I got my degree results and my cousin got
alcohol poisoning in celebration (she blames me to this day, "I was
trying to keep up with Gillian").
My uncle was occupied with feng shooing their garden, it was still in
the planning stage, my aunty just smiled and shrugged.

By the way … where were you when Elvis Presley died? When Princess Diana met her death?

You probably remember exactly … well ask me where I was when Manchester United won the triple?

"What's 'the triple'?", I hear you ask. Not sure, but it's very clever—apparently.

Anyway we were watching football in the caravan, Scoutman was a fan and I was drinking cheap wine from our new big mugs. Suddenly the final whistle sounded and yer man whooped loudly, then stood up. He ran up and down the caravan, well moved a lot in the small space.

I moved my legs out of the way and watched the show, he was still bouncing about screaming and waving his arms around wildly, he was a bit mad for a bit too long.

I had visions of our mobile home free-wheeling it, across the open field, into the sea.

"Fabulous. Calm down now", I laughed at him. He grinned, "It's football you wouldn't understand!".

I am a stupid woman but still made the comment, "Haven't they won a cup before?".

He paused then sighed and looked at me in all seriousness, "It's the triple!".

Oh yeah. I refilled my mug.

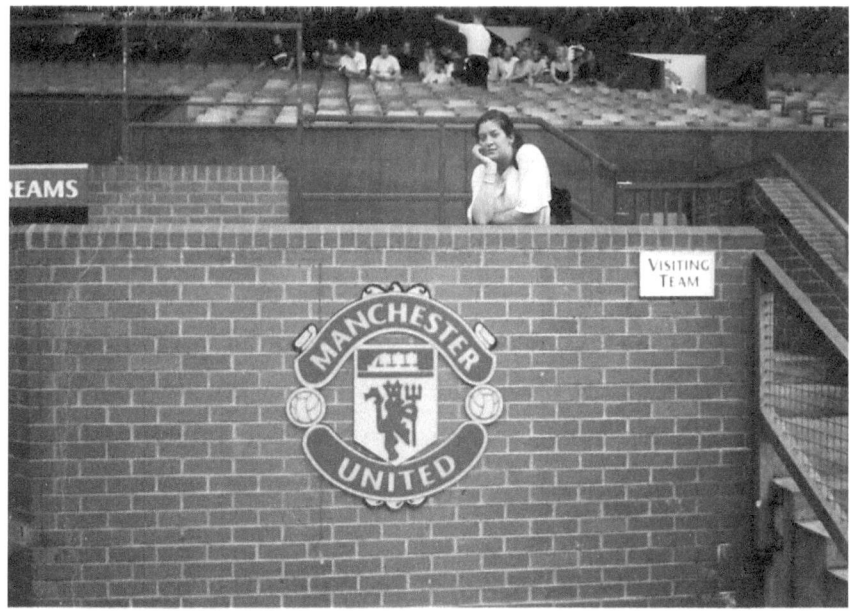

Bored at Old Trafford ... seen the cups ... I want to go home now

When we got back I did go to see the Old Trafford, Man United's home turf, to make a tour of the grounds ... this crazy thing called love. The display of cups and trophies was impressive though, I must admit, almost exciting enough to rip a caravan from its awnings?

Our precious scouts, two hours a week of free baby sitting service—I liked it really, it presented a challenge to my organising and sorting need to make a visible difference.

Remember when I was at the rehabilitation unit? I had stripped and ordered the notice board ... without permission. Even in my previous life, as a teacher, the displays that I did with the children's work were worth talking about. For one theme I made, then decorated, a six foot sarcophagus.
One of the girls that came to the hospital to see me, when she wasn't crying, asked me if she could have the sarcophagus?

As far as I know she took it, I am slightly curious and wonder if it is still around?

I did take photographs of some of my work, they make me a bit sad although they are good, the frustration of such an altered existence becomes a stark reality.

A lot of people have, seriously, suggested that I give talks about what having a head injury means.

Anyway, scouts, we are back, there was going to be a fund raising event and I had a jumble sale head on getting carried away as usual. The felt-tips came out and got busy with treasure maps, the coffee shop prices and details, tom bola enticements got some colour and the huge amount of surplus clothing got attention.

I was having a marvellous time.

For extra money a small entrance fee was charged and a lucky-dip was offered, as a softening ploy, actually it was a way of getting rid of frivolous rubbish. Scoutman and I often went to the coast and would happily get stuck on those two pence shuffle machines. As a result we had bags full of key-rings and other 'useful' oddities, gambling natures were explained away, we were collecting for the scouts!

Beach-side bingo provided a lot of the tom bola prizes, they were quite nice, we had accumulated a worthwhile and eye-catching collection of pretty things. The weather always dictated where we ended up, after we had done the obligatory wet walk on the sand.

On the day, of the jumble sale, the boys were assigned their tasks and knew what they were doing.

I just wandered about, to make sure everything was going to plan, then talked to people encouraging them to part with their money. The turn-out was disappointing but … Scoutman grinned when he had counted up the total takings.

The troop had excelled all previous records, it was the best they had ever done!

Brilliant, I felt responsible and smug ... as the arty things were rolled up to be put away into storage.

When I had my accident there were a lot of get well cards given, which I wanted to keep, so a scrap book was utilised to keep them tidily and this is when the habit started. Of ritually collecting memories.

The reason I mention this is because I am using the scrap books as an aide-memoir for Typically Gillian, who is still a bit rubbish on the memory front and it has been a while. There are still times when people smile and say 'Hello Gillian', as they walk by.

Sometimes I recognised them, if Spruce Girl was with me she would help if she could, but always I grinned and said, "Hello", back ... so whoever they were they wouldn't think me ignorant.

A smirking imbecile maybe?

The local paper is good and it told the community about my latest busy-body adventure, this idea came to me when we were planning questions for the scouts on an observation walk, I had noticed the litter and rubbish on waterlogged ground. The unused area is positioned just off the town centre, I remarked with disgust, it is a visible dumping space and people have no respect.

Reintroduce real punishment I say, make the slackers in our midst pay for selfish and thoughtless behaviour, crap attitudes must be brought to justice.

Start young and bring back caning to schools, consistent disrespect must be curbed, I'd do it.

Those parents that are spitting at the book now ... just stop it! If your child knows how to behave, is a normal and descent little person, then what is the problem? You should be cross with parents whose offspring mouth at figures of authority, you too must be horrified by things you see on television and in the papers. The police should be allowed to carry truncheons, and then encouraged to use them!

Spit at me if you want to, grey people introducing weak areas of forgiveness hasn't really worked has it?

But never mind eh?

The working crowd that pay their way with numerous taxes and behave themselves are ignored, those that get on with it and keep their noses clean, but if you are outrageous/loud/disrespectful you get media attention?

It all comes down to money, yawn, it drives me to despair how can it be?

No really how can it be?

Even a prison sentence makes no difference, no a custodial break means that you have time to write another book and make more dosh than you stole.

I'm not bitter, even when titles aren't stripped and monies are not paid back then you get praised with media attention?

No perish any unkind thoughts.

Flogging and stocks do spring to mind, it has to be said. But, nobody listens.

Whatever happened? Blimey.

Bring it on. I'm off 'on one' now!

Death penalty bring it back, that will sort out the prison crisis, there will be no re-offenders either. Three drink driving offences gets your car crushed and you can pay for the privilege, then you do community service. You can't and won't drive again.

Castrate rapists and paedophiles, you won't be doing that again either. I'm sure that victims and parents would agree. Time is very short and criminals should be accountable, deal with the consequences of free choice, then there would be no need for compensation and counselling.
Sorted.

On my high horse I decided to approach the local council, with my thoughts regarding the 'tip'. They were all for the free labour and supplied tunics, with rubbish bags and these brilliant litter picky things.

So a date was set, for the clean-up, that happened to coincide with the Keep Britain Tidy week and my brother's birthday.
It was a good thing and the important people that cared came—my mum and dad with Bro celebrating his birthday, a single father, even the council chap arrived and stayed the whole time. This was a bit of a shock, we had a can for safely disposing of any hypodermic needles and we actually found quite a lot.

Fruitcake arrived with a video camera, so we have footage of me attempting to get litter into the bag and missing (quite a few times!) then happily just stumbling about … I kept getting my feet stuck in the tangled undergrowth. Walking in this quagmire was a little precarious, I'll say, but we were all totally absorbed with the task.
One of the scouts waded into the water and I told the audience, to camera, "He's been told, quite a few times not to do that!". He was wet through with dirty and smelly water—bet his mum was pleased. But it was an amazing day and I was surprised how involved everyone was. There is video evidence of people filling black bags, one of the boys called me over as instructed. He was pointing to the floor, "It's

a needle!", I could not see it, "It's a needle", again I looked at him and smiled with a shrug. "There!". This time he pointed so closely he was almost touching it.

About ten hypodermic syringes were found and we filled nearly twenty bags with rubbish, Sommerfields did us proud and supplied a fabulous spread of food, but the newspaper and our wonderful MP didn't bother to support us.

This was the only disappointing part of the Tidy campaign.

But they missed out on a brilliant day and we all made a huge difference, the patch looked smart, just a few weeks later though you could see the evidence of lazy slobs that eat fast food and drink cheap lager.

Meanwhile the local rag did good, for me, a free-lance journalist had scanned local papers for potential stories of interest. He saw the bit about the self-published Darlink and followed it up, he called me to arrange an interview. I jumped at the opportunity—well made myself available then.

He came to the flat and I took a book with him.

Now the stranger was armed with all the bare facts, he left with his scribbles of extra information to pass on, his wife was writing the story. The next time he spoke to me Gillian Mk 2 had been devoured and had made its mark.

He told me, "It will be a bestseller". I hoped so, looking at the pile of books in my front room waiting for attention, apparently "it was a good read if it could make me laugh aloud".

Praise indeed from another stranger, even better they were getting me the needed publicity. I was particularly hyped up about this and began to have notions of grandeur, with visions of recognition.

Being in the local papers was brilliant, don't get me wrong, but I was a bit blasé about this now and wanted bigger things with the appropriate credit for my achievements.

But of course I still had a normal life to be getting on with and it was time for the scout leadership training.

The first weekend was a load of adult kids, with big woggles, doing important stuff. A few of them sported impressive badges, 'woods' and other emblems, to show they'd been dedicated for eons. But the rest of us, for the good of our troops, bonded like true leaders and then found a local pub to celebrate the union.

At the end of a tiring day, making a selection of useful things, we had real beds under the sleeping bags that were indoors in a dormitory near to flushing toilets.

The fun-packed time was over and Scoutman picked me up, he asked me about the weekend as he was driving. "You should have done it!", I nodded in response and told him about the activities we'd completed, with gossip about the other leaders.

He agreed, "I will, one day, when the time is right!". I sighed in answer because it was obviously never going to happen.

I shivered involuntarily, when contemplating the next part of the course, then announced "I'm taking the camp bed with me, and my hot water bottle, on the next jaunt". He sniggered and looked at me in disbelief. "No really I am!", I insisted, it was camping outside. Scoutman was laughing now and shook his head, "Wuss".

Not rising to the bait I huffed, with miserable memories of trying to sleep on the cold and hard floor, "Well at least I'm doing it and then I'll have a bigger woggle than you". Now he couldn't respond and I smiled smugly in the strongest position.

Bless him. Nah.

Time passed and the second weekend crept up, I took the ordered books with me, it started well and I was happy to see familiar faces. The tents were erected and the camp bed was installed immediately. I was definitely determined and was going to get this camping lark sorted, but let's be honest—I would still rather be sleeping outdoors in a more favourable climate.

This has reminded me that years ago I did sleep outside, as a smiling and happy with no problems adult, when I was volunteering on the kibbutz in Israel and it WAS better.

Alright I was younger and fit but, it was better.

Hey call me a girly wuss I don't care, central heating and beds now have their place in my life, at least I was there in cold body and anxious mind. Unlike some, being fed by their mothers and then tucked into a warm (albeit skinny) bed. (meow)

On the master camp the instructive activities were much as expected, as far as training to be a super duper scout leader goes, I mean how many ways are there to make a fire?

But the bonding between the adults was an added bonus, of course there were some that I liked more than others. That's surely normal with a group of strangers, it was a long day, but it was tremendous fun. I'd be sure to tell Scoutman what he'd missed out on in all his years of service. Don't really know how he managed to get away with it, for so long, it was not difficult and was good fun … Perhaps he would make the effort this time because I had shamed him?

No, maybe not, he wasn't bovered.

The last night of the training period was planned and it was going to be a riot, a collection of grubby scout leaders around a fire with a corkscrew. That sounds good so far, not a note of song passed our lips but plenty of alcohol did, we all giggled into the black night like silly children and talked about nothing.

It was a funny time and eventually the kettle was boiled, for my hot water bottle.

Oh yes, it was the first thing that went into the travelling bag along with my supply of drugs (epilepsy! It wasn't Glastonbury).

Did go to Glastonbury once, well I have to tell you now, with another couple. It was many years ago, when there weren't as many restrictions or fences. The other woman, in our little gang, and her partner were only able to do the weekend. They both had work commitments on the Monday, my partner and I were there for the lift, so we had to party immediately to make the most of the time.

The amount of mud, on your person, indicates the length of time you've been camping and there is always a long queue at the portable toilets. I was waiting in this queue and an open door was spied, had nobody else seen it? I remember looking around before rushing over to claim this cubicle, I opened the door and stopped.

There was a conical pile of excrement, protruding at standing height from the toilet's bowl. When I groaned to turn around people were laughing and nodding, clearly they had done the same thing.

Time to go! After hours of searching we gave up—the car had been stolen.

Three of us saw my cousin at the train station, she had been there all weekend too, the other man from our group had stayed to help with the clean up. Knew he would—consequently the silly man lost his job, he knew he would.

Back to treacherous disabled/adult/scout camping, with a big woggle, in the woods somewhere.

I remember cautiously stumbling, in an alcoholic daze, to my tent alone—even though I was sharing.

To then deposit the hot water bottle, safely in the right spot, but making sure I stumbled and tripped clumsily behind the tent to empty my tipsy bladder.

Job done so now, ready to retire, it was time to tackle the sleeping bag etc without waking up the snoring woman.

Bloody hell, this is brilliant, I congratulated my genius, a warm and deep sleep quickly enveloped the happy camper.

I woke up.

Suddenly it was dreadfully cold and uncomfortable, shuffling around made no difference when I realised, it wasn't because of the silly bed. Then the reason for my dilemma came to me, with a groan.

I was lying in a puddle.

Baffling … the bottle was now cold but it was still full?

Scoutman had loaned me his posh and clever sleeping bag, it was a good idea and it worked very well, but it was now full of urine and my pants were wet again.

The snoring woman hadn't moved an inch, but I had to, goddamn. I was really pissed off (ha ha—whatever). I was not at all happy but then grinned, as a good bit dawned on me, this had saved me a trek outside into the sightless cold and it wasn't my sleeping bag.

Happy days, no stop it! I'm kidding

Well he didn't smile either, at all, when the bag was returned.

I did pay loads to have it dry-cleaned, thought I should really, it was unfortunately the right thing to do.

Warm and dry we are back to learning new skills but at college now, where us students are starting to cook for the unsuspecting and paying public, next door to the learning kitchen was a real/mock restaurant. This was also used to educate students with correct waiting techniques, there was a small bar too.

Our tutor in the kitchen, a real chef in his previous life, was in his element.

When we had been learning and practising the basics, everything from hygiene and safety to actually cooking, he would come round and chat to us all. Usually sharing, distracting us with, his stories of cooking for large groups. Fascinating stuff but he did go on, that's maybe why we were always making silly mistakes in his company … when concentration wavered?

Anyway this chap was fab and expected the best from all of his students, he personally checked all the meals before they went out of the kitchen, his standards were quite high.

On this day, he was standing near the grill and noticed that the garlic bread was burnt around the edges. A piece of the offending article was in his hand, he shouted at anybody, "Who the *, did this?". We all looked around silently, the young cook responsible stepped forward.

In his new checked trousers he started to voice his excuses, but was smiling indolently, the big man was furious and having none of it.

The chef bowed his head to speak at the student, he glared with hard eyes over the rims of his glasses,

"Do it again", he commanded fiercely and then he threw the ruined bread across the kitchen.

I have omitted the real words that were used, he wasn't that calm, the rest of us cowered quietly and were just pleased that it wasn't us.

I amazingly still have some free time and was told about a well known head injury charity, it caters for people like me … those that have suffered from TBI, it mainly deals with the after effects of a head injury and helps you to get on with a changed life.

How exciting?

Spruce Girl and I discovered where the nearest group to me was meeting, we got all the information needed about dates and times. We called the number and it was a surprise to hear the familiar voice of a friend's mother. A few of the members were old pals, that admittedly I had failed to seek out and follow up, from the rehabilitation unit I'd spent a year at.

Old acquaintances that had indeed been, temporarily, forgotten.

Now I was eager and it would be nice to see these people again, under different circumstances, out of 'hospital' and in a social setting. They met up once a month, in the bar at a bowling club.

It would be interesting to catch up with these people, to find out where they were now, to see how they had progressed and what they were doing with their time. But instinctively I knew, that for some, the movement would be negligible.

It was discovered that most of them were still in an out-reach situation, that's when you live in a shared house and always have a member of staff present. This is alright if the staff are pleasant and good at their job.

Not that I'm at all bitter or scathing, if you remember my stint with this 'progression' was not brilliant. I was hiding vodka in my knicker drawer and laundry basket, so was always drunk in my free time. But it was obvious that I was struggling with such regimented routine, they put it down to " … a clash of personalities …" (if you say so). I had to go back to the unit's bungalow and then the flat was found for me. (Yipee!)

At the meeting the ex-clients (not patients) remembered me, good start, though the carers and drivers didn't know who I was. But I also had a chauffer with me, Spruce Girl was happy to drive and deliver me to the venue, the staff gathered and chatted amongst themselves. My support worker had a marvellous time, talking and moaning about work, with new colleagues. Such was my intrepid eagerness, to get involved and do something worthwhile with my difficulties in mind, I did attend a few meetings and then joined the committee.

Nobody was shocked or surprised, I have got a head full of loose electricity that needs channelling. It is known I am impatient, to make a mark and be heard.

I was on 'entertainment' and was quite happy to tackle the trains, when Spruce Girl was not with me, to arrive on time and get to meetings. Then taxis got me to the venue, to represent the injured faction on't committee.

Loving this—having a meaningful purpose and with a reason, doing my bit for and with people that were like me.

Survivors! Don't know what you were thinking.

I was happily spending a lot of time writing quizzes, Scoutman was coming to the social meetings with me and often helped to compile the questions, ripping up a lot of magazines for the photo-fit rounds too. The raffle was a bit of fun, it was scouts all over again.

Basically the members brought in unwanted gifts, or discarded tat, but it was appreciated nevertheless and it made money. We still had a supply of beach bingo prizes, cheerful tat, to get rid of.

As I was responsible for the entertainment I organised a talk, it was given well by my acupuncture lady—who was helping to alleviate my blinding and disabling headaches.

She was welcomed and applauded by all present, her talk was interesting, then to top it all off I think she won a dodgy raffle prize. The group had to pay a well known head injury charity a lot of money, insurance and stuff, but we were doing OK with our raised funds. Even better us members looked forward to something fun and different each month, with friends and familiar faces.

As a result of my head injury I am still under consultancy with my Head doctor, who has wisely remained beardless, after talking to me and consulting his notes he advised me to increase the dosage of my epilepsy medication. Which I consequently did and took his advice but, not really listening, I was sitting with a stupid grin on my face and was proudly clutching a copy of Gillian Mk 2. Being eager for him to buy the book because, a) he's in it b) he knows me and c) he's a specialist on these brain/head injury/epilepsy things   so he should be interested?
He did let me sign the book, whilst telling me he didn't read, then took it off me. I was cross because that was bloody hard work and it shouldn't have been, with hindsight I rather fancy that the consultant thought it should have been a gift! Well.

He didn't give me any money and the book was returned, he laughs now but I think he should be embarrassed, the tight and clever arse. I was disappointed and oddly offended, but had to go and pick up my next print so this annoyance was short lived.

Talking about hospitals I've got to tell you about this episode.

I woke up one morning and had to get up to go to the bathroom, or wet the bed and Scoutman, on the way back to bed I kicked the bedroom door.

I'm always doing that, the way I walk now means that my toes are always being stubbed on furniture and the like, I have nearly always got one or more black toe nails. One chiropodist suggested my nails may be an indication of larger medical issues, then told me I should make an appointment with my GP, I blinked with surprise and coughed my reply, "Na, I'm just clumsy".

This day I yelped with shock and in pain, the door should have swung back and absorbed the impact, the large chunk of wood had so much junk (bags, a dressing gown, two umbrellas and yesterday's clothes) hung on the back that it didn't move at all.

I looked down and expected to see blood, but gasped at what I did see, wish we'd got the camera and taken a photo for you.

My little toe was sticking out at a right angle to my foot. Must be a bit freaky when a larger bone is broken, if the limb is bending the wrong way. Can you imagine?

Scoutman was here and he was lying over the edge of the bed, looking at my foot, he groaned and sucked in breath, "I think you've broken your toe, we'd better go to the hospital", Now he was shaking his head and laughing.

I was being miserable and vocal because it hurt, more so because it was a visible pain, then I didn't know what shoes to try and force on. No footwear would accommodate such a distorted foot.

Boots? No.

Shoes? No.

Woolly blue slippers!

My toe was pushed back into place and forced into the soft footwear, ouch ouch ouch, then I limped to the car and stumbled into the hospital.

Sporting two rather big pom-poms, the slippers were a Greek holiday present from my parents, Scoutman had a brown pair exactly the same. In fact my brother and his kids have got pairs as well.

I had asked my dad, "Did you just get everybody the same slippers?", he had laughed to answer, "Yeah".

Anyway a familiar nurse smiled at me, "Hello again, what you been up to this time?".

She laughed as she messed with a splint and sticking plaster.

A few of the nurses, at this hospital, have got copies of Gillian Mk 2. Now they all greet me by name, chatting to ask when the next book is coming out—I'll have to break my toe again so I can tell them it's on it's way. The other patients must think I'm a clumsy hypochondriac, eager for attention, because I know most of the staff.

This is proving to be more difficult than I thought, or remembered, complete respect to the likes of grr … who was that female writer that wore pink all the time? Well her, she had a pink poodle and just rattled books off willy nilly. Anyway, this is not easy and I have no idea how Gillian Mk 2 became a finished book. Just get on with it, I hear myself say—and I will.

Do a bit more when I've had a coffee.

When full-on (possessed) with writing Gillian Mk 2 I had this BRILLIANT idea, that's what us writers do Darlink. Buy a coffee percolator! What a stroke of genius, I thought, caffeine on tap so I won't have to stop typing and the 'flow' will not be interrupted.

In theory this notion cannot be faulted, so I sent Spruce Girl off to get the machine and some filter coffee.

Then found a space near the computer armed myself with a soup mug and milk and I was well away.

The first round of 'posh coffee' was nice and I congratulated myself, Spruce Girl joined me, even messing about with a refill when the jug was empty was not a problem. But it's an untidy pain because it's new, I'll get better with it after a few more tries, I was convinced … with a full cup.

It wasn't until I spilt coffee on my keyboard, being disabled and clumsy, I jumped with realisation, then panicked when I knocked the same cup again and nearly blew myself up.
The hot liquid danger was banished, to the kitchen. Where it was supposed to be …

Well at least I didn't have to keep boiling the kettle, so it was still used but less and less. The machine was cluttering up the workspace, collecting dust, when I got fed up of cleaning away all the coffee dregs. It was used occasionally when that little bit extra was called for, usually with cake, entertaining visitors I was trying to impress.
When the effort was made it was always pleasing, in that I do like filter coffee and would happily drink the whole jug, what I didn't like was all the fuss required to get it going and then to clean up after it.
Months later the bloody thing stopped working so I invested in a replacement, don't ask me why, I cursed this for a little while and then the glass jug was dropped. That sorted it out, pain in the butt.
I didn't get another one, but there are still packets of coffee and filter papers in my cupboard. It was decidedly easier and less fuss to go back to instant coffee.

Just maybe I won't drink so much? That would be easiest, I really should never be asleep with the amount of stimulating caffeine in my system.

So my life was good, full of interesting activities and busy with my love, when you sustain injuries like this people generally don't stick around—even though they often say that they will. Better off without these fickle people anyway, the friends that have stuck around, those that accept and like me as I am now are the only people that I bother with. Life is too short to mess about with idiots, wasting time and energy, make moments for good people.

One friend in particular springs to my mind and she will curse me if I don't mention her, Betty Boo you got in there, we met in Germany when we were six and she will always be my true friend.

Love her.

A lot of people I have met and know will buy this book, to see if they are mentioned and will be curious about their code names, if I remember to mention them all this book's already a best-seller!

Ooo … get me.

Still on the catering course at college we had a trip to The Good Food Show, at the NEC in Birmingham, the coach journey down was reminiscent of school outings but with a lot of excited big kids. My mum came too, to support me, not that she wanted to go and was looking forward to it or anything. So our Head Chef had a new and captive audience, wasting no time he was recounting days past, sitting next to him my mum was a nodding mute but she was still smiling You would never guess, from the gabble of noise, that any of us had ever been on a mini bus encounter before.

When we had parked up and were ready to go in, we were all given tickets, with the understanding that we were to be in the audience at the recording of 'Ready Steady Cook'. It's huge and was very busy, so it's a good job my mum was with me … otherwise I would have been stumbling about and lost all day.

We wandered around most of the many stalls at the exhibition, displaying different foods with a selection of wines and various cooking implements, I was stopping at the 'bars' to try the free samples of wine. I'm sure that these stalls would not have missed my attention, had I been on my own, mum kept pulling me away to look at food! She spotted the TV personality Chris Evans, he was walking about on his own, he is taller than I imagined him to be and looked like he could have done with scoffing some of the food samples. "He's a bit scrawny looking", mum commented whilst I sampled some port.

So I was only a bit cross when the show was changed, last minute, so we ended up watching something else. Which fails me on the memory score, it was something about Xmas cooking.
Well it had a turkey or two in it, I'm sure, the edible and boring big bird not the presenters.
But we enjoyed the day immensely, my carrier bag was full of rubbish and I still haven't broken my 'Good Food' wine glass—that's because I use and smash my other ordinary/plain/cheap glasses instead. I have decided on this day, having just read the last few paragraphs, to stop drinking!
Just cut it out.

Not because I don't like and can't cope with the colossal, nay evil, hangovers … that must be an age thing. But because I keep falling over. So far I have escaped with grazed knees and buggered tights but I am aware, usually the next day when I count the visible injuries, of how close I am getting to broken bones or really hurting myself—and let's face hospitals are boring.

Anyway the journey back from Birmingham was quieter, my mum was asleep and everybody else had been partaking of the free alcoholic samples on offer throughout the day, I don't recall seeing the said television show again either.

When I was in the sixth form, at high school, we did a weeks trip to London. It was full on with planned activities galore, I'm telling you because we watched a live recording of 'The French and Saunders Show'—never saw this again either. When the same joke is repeated a few times it isn't as funny, but it was still better than cooking turkeys even with the trimmings, I'm sure that 'Ready Steady Cook' would have been good though.

I mentioned London so I could share this with you really, we went to see 'The Pirates of Penzance', my claim to fame and a most precious memory. We had a bunch of seats on the last rows downstairs, about as far away from the stage as you could be, I was next to a central aisle. Sitting for the performance I moaned that my seat was lumpy, to sit comfortably meant that I had to sit sideways and stick my long legs into the aisle, my small friend to my side would not swap.

During the performance there was a loud and booming voice behind us, we turned to see Oliver Tobias (some of you may be saying who? A stunning, swashbuckling, six footer—that's all you need to know) he started walking towards the stage and stopped at my protruding legs. Oh my God … he was a handsome pirate and was looking at me!

He bent and gently picked up my leg, which was in his path, he stroked it then looked into my stunned face.

A smug teenager grinned widely for the rest of the performance, clapping too loudly and for too long at the end of the show. I wouldn't stop talking, "Oliver Tobias! The sexy and big man caressed my leg! Oliver Tobias touched me! Told you to swap seats!".

My friends eventually told me to shut up, but I knew it was because they were envious. Well, who wouldn't be?

I didn't get a T-shirt printed, but still snigger stupidly today.

That's enough about that because now we are being a responsible adult and washing my chef's whites. Spruce Girl was not with me on weekends, I had to have my uniform clean and ready to be ironed on Monday. Easily done and not a problem, the washing machine has a hot wash cycle, just add washing powder then put the kettle on, simple. I had even filled the machine with other cotton items to save water and time. I am of course living in Gillian's world, with coffee and a cigarette, cleverly putting denim jeans in with the load because they can withstand a boiling round.

The machine clicked off and was ready to be unloaded. It was then discovered what a complete moron I am, no honestly, the COTTON and DENIM jeans were BLACK?

The chef's whites were not white anymore, I couldn't believe my eyes, the essential and costly uniform was a sickening shade of streaky grey. I called my mum, immediately, to tell her what I'd done.

I was still shaking my head, with disbelief at my stupidity, as far as I could see they were ruined.

"Why on earth did you put BLACK jeans in with chef's WHITES?", I wailed foolishness in my response, "Because they're cotton!".

Well they were.

I didn't think for one moment that the colour might run, my mum took all the grey items away and rescued them, needless to say greater care is taken now and I haven't done that since.

I'm very careful now, so I don't know how this happened, Scoutman was now putting his soiled clothes into my laundry basket? Cheeky, but I didn't mind. I was allowing his clothing to fill the machine with mine, it made sense.

I didn't know I owned anything red? But I did and this day it got into the white wash, I sniggered as I retrieved a pair of pink underpants. Scoutman snatched the ruined garment off me, "I'm not wearing them!", then he put them into the dustbin.

I was mortified, "Nobody will see them—I hope". He shrugged at me, "I'll know … and I'm not wearing pink underpants!".

I laughed and fluttered my eyelashes as I looked at him sideways, "They're quite nice, a subtle pink?", he growled at me, "No!".

I carried on emptying the washing machine, "If you keep doing that, or if I do, you'll have no pants left", he laughed, "I'm NOT wearing pink underpants, you'll have to buy me some more".

I snorted at his weakness as I continued the task, "I don't think so … you can wear mine", then I found his lone red sock sticking to the drum.

Spruce Girl is going to get remarried but she's going to Mauritious, so she will get fab photos.

There is one photograph, taken at my wedding, that makes me scowl. My new husband has me held high in his arms, the photographer has a frontal shot, the pleated skirt of sheer nothingness falls freely exposing my outstretched legs crossed at the ankles. My lacy stocking tops are visible, with the borrowed blue garter, then quite clearly you can see the sexy tampon string.

Gawd.

So we are not invited and she's having the honeymoon at the same time, that's the way to do it eh?

But that's not until April 2003.

We did keep-fit things at the gym for a little while, but it's boring so regrettably I stopped going, I was so sure and promised myself that this momentum would continue at home. Mmm

Scoutman gave me a second hand exercise bike and I can hook my feet under the radiators to do sit-ups, that was the plan of mice and Gillian—in Gillian's world. But I bang my knees on the handlebars of the squeaky and stiff bike, my legs are too long, anyway my stomach's not REALLY that big yet!

When it is, sign of the times, I'll save up and have liposuction.

I got a card in the post, from a disabled friend's mother, she was telling me how the book Gillian Mk 2 had made its impact. Again I was surprised that a) the written statement emulated vocal opinions b) that she had bothered to write it down and now I had visible evidence c) my work was seemingly making a difference and d) how chuffed I was with this unexpected praise.

"You made me laugh, then cry and then you made me laugh again", I have still got the card and it became the first in my collection.

Another mother telephoned me on behalf of her disabled daughter, to order a book in response to a newspaper article, they lived locally so Scoutman drove me there to hand deliver a copy of Gillian Mk 2.

She has unclear speech but tackled the phone, to tell me that she had finished reading the book, she gabbled excitedly and had to be stopped mid flow so I could understand her. She was full of admiration and identified with my words of frustration completely. The conversation was engaging and I was intrigued, subsequently I invited myself for coffee and a chat, it was a chance to share a disabled reader's viewpoint. At the same time having my fragile little ego boosted, again Darlink.

She has remained part of my life and has become a good friend, I called her whilst I was writing this and asked her if she had any ideas for a code name.

She has a penchant for chocolate and likes baking cakes.

"What kind of cake do you like making?", I quizzed her. "Chocolate cake", she answered.

"Ok …", too long, "What is your favourite cake to eat?", I tried again. "Chocolate cake", she laughed.

"Nah … that's too long to keep typing", so after thought my friend is now called Truffle and she likes this. That's handy, I was going with this anyway.

In the meantime Scoutman was made to apply for a passport, so now we could go anywhere—well not quite it had to be cheap. He had only been to Spain before, with the lads when he was eighteen, but had just been drunk for two weeks which must have been boring. Well it isn't if you're an eighteen year old lad and that's what you went for I suppose, but now he wasn't a teenager and was with me.

But I didn't have much money either, so the choices were limited. Not to worry though we have love we don't need the Caribbean! I was happy to go anywhere, as long as you didn't have to wear layers of clothing and then have an umbrella to hand! We need some sunshine, I'm more than happy to bare my skin and overdose on vitamin D. Getting everything together and packing for the holiday is part of the fun, I love travelling. Don't get me wrong here, not travelling per se but a journey overseas, long coach or car jaunts just bore me and get on my nerves. I recall doing the cheaper option to get home as a student once, literally once, hours on a coach pretending to be asleep (I tried reading but that didn't work). To avoid talking to the aching bore of a man, sitting next to me. Ugh.

Anyway I'm more than happy to make the journey, even sit out the numerous delays … which seem to be inevitable now, if the hours invested result in a different climate/culture/cuisine with sunshine as standard.

Everybody agrees that some of our own coastline cannot be beaten, there are stunning areas, but, that isn't my point being on holiday for two weeks in the rainy/cold/grey is pants. Anyway I did all that as a kid, eating gritty sandwiches and drinking soup, whilst sitting on the sand with my brother under dad's fishing brolly. Now I'm an adult and can get onto an aeroplane. Thankfully no longer needing a wheelchair or assistance, but I did have Scoutman to carry things and help me so I wasn't on my own.

So Europe, near and affordable, was calling to us loudly.
Thank goodness for the scrap books because I can now tell you exactly where we went, Portugal,

Olhos D'Agua in Algarve. It was a nice place to be but had a bitch of a walk, downhill, to the beach.

I cannot find any photographs, I was hoping they'd help to prompt more memories to share with you, Oh well I have still got the scrap book.
One thing I do remember, Scoutman's mum was on holiday at the same time—in the same country.
So she was just down the road, in England and, in the neighbouring holiday resort here in Portugal. No I couldn't believe it either, but we had to work out the local transport to go and pay her a visit.
I'm not saying that it was a waste of time, meeting her friends then sitting and drinking coffee in the sun was quite pleasant, but I'd rather have gone somewhere else on an adventure as we were only there for a week.

One evening we got dressed up and went for a meal at a posh restaurant, we had steak cooked on this hot stone which they brought to the table, a romantic dinner away from home with a sexy sun tan. Well I had some healthy colour. Scoutman would sit in the shade under the umbrella, smothered in sun cream, he was adamant and petrified that he would burn.

Under cover and shaded from the sun, with factor twenty protection on any possibility of exposed flesh, then wearing his baggy knee length shorts. Mmm.

I don't think so, really not in like a million years.

No amount of ridicule or coercion, with loaded sarcasm, could persuade him to soak up the sun's energy. He went home with a brown head and beige limbs, which was from pandering to my whims, unavoidable on walkabouts with my need to explore. Mainly the head tan, I'd say, was because he couldn't carry the beach umbrella with him.

I love Port and it was relatively inexpensive there, of course, we were now getting good at a bar in the bedroom and now it was a Tawny variety Darlink.

I cursed myself as I saw people sitting outside, around the pool and reading in the sun, holiday makers with spare expendable cash and time to kill. It was an open opportunity and I had no copies of Gillian Mk 2 with me! I was annoyed with myself and vowed to have some of the books with me on the next trip.

So back on soggy soil and Xmas was around the corner again, even though Halloween is still on the shelves and we have bonfire night to think about, it's all commercial rubbish now anyway.

Yah boo humbug?

Actually I love December as much as Port, it's my birthday on the 9th, I have had a lot of practice and can make the festivities last from the 9th of December to the 2nd of January. No honestly I can, my elderly neighbour was right too—she told me when you're 69 your birthday comes every week.

I'm not that old, but when I tell people my age (which I have to think about now) I'm shocked. Then one is surprised and disappointed, if they don't tell me that I look younger or good for my age.

It must be a woman thing? Bloody hell.

I now live in the centre of a town, so am conveniently close to everything, which is brilliant when you're always forgetting things, this is very handy for Xmas shopping too as it happens.

It was the first Yule Tide with my new partner Scoutman and it made me very happy, I have saved my nice and special celebratory cards. One of the cards he gave me was sloppy and soft to 'My Girlfriend' (ah) and the second was to his 'Crimbo Totty' (funny).

I love the way you wear your hair

I love your gorgeous botty

So get here with that mistletoe

You scrumptious Crimbo Totty

I can't remember what presents were bought for him, there must have been something nice amongst all the cheap and cheerful thoughts (surely), but I do recall my disappointment when I had opened my gifts from him.

A big bumper crossword puzzle book was one, I'd like to think that my disenchantment was not obvious, but it was a present and better than nothing? Not much thought and my thanks wouldn't have been very enthusiastic, I'm not very good at hiding my feelings and I don't tell lies, but I smiled and shrugged because it was Xmas.

The end of the day was the best bit and reveals my greatest memory, we were full of good food and cheer but now ready to sleep. Scoutman grinned and gave me a small parcel.

It was some kind of jewellery, I held the unusual gold necklace and laughed, what a lovely surprise and I really did like it!

Now I could give the crossword book away, without feeling bad, I was happy and knew he loved me. The chain broke a few months later, it was put into a labelled envelope … which is somewhere.

Lunch that year was at my parents and it was very nice, with all the extras, my niece and nephew were there being loud and kid like. But it was only one day, then we went home, I'm not a very enthusiastic aunty … sorry. My new partner was good with them though and they loved him, he made up for my disinterest, they ran to him and he threw them around. Kids like that eh? Well they were lucky that I didn't try it … one of us would have got hurt and broken.

We went to Scoutman's family for food and presents on Boxing Day, which is what couples do.
I seem to have avoided cooking turkey and Xmas pudding etc most of my life.
Nice one.

Now we party into the Millennium.
I have a load to tell you

CHAPTER II

Cracking On 2000

This is strange—being on chapter two already and not really knowing what I'm doing. As I'm typing this the enormity of completing Gillian Mk 2 is becoming more apparent to me, blimey what an achievement, even though people did tell me at the time.

I do know this much however, that life is unpredictable and a pain in the backside—when you are 'fighting' with a real life disadvantage. The ex teacher of mine, that I mention on the first page of Gillian Mk 2, who often fancied himself to Elvis Presley, has asked me to speak about disability as part of a social awareness course.

He wrote to tell me that my, "refreshing … stimulating … enlightening approach would be interesting". My mum was impressed, but that's maybe because she rather liked him when I was a pupil. It will be nice to see him again though, it will be strange going into the staff room, hopefully some of my other teachers will still be there. My head is brimming with ideas and going back into teacher mode, but we will see, I'll tell you about it when it happens.

Incidentally I parted with two books last night, one with a red lipstick kiss on as requested—honestly I'll do almost anything to keep my public happy Darlink. So things really aren't so bad, but of course there are still crap times.

I mustn't keep doing that—these jumps of text that talk of the present times—confusing little party animal that I am.

Anyway we glide happily into the new century with Typically Gillian, it feels exactly the same as last year, it's easy to forget it's supposed to be special when the party banners come down. There is yet another new pile of monochrome publications in my front room—by the way—they are being trashed by Joey.

My collection of fan mail, from impressed readers, is now becoming quite extensive. I was gladly saving them all, they were starting to get in the way, the letters and cards were getting mixed up with other jots of paper. Spruce Girl and I would often have 'blitz' days the flat. Essentially this was both of us going on a tidy mission, to eradicate and file the messy paperwork, numerous lists, bills, letters, cards, book orders and scribbles of literary inspiration.

I forgot to mention, other than being incredibly disorganised and untidy, we are now an encouraged and stimulated writer don't you know.
If speaking to somebody, that had read Gillian Mk 2, I would invariably ask for their thoughts and opinions. I think most Darlinks of authors do this, with need of an ego boosting confirmation of my witty delivery. But on this day the reply was, "It's not very good is it?".

Well poke me in the eye with a quill! I stumbled in thought, then laughed with disbelief, nobody had ever said this to me. I shook my head to ask her, "Why? (shocked pause). Do you think that?".
She looked at me, as though I was simple, then declared rather pompously, "There's too much swearing".
Phew, a sigh escaped, I had thought it was going to be a serious criticism. The nonchalant shrug in response was because I didn't really care, I didn't though.

I do have a bit of an attitude, maybe, sometimes.

But this has been the only negative comment to date, although others have mentioned the healthy dose of blasphemy scattered amongst the pages. Usually with a shocked nod, because I'm not that kind of girl? Then follows the laughter, well the language just spells out how grotty and annoying this type of injury can be.

"… most of us have no idea … very moving … very vivid … four years of frustration, anger, humiliation and pain … disjointed style suit's the subject and punches home the points … flippant style with no wallowing in self-pity …" M. Thomas Swansea. (my favourite landlady)

This quote is taken from one of the letters (bring it on), I like this kind of comment.

I was becoming complacent, with the unprompted praise. This observation and others like it, encouraged me to pursue my new literary interests./awakening/genius and investigate related events.

Had I found my alternative niche in this distorted life?

So I joined another writing circle, which ran fortnightly, but this involved a car journey. Spruce Girl came to the rescue again, it was on the right day, as a happy taxi driver. She is always smiling, she's got a new man who gives her lurve and of course she is MY support worker!

By the way. Could it be any better? Eh, I ask you?

Being assistance to the aspiring author, who's always in the paper, local people know my face now and therefore will be aware of my exploits. They may see my picture and think 'Bloody hell she's in AGAIN! What's she up to now?'.

I don't know but, all the cuttings are filed, I am getting noticed Darlink and it's not because of my physical demeanour for a change. Some people do comment, often stopping me in the street, that they saw the article and say nice things to me.

So, in this writing group the meeting was organised and implemented by an author, literary exercises were set in class and you were given homework which you read aloud at the next meeting.
Spruce Girl would just sit drinking coffee and eating biscuits.
I moaned at her, well that's new. Saying, "You should write something too! Just sitting there for two hours must be boring?". She smiled and told me she was alright then shrugged, "I'm not a writer like you".
Well no, Lovey. But I was insistent that she try doing the homework, then pointed out that she had two weeks to complete the task.
Love her, she did it and it wasn't bad. But she still wasn't as good as me.

Having said that my writing can be construed as tedious, no matter what the outline or topic was, I can and do always twist the words to end up tackling disability issues. Obsessed or consumed?
Well, unfortunately, not being able bodied is a big issue in my daily existence and I can't get away from it. Physically or mentally.
But in these sessions we were encouraged to explore the written word, in its many guises, I was enjoying the opportunity to tackle an audience and discovering that my sense of humour was appreciated.

Writers came and went, until the group had the regular stalwarts and diehards waiting for recognition, there were one or two people with whom I took exception. But held my tongue and didn't react in the class. I would gripe and bitch with Spruce Girl on the way home.

You know the kind of people that whinge and complain all the time? About nothing, but their own miserable and sad lives? Well just keep it to your-bloody-self!

One of the members would burst into tears regularly, if you said anything derogatory about her work, boring melodramatics maybe but I actually do like her.

I would look at Spruce Girl, who would be contemplating the Jaffa Cakes, with an eye-rolling shrug indicating another interesting journey home.

I was told about a BBC 'Telling Lives' project. Exploring and utilizing story telling technology, with guidance, you had to complete an extensive application form to be accepted.

My attempt for approval reached them on the closing date, I crossed my fingers and firstly hoped it had got to them on time, anticipating that they would be impressed with my reasons for wanting to do this.

It did get to them and they were happy! I was in and part of this scheme. Brilliant!

Later I found out that only six places were available, for this adventure, mine was the sixth application form that they had received.

Mm, Oh well. It was still brilliant.

I was really really pleased and committed for six weeks, but realised I had no support—as it was on the wrong day, it now involved dealing with public transport and catching a bus.

This meant that I was responsible for myself, in that if the right bus wasn't caught on time I simply missed out. The thought of this was daunting, it was my problem and I was paranoid about messing up.

Spruce Girl to the rescue … a thorough investigation was required, regarding the bus times and which bus I should actually get onto to. So I was eventually armed with a pocketful of lists again.

Incidentally you should see the paperwork implicated with a train journey, the rail system is generally a pain in the arse—if you are lucky enough to get a seat.

In the interim, one's coming, the scrap books have provided and prompted these memories in the life of 'Typically Gillian'.

On one of my treks on the rail-service and the journey was discontinued—probably paranoid leaves on the line—which meant everybody had to get off the train and wait for the next link.

Imagine, if you will, when the replacement train arrived. There was a packed platform of grumbling passengers all pushing and rushing to board the already full cabins.

After a mad and unpleasant jostle at the doors, the remaining seats were quickly taken, one passenger found his pre-booked chair. It was occupied and he pointed out the reservation ticket, the seated woman looked at him, the occupant squinted her eyes then growled, "I've been working all fucking day".

Well? What do you say to that? I didn't bother mentioning my disability, or preference for a seat,

Oh no.

People around were quiet and the chap just stood in the aisles with the rest of us, as he realized that she was not moving, a bit of rail rage was on order to make the journey even more distressing! Nobody said or did anything … except moan about the service.

By the way I have an annoying habit, well quite a few I am sure but this one was mainly because Scoutman was able to drive, I kept dragging his mind into Gillian's world and encouraged him to explore further than the end of his nose.

Even though he knew me, and said he loved me, this often lead to unpleasant episodes in the car. As the whim of mine was sated. I am a grumpy passenger, reacting badly if we were moving at speed or if we were lost. In the eventual screeching matches he would defend himself and argue, "Are you saying I'm a bad driver?", then, "We always get there, don't we?".

Well he did drive better than me, but I would answer tersely under my breath … "Eventually". It always surprised me that he wasn't that good with maps, being a Scout leader and having related badges of merit and all.

But we did get there, at last, the printed information had been filed safely and had just been discovered then used. Beamish was interesting even though, we went at the wrong time in the year, some parts were closed.

Wensleydale was a good day and I love cheese. Shortly after my accident I could only distinguish sweet, savoury and the taste of cheese, very strange. But it's back to normal now.

You know that I love the theatre, I am partial to comedy though have enjoyed an array of productions. (Did I tell you Oliver Tobias touched my leg? At a London theatre?).

But getting to the venue and getting home, from where I live, using public transport means that you have to leave the theatre before the show finishes.

Teef Geezer and I had to exit a show early, to catch the last bus home, in Gillian Mk 2 days.

I moaned all the way back, about missing the end, and have never done this since.

By the way he remains a star and we are still in contact, but I haven't seen him for years, I don't think he's read my first book yet.

Other characters, in Gillian Mk 2, have shared their opinions and have been flattered with their code names. That's good, I didn't want to offend anyone.

This day with Scoutman I had the advertising flyer in my hand, for an amateur show that was local, "Let's go and see this", we have been to this small theatre before and left smiling.

Scoutman looked at the paperwork and shrugged, "Yeah—Why not?".

Off we went and it all started well, the atmosphere was buzzing, a bunch of confident teenagers warbled and strained to entertain us. Then the audience went into raptures and exploded with applause? We were quick to realise, as we clapped politely, the rest of the audience were the relatives of the young performers.

They weren't that good and we left in the interval.

Scoutman vowed to me, "I am never letting you do that to me again", so we'll just not do anything then? That is easier though eh?

Just found a letter from my head doctor, who remains beardless, he comments, " … notably your memory centre for remembering jokes appears to be fully intact …". Well you've got to laugh haven't you? Wonder how much he gets paid to make these observations?

Not enough to buy self-published books.

Anyway this has reminded me to tell you the only joke in my memory bank at the moment, he must think I'm a bit mad, I have to tell you now.

Noah is watching all the animals disappear, two by two, up the gangway into the ark. As the droppings are cleared from the walkway he nods his head and sucks in breath, "It's getting too heavy, we're going to sink!".

At last the polar bears board, they have the furthest to come. Noah panics, as he thinks of all the animals doing what comes naturally, then he makes an executive decision.

He stands before them and announces, "We cannot have any extra weight, so you cannot make babies, all the boys must hand in their tackle. Don't worry you can collect when we arrive". In the noise the rabbits fainted.

The others nod, "Well he is saving our lives", then do as Noah directed. Days and nights of darkness pass, then one day the sunshine pierces the cloud.

Noah gathers the animals and grins, "We have arrived! The way is clear and you can collect your tickets, for your tackle, at four o'clock". The animals roar and squeak with excitement.

Later Mr Mouse whispers to his wife with anticipation, "I am going to make love to you tonight like you have never been made love to before. The earth is going to move for you my little rodent".

Mrs Mouse blinks, "What's come over you?". Mr Mouse smirks, "I got the elephant's ticket!".

In the meantime the BBC assignment had started and the chosen six met the team, Rupert, Olivia and Annie (OAR—as in they guided us through the sea of video tape and equipment). It was a joy and it was strange, we were all taken over, from that moment on the six of us were totally enthralled.

Enraptured and fascinated by the whole process, from the team building exercises onwards, they provided coffee and food too—we all love buffet grub—brilliant.

OAR were a comprehensive team and their input was invaluable fun. We did everything that was needed, but had help where necessary, my story was titled Gillian Mk 2—quelle surprise?

The whole lot was tackled by the individual story tellers—from the story board, the script and voice-over, artwork and banner, copying photographs and choosing the songs/music.

I even planned to do the running. Yes, I RAN on my video (kinda).

One day, at home, I had just completed writing the script when the intercom announced the insurance lady had arrived. She had come to assess my damaged living room carpet, she looked at the paint stains (I had dropped and kicked over a FULL tin of emulsion) and the triangular iron burn. The good thing is that I didn't try to catch the falling and hot iron, the bad thing is that it burnt a triangle on my carpet in the middle of my front room. Anyway I asked this stranger (to become Lill) to do me a favour, to sit and to be my audience, then I made her coffee.

She listened to my words and smiled, "That's really good. Where do you get the book?".

Well.

The day of filming came and I made the big 'FINISH' banner, it was held high by my fellow artistes, I geared myself up and 'ran' through the paper sign. As I was grinning and catching my breath R was looking at the video camera, then he shook his head and mumbled, "I didn't get that, you have to do it again".

We all looked at the paper banner, now in tatters on the floor, then I groaned in discomfort and rubbed my knees.

OAR teamwork saved the day, O had rolls of black tape in her car?

So the paper was haphazardly stuck back together. When you look at the video (www.bbc.co.uk/tellinglives : Humber region : Gillian Mk 2) you may be able to see this handy work. There was so much of this industrial black tape that I had bouncing visions, feeling that I would ricochet off the reinforced sign and land on my backside, so I 'ran' harder with determination. Then almost crashed into the cameraman when I couldn't stop.

The end results were a credit to the team, the stories were brilliant, they were all individual and varied. My mum, dad and brother attended the debut showing of my work. It was weird, people in the audience were reduced to tears.

I was grinning at the reaction and bursting with pride, I was glad that my parents saw this.

To close this chapter the six of us and other story tellers were invited to a special showing, at a big hotel with an opportunity to do posh with mascara and Scoutman made an effort too, he drove so we got there eventually and it was very impressive.

What an eye-opener, we sat and watched a selection of works, sharing personal stories and achievements by a variety of people. The applause was genuine, as we all knew what it had taken to get here, and OAR deserved the heartfelt recognition too.

The best was yet to come—Gillian Mk 2 was shown as the conclusion to the evening—I was bursting with grins again.

We were all given a video, of the six stories in our group. I was showing everybody my video at home, it was also made available on my website— www.gillianfirth.co.uk.

This remains, one of those events in your life, a constant smile and I am so pleased that I didn't mess up with the transport. Having too much time to kill was beneficial for a change, the timetabled six weeks guaranteed a result, it was worthwhile and my video story is brilliant— you should watch it.

Talking about worthwhile activities leads me nicely onto my next memory, it involved making lots of lists to add to my collection then getting organised and excited, we went to Pissouri in Cyprus for two weeks of jollydays.

This time there was only the two of us and I was happy with that, no burdens or distractions down the road, Scoutman was made to take his driving licence. At first he declined the opportunity, with irrational reasons and a vocal fear of the unknown, you can imagine that I was very understanding. I pointed out that they drove on the same side of the road as us at home, he sighed defeat agreeing to take the essential document and I was now happy.

This of course meant not having to sort out, then tackle, foreign public transport. Though this in itself can be fun, I have recently discovered that my ridiculous fear of being lost is my mum's fault. My dad always drives any long distances, on any unfamiliar roads, uncanny he can locate most places by recognizing local pubs on many horizons. A useful skill, as proven on many a family excursions, perfected in his army days I believe.

Clichés of old are coming true! I am turning into my mother: you never know what you've got until it's gone: your body does head southwards with time … I can't remember anymore now I've started but you know what I mean. This aging and rubbish memory thing's a bugger isn't it?

Anyway we are back at Cyprus and we arrived at the resort, after a brilliant flight—I love flying.

I collect souvenirs of events, trips and outings, for my scrap books now. I used to hoard reminders, tickets, programmes, beer mats and the like. But they get moved from space to space then, unless you actually do something with them, they get tatty and eventually you throw the memories away.

The resort was small and nestled at the bottom of a steep hill, here there was a swimming pool with an outdoor bar then toilets and the accommodation. There were stairs up to our first floor chalet, which was worrying, but there were handrails so it was manageable. Scoutman carried everything up to our rooms, I was coping with me, an item of hand luggage was about my limit and I didn't attempt to help with anything else.

He was doing all right on his own, what a hero.

There was a terrace of white and two-floored houses, with a bar next to a pool on our doorstep, it all looked like a holiday brochure—how brilliant!

On further exploration there was a supermarket further down this road, towards the small beach, then an outdoor restaurant opposite, this place just got better.

We bought milk, coffee, sugar and cigarettes, which were the basic essentials and probably some bread and things I imagine?

Onto the holiday itself—Scoutman would get annoyed with me, when I always seemed to be telling him what to do. But I was determined to explore and take advantage of the fact that a) we were in a different country b) we only had two weeks to fill c) the weather was gorgeous and d) we had saved up the spending money—so spend it I say.

I am a little controlling and had all the brochures laid out on the bed, then told him what we were going to do. I'm not actually saying that he was indecisive and unimaginative, he could be, but each day was planned and I talked through the subsequent list with him. He would nod and just go with the flow, he probably knew that we would do what I wanted, mainly because he had nothing better to offer anyway—not that he was given the chance.

Best laid plans of mice and Gillian: an irritating aptitude from my previous life that is exaggerated in the new existence.

Scoutman was a lucky man, I compensated for his misgivings, because of my affected impatience we actually got out and saw a lot of Cyprus, thankfully we were in an interesting and beautiful country.

This morning we were up early and ready, then sat waiting for the transport—that would take us to Troudos a trip that was paid for already. We were at the bar drinking coffee when we discovered that our lift had been here for us already.

Further investigation revealed that the driver had been given the wrong chalet number, he had knocked on the door and woken up another couple apparently, a confused and unimpressed chap with holiday hangover had opened the door then sent him away.

We were horrified and feared that we had missed out on the day, but the tour company was called by the bar staff and they came back for us.

Chris the driver apologised, profusely, for the simple mistake. But I shrugged at the handsome man and smiled widely, "Don't worry. You're here now".

The drive up into the mountains was interesting, the new scenery was stunning and Chris was incredibly chatty about everything, our driver pointed out the curry plant and the Moufflons—a rare and wild sheep—amongst other things.

We stopped at the Caledonian waterfalls, this is where it started to get worthy of note in my opinion, the lovely man Chris held my hand to help me on the steep uneven footing. I didn't want him to let go—I had no idea where Scoutman was at this point.

Chris picked a pretty wild flower and gave it to me, I am grinning widely with the memory as the letters hit the page, ah. The flower is stuck in my scrap book, although it is now dry and brown, it still makes me smile.

He was luverly.

Kykkos was a monastery that we just had to go into, but shorts and bare shoulders were not permitted, handily outside there was a market stall that hired appropriate clothing. This was where all the charity shop rejects ended up I'm sure. But needs must, I got a big pink nylon skirt and Scoutman got some mank trousers, Chris took a fashion shot of us for future reference.

The religious building itself was amazing, I have never seen so much gold, anything that was still for any amount of time was attacked with a layer of gold leaf.

Spectacular and well worth the fee of a pink blancmange skirt, paired with the old baggy trousers.

This day was packed with activity and a wild salmon farm, somewhere up in them there hills, was next. Chris held my hand (!) to help me up the steps and I was happy to have lost Scoutman again. No really, I was.

We went further up Mount Olympus, the views were amazing and I was at the front of the jeep with Chris now, we stopped in a small but busy village. Here we spotted a familiar face sitting with a woman and drinking coffee, can't remember his name, they were filming for a holiday/travel programme. We tried, unsuccessfully, to get into the background but then got bored and went to explore.

Found the glass blowing chap, I fell in love with almost everything he had on display and told him so, if you see my front room my penchant for glass objects is obvious and collecting dusty spiders.

I gushed appropriately, but explained that what I liked was beyond my budget, when I am rich he should be sought out. As we left a yell was heard, we turned to see this artist running towards us with something in his hands. He smiled at me as he handed over a piece of his work, it was a reject and a little flawed but nevertheless a beautiful chunk of glass. I was incredibly touched and I kissed him thanks, he grinned then turned away and ran back to his studio.

Now it was time to go back to the resort and I was talking to Chris, he was funny and he made me laugh, but he had other passengers so left. Back at our digs we showered and changed to go to the bar outside.

To finish and end a good day a lot of talk and alcohol passed our lips, easily done to quench a greedy thirst with pleasant company and foreign currency. I wobbled precariously to the toilet block, but because I made it without any mishaps, then since my underwear was still dry I went back to the bar. As you do, just one or two more— come on everyone does it! It wasn't until I pushed myself off the barstool, to leave, that the amount of alcohol I had consumed and was filling my legs became apparent. The man engaged with my slurred departure followed my eyes, to the floor, as my legs forgot what they were doing and simply concertinaed under my weight. I was suddenly, with no warning, talking to his knees. The bar erupted with laughter, as strangers rushed to help me back to my feet, I sniggered with embarrassment and fell into Scoutman's supporting arms. Then with relieved bravado I waved them all off, to assure them everything was alright, as we left.

A few steps down and around the pool, thereby avoiding the visions of a big wet accident, then we swayed down the path to get to our apartment. There was a small bush, at the end and this walkway … that continued to the left going behind the apartments. Here we both swerved and fell into this shrubbery, on our backs we started laughing as we gazed at the stars in a clear sky.

Then Scoutman had his sniggering hands on my bottom, to push and guide me, so the final flight of steps didn't result in a local emergency room.

Another day and I had booked us on a shopping day, that included visits to a market then a lace-making village and a free 'blanket tour'. Where they give you a glass of cheap and cheery plonk, then encourage you with a free raffle, before trying to flog you an expensive mattress. Scoutman just tagged along to humour me he really had nothing better to do, it is true to say that these madcap outings were my brain waves. I take full responsibility, but he was good for carrying wacky purchases. I bought a gorgeous sample of hand-made lace from a wizened old lady, sitting on her doorstep in the small village, the toothless and smiling brown face convinced me to invest in her art. Then I left it, forgotten, on the coach.

I told the people at the bar in our resort, they reacted and rang the tour company, but I never saw the lace again.

We bought some sweet red wine and looked around the small cottage, where it was made, this was supposed to be saved to take home. But it got consumed in the bedroom bar, we had to buy yet another corkscrew from the supermarket down the road.

The woman behind the counter was always chatty with me, in the shop that sold everything from food to cheap wine and beach ware, she told me to stop smoking then I could save money and afford to come back to see her. Good idea.

This has reminded me to tell you more about a chapter in my life, that continues to haunt me, I started smoking when I was nineteen and fell for a dashing smoker. My parents had been nicotine addicts themselves, but had managed to stop the habit, both of them became ex smokers.

Unfortunately their daughter (me) had a new partner, and a new pastime. Went off to do student things for four years and he was still with me, then a month before my FINALS he ended the relationship on the phone. Confused? You will be, he turned up from miles away the next evening, he gave me a huge bouquet of red roses, then declared that he had made a mistake and he was sorry.

He left the next morning and I never saw him again, not sure how I know but I believe he married someone else six months later?

I was devastated at the time, but still managed to sit my exams and got my degree, "All men are bastards". My tutor was right, I should have become a celibate nun or something then.

Anyway, I obviously had no idea where he was now and so sent an advert for my book to his parents. Thinking that they would forward it, but they chose to ignore it or binned it.

Nothing happened, so I forgot all about it and shrugged away the thought, but I'd tried. Nothing ventured and as it happens nothing was gained.

I have a post office box specifically for book orders, to protect the identity of my home address, it was a few weeks later that a letter came and I vaguely recognised the hand writing.

It was him.

But he hadn't seen my letter, apparently in a curious and reflective moment, he had typed my name on the keyboard and instructed his computer to search for me.

www.gillianfirth.co.uk is what he got, then he was slapped hard with the surprising news of my devastating accident.

In response he ordered a copy of Gillian Mk 2, writing with his thoughts when he had poured over my work, by all accounts he was impressed, " … a triumph … compulsive …". Then I was secretly, nay stupidly, harbouring romantic thoughts of reconciliation and long lost love.

By odd coincidence my ex husband had the same name, also they were both graphic designers!
Told you I should have become a celibate, putting it out of circulation, nun.

I now had his telephone number and couldn't resist the temptation, against better judgement, it was an odd thrill to hear his voice again. The memories of being a young student, carefree and in love, waiting for the arranged public phone to ring, were in my thoughts.
He even sounded the same, after all these years, then my brain was thrown into a time warp as he uttered in a grin, "One two".
His nickname given to two freckles on my right breast, I stammered in thought and giggled like silly a girl, "You remember?".
"Of course", he laughed, this is when and why I was intrigued/ conceited enough to follow this innocent remark up.

In my defence I also wanted him to assist me with my latest idea, for more publicity, it is who you know not what and he might be able to or want to help me?
Incidentally I didn't mention my bosoms, he did and therefore was responsible … inadvertently—whatever … for my needy reaction.
Eventually he text me and requested that I stopped all contact!
How embarrassing, I was dumbfounded by the rebuttal, but deleted him from my mobile phone and life. I only called him once or twice too.

It has been an absent characteristic for many years, but I now dream in my sleep. Not only about literary world domination—Darlink, they are usually connected with life events that have rocked my boat and disturbed me.

So anyway waking up in Cyprus was a good memory, there were days when I hadn't planned anything to kill our free time, I was happy just sitting on the beach in the sunshine. It has to be said doing absolutely nothing on holiday is a good day out too—we had marched down to the beach which was going past the supermarket selling cheap cigarettes. Method in madness … brilliant.

I had fallen asleep and I am just trying to imagine this picture, of that glorious feeling when you are stretched out and the sun is warming your skin. But it is grey and miserable here, the central heating is gurgling as a distracting reminder, the jumper and the woolly tights are not conducive to sunny thoughts either.

Scoutman had surfaced from under the large beach umbrella, then gone straight into the café, I sat waiting for the milky coffee and lit a cigarette. A couple of men arrived and sat near, they both started chatting to me, when the caffeine arrived a few more men were in the group and I was enjoying the attention. They turned out to be soldiers and didn't move, when my man in big shorts came back

They wanted us to make up the numbers, on a banana boat ride, my immediate reaction was yippee and then my brain caught up. I swim like a brick and the sea is deep, as in there's no tiled floor to stand on, when you fall or slip in the water. I was experiencing a moment of foreboding panic. The boys all reassured me, that they would dive in to rescue me, then told me I could wear a life-jacket. They were laughing with anticipation for the ride, so would they think about my dilemma, when we all climbed onto the big yellow banana.

It was a real buzz, when abroad if you have the opportunity I highly recommend that you take it, had the inflatable been any smaller it would have shot from between my legs. I was squeezing so hard with my effort to stay on.

One person did fall off and was temporarily abandoned, out at sea, it wasn't me I had to be prized off the yellow plastic. My legs were seized up, in gripping mode. Scoutman was the weakest link, I laughed too much with relief, when he struggled back onto the banana and everybody was sniggering at him.

Just sitting and resting in a castle ... because I can.

We met up with these men that evening, at a resort of a village in the hills, it was a loud and lively spot.

The entertainment was an added bonus and the alcohol was flowing, into my wobbly legs again.

I always manage to get home, admittedly I often need a little too much help and guidance, then with the precautions taken in the underwear and urine department I even had dry pants.

These safety measures are christened my 'wee pads', a non too sexy and bulky protective layer in my knickers, for those moments when I have drunk too much then invariably left it a little late: to locate and tackle a strange toilet. A catheter would come in useful at these times.

But no I have to stumble to the chore, finding the toilets means kicking almost every chair en-route and clumsily knocking into people holding drinks. I'm still controlling my bladder at this point. I should imagine that I look very stupid and deserve the sneers, the looks of pity or disgust and the snide comments about my alcoholic state, generally I take little notice. Partly because I've heard them all before, even when I'm sober, but more so as I am on a mission to get to the toilet before I have a real accident.

But when I'm getting near, or see the word toilet, the trouble begins.

My fuddled brain jumps ahead, to start thinking about the mechanics, fumbling with buttons or zips and not wetting myself are the foremost thoughts … not walking.

It's when I get behind closed doors … all is forgotten, to clench and to hold everything in check. The ensuing panic is onset with a wail of anguish, through gritted teeth, as I wiggle and rip at garments frantically in desperation not to wet anything.

I always get there, quite amazing really considering, then crash around appropriately in the usually small cubicle.

I no longer take much notice, of what thoughtless and crass people say, the ignorant remarks are largely ignored, unless I am meant to hear their educated and clever observations. It's too rude and ignorant to even acknowledge.

"Look at the state … how pissed is she?", that's one of my favourites and makes me want to reply, "Have *you* got an excuse? Or a mirror?". But I know that at best I'd be wasting my time and at worst I'd get a mouthful of drunk abuse.

So it really isn't worth the effort and I just keep going, getting into silly and unpleasant discourse isn't my idea of fun really, sometimes wishing that I still used a walking stick.

If I'm out on the town with Truffle it's a different story, she will sometimes be on my arm—blind leading the blind, I have to physically guide her away from confrontation: as she verbally reacts and tries to explain to these morons. Her speech becomes an angry, incoherent garble. Bless her little socks, for trying to enlighten the masses. "Ignore them, ASSHOLES!", that's how I react, then they are dismissed and we get on with our lives—I forcibly move her onwards.

But I am a yellow belly and don't say this to their faces, it's for Truffle's ears only.

But we are still on holiday and there was a Cypriot night, at the local restaurant, we had to go. A selection of food was delivered to the table, until it was covered almost entirely with little dishes. The entertainment was a wailing blur but we had to stay and watch. We, I can speak for both of us, had eaten most of the table and drunk so much that we couldn't actually move!

We rolled and swayed back up the road, eventually getting to our apartment.

It was on the beach that I was shocked, to suddenly be made aware that I was becoming comfortably round with feet. A rude awakening, the bikini had been bought and worn last year, the top had exploded to hit Scoutman in his grinning face. I groaned and modestly covered my nipples then noticed the boobs were getting bigger, nice one … but, so big they were hiding the extended waistline.

This was a problem, my weight had never been an issue before, I didn't like it and would do something on our return.

In my previous life, when I was fit and active, it had been easy. I was able to do various activities that burnt off the calories.

Not anymore, the odd sit-up here and there would be like the proverbial chocolate fire-guard, I knew I needed help so joined a slimming group. First time for everything.

At the initial weigh in I genuinely gasped with disbelief, then laughed and shook my head in wonder that I hadn't really noticed until now, eleven and a half stones. Blimey … I have never been more than nine and a half before.

I was given the book, bible, detailing the weight loss eating regime. One chap there had lost five stones and was still going (he ate five chickens a day … free food) so the routine of green days and red days alternated worked.

It was quite straight forward and didn't take long to translate: free foods … salads are good, sins … fast food is out, stick to the routine and don't cheat.

I was surprised, you were allowed to consume a limited amount of sins to keep life interesting, whilst working out what I could have as a treat it was duly noted that one fast food burger was the same as three glasses of wine. So I saved all my sins for the weekend, for the rest of the week the plan had been adhered to … rigidly.

At the meetings it does get a little predictable, as in awards were given in recognition of high figures, but she didn't shout it out or make a big fuss if anybody had gained a few pounds.
One week I was two pounds more, I was gutted, it really upset me.
Bro told me to go to the toilet before the meeting.
I did lose the extra two stones, then because I thought it had been sussed I stopped going. I put weight back on, of course, but not that much and I could wear baggy clothes or suck it in.

My last and rather poignant thought, regarding this beautiful country (I'm talking about Cyprus), involves a visit to Nicosia the capital city.

We were walking around the shops and cafes, in the sunshine, the loud brightness was energetic with locals and holiday makers. In the middle of all this was a built up barrier and it was effectively making one part of the town inaccessible.
It was the Green Line?
This had to be seen and demanded closer inspection.

There were a few steps up to a platform, then you could look through the windows in this wall, to see a different world. My shocked silence was the response.
I had to turn back, firstly to look at the tanned and smiling faces behind me, then to confirm that we were still in a happy holiday zone. What I could see on the other side was a cold and grey pile of devastation. The scenery was still and haunting, like the stage set of a ghost town, here in black and white were the visible results of violent conflict. Where you could only imagine that lives were taken, quite

unreal when behind you there is such a direct comparison, the noise of normality becomes blinding and pretentious.

I found this quite disturbing and was reduced to pensive thoughts. Then got off the platform, to rejoin the throng of talkative shoppers, 'lest we forget'. But, as I agitated the froth on my cappuccino, the holiday mode returned and the lessons were put out of mind.

This did remind me of an equally tormenting image, stored in my memory bank. It's an enlarged photograph of a pile of gold fillings—removed from Jewish teeth in the second world war.

Seen at the holocaust museum, Yad Vashem, in Israel.

But with modern world distractions, retail therapy with coffee and cakes, we do forget.

Look at the daily news bulletins, our world is in a selfish and greedy mess, I should be a leader putting my money where my mouth is!

Anyway, enough of this maudlin talk—after all Scoutman and I are on jollydays.

As usual when we got back to our home turf of grey land, displaying the variation of our off white complexions, we were asked if we had actually been in the same country?

Then, after I had explained about Scoutman with his big shorts and lashings of sun cream, I was complimented on my healthy glow: he wasn't as he didn't have one. So I am turning into a leather handbag and he's happy, well he might have burnt his delicate skin sitting under the big umbrella, he is of course right and you do have to be careful.

Back to routine and donning my chef's whites I took control, to get the scouts organised, we set about the required elements for their cookery badge. It was all taken, then delivered, very seriously and the boys did well. I was in my element and was happy to perform, in the teaching role, they were enthused enough to plan a menu and cook a three course meal for their invited families.

They actually did a good job, my mum and dad paid compliment to the giddy boys, I just made them clear their mess up to finish the task. I didn't have to lift a finger with a big woggle, they all got their merits to sew onto their uniforms ... they all did well.

The dinner party was held in the main hall and the guests sat under the mural, it was a large and imposing depiction of a scout camp.

At one meeting I had the boys drawing on lining wallpaper, then it was all pasted to the wall, it was good and messy fun. We made it part of the artist badge requirements, well I'm not too sure about my interpretation but they enjoyed it.

A few of the parents had my book, one particular mother has a mentally disabled daughter and now makes a point of snubbing me in the street? I don't know why nor do I care, the others are fab and compensate in buckets for this woman's weird behaviour. Odd.

So Scoutman and I were working out to be a good team, we performed well together, well he simply followed the orders: but it did get him off his stagnant bottom.

Occasionally he bought me flowers, typically as an apology for him being crap, sometimes because he loved me and I was good for him. But he was good for me too. Not because I dropped massive hints, or occasionally and poignantly moved the empty vase.

On a whim I took him to Amsterdam, for a long weekend, I love it here the diversity of scenery and life fascinates me. We travelled by ferry, for this trip, and chose to occupy a reclining chair to snooze the journey away.

This made financial sense at the time, never again, seriously I am never doing this again.

Firstly we had to get there and pay to park the car, additional costs already, then on the big boat we had a couple of drinks at the bar to kill a few of the evening hours—sailing in black sky on black sea.

The crossing was rough and I could not walk at all well, across the moving deck to locate our reserved chairs, Scoutman had to carry both of our rucksacks and support me. Only then you are thinking, that just maybe the consumption of alcohol was not the most brilliant of ideas?

Trying to sleep or even doze in a space full of giggling and talking teenagers, all eating bloody crisps, was not a good idea either … just silly. Not at all disastrous if you are one of the youths, we grumbled and concurred that we were too old: to be messing about with communal sleeping arrangements in chairs and with the cumbersome baggage. Next time, we decided, a cabin would be utilised.
No. I disagreed vehemently, when I had crashed back from a trek to the bathroom (which I swear was on the other side of this floating roller-coaster), we are flying next time.
There was no argument, from the bloodshot eyes and sleepy head of Scoutman.

Standing on the motionless land we still had to get to the train station, to catch the next link into Amsterdam, we were still miles away. For some reason we actively dismissed the waiting busses and Climbed into a taxi. Nearly twenty pounds later, the driver may have seen us coming, with our tired eyes and 'tourist' stickers on the forehead. Now we were at the busy train station and my walking had deteriorated to a limping shuffle. Why I wore and travelled in those stupid boots, vain and heeled, was beyond me, obviously I had not really thought about at all: but it didn't cross my mind that we would be drifting about and walking for so long!

In Amsterdam, the city of waterways, at last. But we had to find the cheap and pre booked hotel. When on the phone I had asked if the room was en-suite? They had said yes, this was ideal, so I had booked it: note it had nothing to do with Scoutman.
We had to get another taxi, to find the building, it took us on a tour around the city's one way system. Then it stopped: outside the hotel. Blimey, what a pain, we could see the train station from where we were standing.

The hotel looked alright, well it was a bit studenty, until we were shown to our room.
The requested double room had bunk beds, the en-suite was a sink in the corner, with a rubbish bin, the wallpaper was peeling off the damp and dirty wall.

Well. We were horrified and screwed up our noses, but it was cheap, the sheets were clean and breakfast was included.
So with a shrug we threw the mattresses together, they just fit on the floor, it was no problem and we coped. I used the plastic bin to empty my bladder in the night … well … it was better than stumbling around the strange corridors and trying to find the shared toilet

We emptied the bin into the sink in the morning, then went downstairs for breakfast.
The young chap, waiting the tables, smiled and asked me, "Do you want eggs?".

I nodded and asked him if there was anything else? He smiled at me again, "Fried or boiled".

So eggs it was, with plenty of bread and milky coffee, a fine way to start the day and you couldn't really expect anything else for twelve pounds fifty.

We visited many of the art galleries, when we found them, I cannot believe that we were so lost all the time. Scoutman has got badges, the city is all grids and canals so other than direction signs (in Dutch) it could not be any easier. It wasn't until we had been walking, for what seemed a long time, that I stopped the man holding the plan. I now sighed deeply and glared at him.

"Where are we? Are we nearly there yet?". (bloody annoying child)

I had my whining and fed up of walking voice on, he too sighed heavily and looked at the paper then at me. He thrust the details in my face and with his finger traced our steps, "We went down here, across here, down here, round here and down here".

I stopped him and shrugged, "So where are we?".

He sighed again and dropped his arm then rolled his eyes, "We're here!", he shook the map in his hand.

Now I sighed sarcastically and looked at his clueless face, annoyed that we had been walking and stumbling about for so long, "You don't know where we are do you? You've got us lost again haven't you?".

It should and would have been funny, if I wasn't so demanding and impatient. Horribly so ... well we'd been on foot a while.

We did find a few of the tourist attractions, usually by mistake, as we walked past them trying to find something else. Amsterdam certainly has a lot to see, for a relatively small city.

We wandered around Madame Tussauds, the waxwork museum, where we paid for a photograph taken with Pierce Brosnan—on inspection it looks like I have his gun coming out from the back of my head. Another attraction we chose to visit, being responsible adults we just had to, the Sex Museum.

Well!

It begins by showing the Victorian depiction of pornography, the odd titillating shoulder led us onto more modern interpretations, around the corner it became more graphic: I am quite literally an ignorant prude. I had to laugh at the fetish section, as the rubber clad bodies had goggle eyes and breathing apparatus, then was shocked and disturbed by the next entries that seemed focussed on pain?

This exhibition of pleasure through the ages was now lost on me, we made our way out but not before seeing the final picture—I think it's called beastiality? The computer's highlighted this as an error, so maybe not? Whatever it is, enough said.

Really.

Then we went straight into The Bulldog to partake of coffee and things, also to warm ourselves, each time I have been to Amsterdam it has been really cold and it's good that there are a lot of cafes.

A memory for you, one visit it was so bitter that the canal was FROZEN! Bro and I were wearing our bath towels, tucked under our coats.

I have lost the photograph taken of the canal, so can't show you but believe me it was not the appropriate temperature to be stumbling about aimlessly.

My timing was a perfect pain in the arse on this trip, I have the joy of a menstrual cycle now, unfortunately I am never prepared and do not have an organised memory.

I sat in the hotel, packed with a mattress of toilet paper in my knickers, whilst I waited for my poor brother to firstly locate a pharmacy and then to purchase some tampons for me. I do love him and am lucky he is so bloody good, the weekend away was his twenty first birthday present from me and he bought his sister tampons in Amsterdam Mmm that's a good one to store.

Incidentally, I have never had any rude stares or hurtful comments at any time here, I love the place. Probably because there are so many distractions and sights, variety is the spice of life after all and I just blend in, nobody takes any notice of me or my disability …

The finale to this year, basically a celebration that Scoutman now had a passport, was another end of season holiday. Spain was convenient for a week—self catering and cheap of course.

Roquetas De Mer, shan't be going there again. The travel agent had said, "There's not much there", but we ignored her. We were convinced that we'd find something and it would be alright.

On the day we arrived there was a gale, we watched the crashing waves from a safe distance, it was fortunate that we travelled in coats, by avoiding the rain we discovered that most of the shops were closed. We admired the building site(s) from our balcony, noting that you could almost see the sea but had no chance of a picturesque coastline. Then I turned to shrug at Scoutman, he had developed a cold sore the size of a dinner plate, fabulous.

It was the end of the season and so the in-hotel entertainment was limited to bingo, honestly that was it.

We did go down for this and were surprised, that not only were we the youngest people there, we were the only British contenders. Holiday bar bingo, you know what it's like, I had to keep asking my partner what number had just been called as the French and German then Arabic kept distracting me.

I kept thinking that I'd recognise the numbers, did two of the languages at school and have lived in Saudi Arabia, but no. Then I kept missing, or forgetting, the English.

We didn't win and it took ages.

The bar across the road did Tapas, basically bribed you to stay and drink more alcohol, offering little tit-bits of food with each purchase from the bar. The theory worked and we consumed most of the proffered menu.

Which meant a rather precarious weave back to our rooms, thankfully there was a lift to stumble into, the grommet on his chops was not particularly appealing and so our state wasn't so important or disastrous. We found another bar and the Tapas offerings had to be explored, but it was a bit of a trek which wasn't a problem at the beginning of the night, against better judgement we did hike there again in the week but mainly because there was little choice and the Tapas was nice ...

Bathing in the glorious sunshine was not on the agenda, nor was frivolous shopping for needless keepsakes or unusable gifts, we had to find something else to do .

Planet Hollywood was still open, so it was booked for a day out, the movie capital past the sea of plastic greenhouses. It was where Spaghetti Westerns were filmed, but was now reduced to a money making tourist attraction. It was quite good, well it was the best and only thing we did worth mentioning. The photographs were a little limited, but all in all it was nice to have a change of scenery—even though the weather was much the same. How annoying.

But thankfully it did improve, not much, so we didn't have to wear our coats all week.

The only other thing we did, just remembered, was one night we went along to a car show?
I know, but there was nothing else on and it was different. I'll say. Ordinary cars balancing on these massive wheels, the vehicles bounced around at high speeds, travelling up and down the arena, then the show was over.
Mm.

An interim: Watched something on television last night, about nuisance telephone calls, it reminded me to tell you about this.

Gillian Mk 2 was finished and I was sitting at the computer, being a writer Sweety, composing my homework to be read in a writing class the next day. When the phone rang. A male voice told me that he was doing an interview, for Woman's Own, Darlink. I immediately got giddy: automatically thinking that this was in direct response to my work—which was out and in the public domain.

He asked me if I had time to answer a few questions?
Bloody hell yes, already fired up and raring to go, I would do anything to get recognition, world domination thoughts were buzzing and nodding clearly in my head again.

"How many sexual partners have you had?". I flinched with surprise, what a strange question.
I wasn't expecting that—but answered him anyway, "One or two". I laughed.
High with discovery, with a scatter-brain nature, I started waffling about the book—extolling it's virtues and popularity.

He interrupted me, "Have you had sex with two or more people at a time?". Although taken aback I did reply again, I was blasé with my answer as this was really none of their business, but now I was shaking my head and losing interest.

I wanted to talk about Gillian Mk 2.

He would not deter me, I even asked my interviewer if he'd read my work?

He came back, "Do you like anal sex?". I snorted now with thought … these questions are a bit naughty and nosey for a woman's weekly? But again I responded, "Ooee. No", bloody hell.

There was a brief pause then I carried on, "You really should buy the book and read it yourself".

I was still talking when he blurted, "Gillian I want to f*** you!".

Still I was chatting, "I get a lot of praising letters from my readers". Told you I would not be put off and he groaned, "Gillian did you hear me? I want to f*** you".

I gasped as the penny dropped.

"Oh no!", I suddenly felt sick and stupid, "I've been scammed".

He simply repeated his desire, slowly, with a sneering and creepy voice.

In reaction I blurted, "Give me your name and number then I can call you back", I couldn't think of anything else to say. But that was good enough, I heard him make a guttural sigh as he answered, "David". Then he gulped and put the phone down.

Of course his number had been withheld, I did check and well … I was stunned. I was actually disturbed by this and a little fearful of the consequences. I had given my name and address, but I was annoyed with myself for being so vulnerable and dim-witted.

Alright an egotistical, slow and dozy, Darlink.

When I told Scoutman he shook his head and laughed?

When I professed, embarrassed, outrage he then agreed that it was an infringement of liberty and that I had been a bit silly.

The next day I told Spruce Girl and she too sniggered, "Classic! Only you would try to sell a book on the phone to a pervert!". I nodded in foolishness and shook my head, then grinned at the funny side, "He didn't buy one though".

She allayed my fears though confirmed my rash stupidity, "Your name and address are in the phonebook anyway. But what are you like?".

I could only indicate agreement, well I had got a bit carried away, it was ultimately a disturbing episode, but how dare a pervert call me at my home and invade my space with his filth.

Now the catering stint was at an end, the checked trousers and chef whites were packed away, but when the course was over I had been nominated by my tutors to receive an award. An acknowledgement of Effort and Achievement, presented at a ceremony in the Abbey. It was a good time and my parents were there to see this, I was glad and it vaguely made up for my missed graduation (at the time I was inconsolably gutted and could not be bothered—with this pointless once in a lifetime event? Stupid woman). People were pleased and proud of me, I did posh with mascara and got a nice photograph of me with the certificate.

The well known head injury charity group in York was thriving, we had a lot of members with an eclectic range of ages and skills, the gathering of people was interesting. Their injuries were achieved in a variety of ways, from illness to accidental damage, but we all had something in common. Other than being people coping, daily, with the after effects of an acquired brain injury.

We are human beings that had normal and fully functioning lives once, none of us chose to lead such a changed and alternative existence—by the way.

We individually bumped along and coped with day by day routines, then collided at a bar in kinship once a month.

One of the symptoms, associated with TBI, is an appalling and unreliable short term memory. Quite funny really, we all knew each other well by sight but couldn't remember each others names.

Actually they all knew mine, maybe because I had got involved with the committee and was responsible for entertaining them, but most probably because I demand attention and encouraged them to look at my book?

I loved it and was finding time to write the quizzes and mess about with photo fits, by dismantling numerous magazines. My dad got implicated and joined the committee, doubling with me, on the entertainment side. Scoutman also got involved, albeit grudgingly as in he wouldn't do anything extra curricula. But I too drew a line at the costly courses. Run by experts, I have no patience (true) so it makes me sick and cross. When these amateurs were addressing the implications and consequences of having a head injury, it would be like me lecturing on childbirth

Ask me, pay me loads of money, I'll tell you. Je sait tu sait. (I know you know).

This attitude went down well with our area manager, I'm not being catty when I describe her as a bag with a badge (bitchy is: fat old bag with a badge), who would occasionally come to the meetings and take over with boring waffle.

Once Fat Badge took time out to arrange a beetle drive for us clients, lucky us, incidentally nobody asked her to do this. A friend grabbed my attention, he was writing a book himself, he had asked me to share my experience and help him.

Fat Badge passed me, as I was making my way to the fellow writer, then she asked if I was going to join the beetle thing. Scoutman heard her cutting reply, when I declined saying that I was going to talk with one of the other clients.

Fat Badge looked down her nose at me, "Well don't be surprised when nobody wants to join in with the things you arrange". We were stunned and watched her as she flounced off, with her head tilted back and off-side, in a whiff of bullshit.

Scoutman looked at me in astonishment, then smiled and shrugged, "I'll do it". I laughed in response, "I'm not", then I went to talk to my friend in the wheelchair … who was trying his best to make his mark. Afterwards Scoutman complained to me and shook his head, in disbelief, it had been organised incorrectly. The bored clients were just drawing beetles—without rolling the dice.

Then they just gave up, to wander and talk, when the paper ran out.

At another meeting she singled me out, with her nastiness again. She had the room's undivided and expectant attention, we were waiting for her to get fascinating. She was loving the quiet attention, warranted by the badge, then in her important voice asked us, "Has anybody done anything interesting they would like to tell us about?".

Cue Gillian.

I looked around and nobody in the group had reacted so I put my hand up, Fat Badge rolled her eyes but smiled politely at me, "Yes Gillian".

I blurted out, maybe too smugly, "I've written a book!".

I was smiling-well grinning—and nodding at this point, she flapped her hand at me in dismissal, "Yes, yes, yes, we know all about that".

She smirked at me with clasped hands and then started talking. About what she'd done with her son's brilliant group, then how marvellous she was. I looked at my parents, with raised eye brows, my mouth was open but speechless in dismayed shock.

My dad, who's diplomatic to a fault, shrugged at me and whispered, "Just let her go on".

But I had taken offence and was disturbed by the rude, unprofessional and narrow minded, approach displayed by this stupid woman here, standing before us and representing a well known head injury charity. Gasp for breath. Grrr

On the way home my mum was grumbling, vocally, with a dawning realisation.

Reacting with hindsight, at this woman's comment, "She should have been full of praise for your achievements and let you speak! I should have said something. Told her that you've done this on your own. I should have spoken and told her what I thought. How dare she speak at you like that".

Now it was my turn to act with decorum, but I was still annoyed, "She's a bag with a badge, full of her own importance, I don't need her".

Then we turned to my dad who was the peacemaker, he nodded and agreed, "We need her until we get a new chairman but, she is rubbish".

Initially when I had told her about my book she had shown no interest, explaining to me, "If I bought a copy of everyone's book, I'd be out of pocket". Then she had laughed.

It wasn't funny, nor was she, so I didn't smile or pursue this point. I don't like her nor did I care whether or not she shared my story. Couldn't even be bothered to ask about all these other books on offer? I know of only one head injured author, me.
Silly cow.
Honestly. I don't appreciate her attitude ... at all, not one little bit! So there.

I did talk about the book a lot though, little encouragement was needed for me to go into writer mode, we were picking up reprints regularly. I can't help it, but whatever I'm doing and saying works, I'm not at all troubled if the book is taken to shut me up.
I do feel a little smug, sorry but I can't help this either, when they order more copies of Gillian Mk 2—as impromptu and special presents. (Ha, see told you, the gob works)
Each new batch of reprints made me panic, even though some people were ordering more than one, word of mouth was working but I was still fearful of being stuck with them. They had to be sold.

Oh yeah—we have girls at scouts now, the boys like it sometimes. I'm alright about it, with a more the merrier outlook, and we need the subs money. With equality and as a sign of the times it was bound to happen, I suppose, but there is a girl guide facility upstairs. They too are struggling but, I wonder, will they accept boy guides?
Do they already?

Do you know what?

I thought that writing this book would be a doddle, a walk in the park as it were, easy peasy lemon squeezy, but it's not.

I don't walk with automatic grace anymore and I'm definitely not a writer, so goodness knows where this notion came from.

Oh I know.

When Gillian Mk 2 was ready I was convinced that any publisher would, do somersaults, sign me up to get a slice of the pie. Blame the writer's circle, for laughing at the right bits, the feedback coming to me so far had been exceptionally good.

But after four rejection slips, a writing friend told me he's decorated his spare bedroom with all of his, I got all impatient and determined when I found out about the self-publishing. With nothing to stop me I forged ahead, the rest is history, but the fan mail that has been collected asks about the sequel.

As in, when is it going to happen? I have a few orders already. (ooo)

A lot of readers have said they want to know what happens next, I feel obliged and want to spill the beans, told you I have become a Darlink.

A disabled woman wrote and told me, " … count yourself up there with Alan Titchmarsh, your two are the only books I've read", I did meet her and she is very clever—she often sends me examples of her painting and they're brill.

Another disabled reader, from Scotland, bought the book as it was recommended by her friend. Subsequently the Wee Lassie has given herself the title, "I'm your number one fan".

She and her girlfriend (No 2 fan) are coming down here to meet me in a few months, they're taking me for lunch, I could get used to this. The Wee Lassie has already placed an order for Typically Gillian.

Isn't it strange how things happen?

One thing is certain you just never know, I have an ever more varied collection of people in my life now. Recently I went to see a clinical psychologist, who had met me previously. This person first saw and assessed me in 1995, when I was physically and mentally at my lowest point. She took a professional re-evaluation then smiled at me and said, "You are amazing, just look at you".

That was it. My mum was nodding fervently and grinning with delight again, by my side, the writer Darlink attitude keeps being stroked and encouraged. I disclaim responsibility, for anything, all I did was get on with it and just went with the flow.

There are still days when things are not so good, I am damned by and with a disabled life, times when the frustrations of limited choice and cruel comments by idiots make me physically ill.

The resultant headaches were so horrendous, I would have no other option but to retire.

When I told the head Dr chap about this he referred me to an acupuncture woman, I went along though was a little sceptical that sticking skinny needles anywhere would make any difference. At least would this eradicate these debilitating head pains, she was lovely and got to know me quite well as there were a few sessions.

I still get headaches but nothing like they were, so it must have worked, she eventually bought the book and was impressed. At a meeting she would tell me her thoughts, sharing and asking about the parts that made her laugh, then offered to proof-read the sequel.

Scoutman was pleased that she held season tickets for Old Trafford, Manchester United's home turf, he was more chuffed when she offered me her seats for a match she couldn't attend.

Scoutman whooped and told his brother, I am a good girlfriend and got carried away (surprised?) with face paint, on the train they did sit with me. I had a BIG red U drawn on my face and was sporting big red letters saying MAN as a hand-made tiara. Smart. But no photos were taken.

At the game I missed the action, mm Oh well. But the ball was tiny and hard to follow, I didn't jump up from my seat in time—well at all really .

Then I had to look up at him and ask, "What just happened?". Scoutman laughed when he glanced down and told me, "They scored!".

Then a little later he jumped up with all the other fans and cheered, they scored again!

I missed that one too.

This unfairness of mobility and speed is a tad frustrating, combined with the limitation of choice, to say the least. Wobbling to the bingo hall one day I passed a boy and a girl, they were just standing around and hangin'. They were mid-teens and being confidently loud, but then I stumbled and jarred in astonishment, unbelievable but I was actually meant to hear their sneering commentary.

"You had a drink lurve, you pissed? Or what? You had a few eh?", I was horrified but ignored them and continued walking, then was disturbed when they carried on!

"Pissed enough? Was it good?", they were sniggering like stupid little kids.

Goddamn—I think a growl ensued here—but really this was too much.

I stopped.

Turning back I paused and looked at their surprised faces, then started walking back towards them … on a mission, it was then I heard the boy gasp, "Oh Oh".

Now I was standing in front of the quiet youngsters, with direct eye contact, I explained, "I am disabled".
I tried not to grin, as they both squirmed and fidgeted with embarrassment, they seemed to react simultaneously, the boy pointed at his accomplice and stammered, "It was her … it was her!".
The poor girl was mortified and just mumbled, "I'm so sorry, sorry".

Then I was satisfied and jerked away, to lose money.
I do remember frequenting this entertainment (the bingo hall) whilst still in the wheelchair, some of the regulars often tell me how well I've done and have watched my progress with interest.
Scoutman comes with his own dabbers now but we don't sit in the same place each visit, though some do then get very vocal and disorientated if unbeknown somebody is at their table, we are not that sad.
But we do have winning pens and lucky pants, with a sad array of hopeful trinkets and charms displayed on the table for luck.
I'm kidding.

Back in the flat things were good, untidy and disorganised, with lashings of bird seed but alright. Spruce Girl was still coming three times a week, to sort me out and get me organised: to tackle daily routines and to make sure I paid the bills. Scoutman's rubbish was creeping into my space, giving Spruce Girl more things to clear up. She only said nice things about him and commented how besotted he was with me, I would just grin and nod, it felt good and right.

Nothing was said but I kept rearranging my cupboards, making spaces, to put his junk out of sight and to eliminate his presence. Of course having my belongings scattered and unruly, all over the flat, isn't a problem.

I have to, literally, be able to see the item I'm looking for. If the said item has been put away, tidily and where it's probably supposed to be, I have a slimmer chance of locating it at all or in time.

This dilemma is quite normal, you will find it when you are looking for something else, maybe later a mental spark will flash the whereabouts.

But by then it's forgotten why it was needed (how annoying), so I put it back in the same place—to be searched for again another day.

I have lived here a long time now, I'm getting better and can track down most things eventually.

Nay problem.

Spruce Girl remains invaluable and will eventually locate items, mostly important paperwork, that I am convinced have disappeared forever and may have been binned.

But now the front room needed decorating, although the Devon Custard (yellow and tar stained) still looked fresh and clean—under the pictures, it was time for a change and I had the willing able bodied workforce under my roof.

He was able to move the furniture and could hold a brush, so far so good, I was quite happy to daub paint everywhere and be really useful doing my bit. I was helping, although a little slow and clumsy, but was more useful put in charge of the refreshments.

The high ceiling is still barley beige, or something like that, I refused to let him paint it white because a) it's a time consuming pain in the bum to do b) I actually do like it as it is and c) he's not very good (wuss) with heights and ladders.

I was doing him a favour, he was just being a bloody boy scout on me—he insisted that we prepared everything. Miss Impatient Knickers here just wanted to get on with it, abandon any rational thoughts of time consuming routines, get on with making a visible difference. (Mess)

But I had no choice and did what he said, still managing to get emulsion everywhere. You always spill paint on the floor and drop painty things, it invariably lands on the carpet.

Ah, you say, but Scoutman covered the floor with old bed sheets!

But they move or get dragged. When you walk over them and don't pick your feet up, paint spills always manage to find the gap!

Moan, groan, but that sounds about right eh? Buttered toast and all that.

I'm good at making and creating mess but not so dedicated, it's boring, when it comes to clearing and cleaning up. Scoutman was good at that (handy), but even the boy scout could not get the spilt paint off the carpet, rearranging the furniture hid a multitude of sins and the sideboard did cover the spontaneous art attack on the carpet.

When you decorate and improve one room the other spaces start to look worn and shabby, so you have to keep going, the forth bridge syndrome, unless of course you are satisfied and happy to ignore the dodgy rooms.

The front room looked smart and it was tidy for a while, Joey got his cage cleaned and he too looked good for a short time.

Disability is an issue in most people's lives at one point or another, be it physical or mental though these factors are interrelated, there are days and times when it is more tiresome than others.

Generally I don't let my disadvantaged existence get the better of me, but I am no super hero so of course it's a dreadful pain in the arse sometimes adapting with limited choices, even so I am aware of how far I have come. Blah blah ...
Big bottom, bulbous nose, floppy ears, thunder thighs, whatever, having an obvious and visible difference is not fun. Is it?
Trying to be normal (whatever that means) and out on the town with my man drinking, this always starts and seems like a good idea, there are occasions when too much of the falling down water works and I fall down.

The staff on the cameras in town could have a betting system in operation, will she or won't she?
Yep, thar she goes! Oh excellent, the boyfriend's down too! Is that extra points?

He was drunk as well, some solid saviour he was, being on your backside here is not quite as romantic or funny as abroad under the clear stars. Some of the tumbles have been in my car park, so near yet so far, therefore off—camera but it's still a pain in the bottom—and knees and wrists.
Thinking about it now I have been fortunate.
Not to have had serious damage or breaks to my person, or my escorts as it happens. Up to date that is.

The initial input that I had when I first moved here, from the rehabilitation unit—specifically for acquired brain injury, is less than it was as I have improved But Spruce Girl is still around, thank goodness, to sort any problems out.

Actually they are not really involved with my life at all, I did tell them about the book and had thought they would help me to promote my work. One or two of them did invest in my time—to read about themselves probably. But no help was forthcoming, what a disappointment.

I was toying with the idea of driving again, bugger messing about with public transport, I suppose that means another driving assessment will happen—but it's just got to be better than the last time.

If the instructor hadn't been there with dual controls, able to correct my haphazard steering, I would have demolished and ploughed through most of the front gardens in Derby.

But when bearing in mind the squabbles and unpleasantness with Scoutman, if he was going fast at night on dark roads, then the fact that I still get lost where I live. Oh yeah, then of course there is the lack of coordination and the epilepsy.

Mm. Maybe not.

But perhaps I'd be a better driver than passenger?

Just a thought.

Bandit and Truffle manage to drive with the use of one arm, Truffle's car is cleverly adapted, she's getting better with practice and is generally brilliant.

My thought is not a very good one: cars coming in the opposite direction are a bit of a deadly distraction, the speed and reckless manoeuvres of some simply scares the pants off me.

I have seen the most appalling behaviour on our roads, it makes me wonder how some people get their driving licences. They all cleverly avoid speed cameras, knowing where they are, then the police.

Have you seen the programme that is dedicated to police car chases? It is fascinating at first but eventually it makes me mad, when there are eight cars and a helicopter following one driver! What a waste of time, money and resources. If the police are behind you and stay there, with sirens and flashing lights, it is forewarning that you are expected to pull over and stop your vehicle. If you do not, within a reasonable time limit, then you are either a criminal with something to hide or you have no respect. Either way … shoot the tyres, that will make a big difference. This message should be part of the written test: Q You are breaking the law and the police are behind you. They want you to pull over. How long has the speeding driver got, after the request to stop, before their tyres are blown up?

I've had plenty of time, to become an annoying back seat driver—I'm becoming a 'Grumpy Old Woman' too. That's an extra bonus, with time to be perfected, the lack of discipline and respect nowadays drives me mad, well there's plenty to be grouchy about.

They don't want to be teachers or law enforcers (too dangerous), not when you can sing or go on Big Brother
It bugs me that the news reports let us all know, of the disgusting behaviour, then either blank the faces of these criminals or withhold the names! What's thc point in that?
Do know what's worse?

When the likes of the boys found guilty of child murder, Bulger case— you must know of that, are awarded a new life of opportunity with a changed identity. The parents of the children must have whooped with joy and praised our judicial system highly.

It's not right or fair that Maxine, the girlfriend of the child killer Ian Huntley, knew of his antics then lied in court and withheld vital information. Her punishment … she was awarded with a new life. What's going on?

My new life has not been recognised or rewarded by anybody.

Why aren't people held responsible for their actions and choice of behaviour?

Then why do they not pay the consequences?

Why have we not brought the death penalty back? An uncompromising penalty.

Some would argue, "What if they hang the wrong person?", I say speak to the victims of heinous crimes or to the tax—paying and law abiding public.

Mistakes do occur, I do not and cannot argue with that, shit does happen. But with the use of modern technology, new investigative techniques, that's less likely.

Some are destined to be in the wrong place at the wrong time, that's life for you … I do know all about that.

But still, watch the news, indecisive mollycoddling half measures don't work. Real laws would.

Law abiding and decent people, often struggling to get by, are not given the appropriate credit or compensation. They do not get hand outs or help with media coverage, I speak of people like my parents or my only brother.

Blimey time does fly, he has got a degree and two children now.

But he is not Dippy in Bed with Honours like me. He's got a science based qualification, a BSc, both my parents went to his graduation. So they are happy, at last they have got a photo of one of their smart ass kids in the cap and gown.

(Aunty Gillian—has no thought for their mother, since that day I was looking forward to the party and she told me, "We can't take you, you might embarrass me and I can't take that risk". You don't need me love. Years later she comments, "You mean when you upset me". Whatever … Prima Donna).

I'm not going to say anything else, though tempted, I adore Bro.

Anyway my niece and nephew are getting older, I love them even though they're not so cute now, I am their only blood aunty and so the poor things have no choice. They love me at Xmas, well all children are materialistic, they are very spoilt and have themed birthday parties with hired bouncy castles.

Blimey, what's wrong with musical chairs and jelly with ice-cream? They have to buy the birthday cake, because she doesn't and can't cook. But they have set up a chiropody business, that's doing well by all accounts … nice one, he does all the running around with home visits whilst she sits in their shop. But it's affording them the nice house on a hill, that he is having fun practising his DIY skills on—he's like a little child with a new toy.

He deserves good things he's a good boy, I mean man! He's thirty four now—time runs fast, but he's still my little and only brother.

With time and an improving (still) long term memory you can think too much, about past events and people that were in your life once. I suppose, or hope, this is quite normal.

To reflect on your life, sometimes with a smile, but often with hindsight—which is a luxury that you can do nothing with . As in: dwelling on your past, sometimes recognising mistakes, thinking how you could have done things in a different way and had alternative results. But—you wouldn't be where and what you are today.

That's a sobering thought, I might not be disabled or head injured in another chance, what would I have done then?

But I might not have survived either … I wouldn't be sitting here doing this and letting my forgotten coffee go cold again.

I was the Best Selling Author at the Art Circus, where GM2 was self-published, it was recognized and I was rewarded with publicity.

CHAPTER III

This Crazy Life—
continued. 2001

Now we are rolling and jerking—onto chapter three. I know!

My mum and friends keep asking me: "What page are you on now?". Then they shrug and laugh, "Is that all?", when I answer them truthfully.

Well what can I say? I haven't got a routine, though I know that I should.

I am still a bit muddled and get distracted easily (goldfish impersonator), then forget what I'm supposed to be doing—bugger.

My mum calls me her "flutterby"—others are not so flattering, but I am getting used to this scatty feature of a brain injury, it doesn't annoy me so much now.

It was Truffle's birthday yesterday, oops, I forgot. Not because I'm not bothered and she knows that, she forgets important things too, so it's alright.

What's not alright is the fact that she goes out of her way to point out that I'm older than her, she even told me that one of her male friends thought I was "Fifty two"!

No way! This briefly bothered me, it must be another girly trait. The birthday thing happens each year—funny that.

It's become a vicious circle of irritation, she told me yesterday that I look older and have more wrinkles! Cheeky cow!

If I was nubile and eighteen, or a bloke, maybe I wouldn't mind? I'll stop smoking and drink more water …

But still Gillian Mk 2 is on my mind, partly because I am occasionally stopped by smiling people who talk about it. Maybe it's the collection of fan mail that's accumulated. It could be because I have unoccupied space in my head i.e. it's no longer full of teaching, driving and able bodied life stuff etc …

My mum keeps telling me, "Get on with it … you cannot lay back and lie on your laurels. Your readers want another book, they have told you that and it won't do itself, so just get on with it!".

Aren't mums brilliant?

Enough waffling now I must get on.

The fires were lit under Gillian Mk 2, using the newspaper coverage from last year as combustible paper sticks, now it burst into flames of interest.

The freelance journalist that had covered my story got a result, his tenacious perseverance had paid off, a photographer for the Daily Express came to my home. Scoutman, who does shift work, was here with me and so got in the photograph as well. It was a nice sunny day, so the picture was taken outside, he hugged me in readiness for the camera and it was an event fringed with anticipation.

On the day the paper came out I bought about ten copies—as you do when you are featured in a national. I sniggered aloud, when I noticed the tiny photos of Liz Hurley and Britney Speares on the same pages. The picture of me and Scoutman swamped them, ha, it was a good feeling.

My journalist friend spoke to his contacts and I received an invitation, in the post, it was a time and date for a live interview—on Yorkshire television. Well I told everybody, but only people that lived locally could actually tune in.

It was all getting very exciting and I was expecting, or hoping, for great things along with the selective and high impact exposure. The local newspapers were good to me again, which of course meant more cuttings to collect. Some interest had been shown, as a result of the national newspaper, a woman in Oxford ordered the book. She wrote a long letter, telling me about her head injured son.

I wrote back and sent the letter with the book, each posted order included a note from the author.

Then I got organised, to locate my passport and pack all my summer clothes.

The timing was spot on, Scoutman and I had booked a cruise down the River Nile in Egypt, my debut television appearance was a week after we came back from jollydays.

So I will describe the week of the cruise first, an all singing and dancing float down the majestic river. It was better than anticipated, we discovered the brochure hadn't extolled the virtues of this trip for nothing, the sight of the big ship itself was exciting.

One week of gluttonous indulgence on the buoyant hotel, all the food the sightseeing trips and the onboard entertainment was included, we didn't even have to make the beds.

Not that I do anyway.

I tackle a golf ball of duvet most nights, if left to my own devices I would change the sheets—eventually. If they were grubby or crispy and the make-up smears were obvious on the pillows.

But better still just let Spruce Girl or Scoutman do it, but I am pleased when they do—it must be said.

I do like clean bedding, getting into a clean bed after a bath is a happy childhood memory, "I'm going to change my bed every day when I'm big".

I could talk out of my bum when I was little too.

Anyway back on the big boat.

The cabin boy assigned to us made animals and pretty patterns, with the bed sheets, they all did this apparently

The attention to detail makes for good tipping from happy campers, they were good though, he smiled a lot too and told me I was beautiful. That works as well.

But then he kept talking and told us how many children he had got, which was difficult to believe, he looked much too young.

(Technically I am—just—old enough to be a grandmother myself. So everybody is starting to look too young—to do grown up things).

Our first meal on the ship was dinner, it was waiter service and you had to get dressed up, where you sat on the first night was where you stayed for the rest of the week.

Of course we were late and being last in the dining room does limit your choice, fortunately we ended up near to the doors so we didn't have to walk past everybody, we sat in our glad rags and waited for the imagined gastro delight.

We were opposite a trio of trepid travellers, a married couple with her father, they had been on the same cruise a few times and were veterans of all involved. They were funny and quirky—at the beginning of the week anyway.

It didn't take long for us to hear, what seemed to be, their entire repertoire.

The first course was cream of chicken soup and it came with a sweet bread, they baked this staple onboard daily and it was yummy, then came steak and chips with an adapted tomato. Well.

The steak knife was useful, to saw through the strip of leather that was on my plate, the chips could only just be pluralized and when counted along with the six peas got into double figures.

The wife mumbled as she prodded her food, "They stuff tomatoes every day". She said this every day too, but we soon discovered that they really did. The husband was a big man, his extra weight affected his mobility, daily he contributed, "I'm on a diet". Usually whilst he was tucking into his wife's leftovers.

The old man was funny, at each and every meal, he moaned then growled, "All I want is an egg sandwich!". All this was invariably said with a full mouth.

The deserts always looked so pretty, we were silent with gluttonous admiration, great care had been taken with the presentation. But disappointingly they were just very sweet with coloured bits on.

As we left the table I was not happy, "We've got a week of this! What a nightmare!".

Scoutman sighed and tugged at his collar, "The bread was nice though".

The bar was a sharp shock, we silently perused the price list, "It's a bit expensive". Scoutman was gasping and gawping at the menu, when he had spotted his tipple.

Thankfully the glasses in front of us were the cheap (er) home brewed Egyptian lager, go figure. Even though we were on holiday, spending money was limited, we decided to pay the bar tariff at the end of each binge.

But from hereon we decanted our duty-free gin each night, to top up the bar tonic, hopefully they had already noticed my difficulties but might have wondered at Scoutman's altered mobility after a night of fizzy quinine?

The cabin boy left real flowers—as in not made from the sheets—on the bed for me, ah.
I don't care if he put flowers on every female bed on the boat, nor did I care that it might be a prompt for tipping. Whatever, he didn't have to do it. I'll bet you that all of the recipients smiled when they saw them. Even if they were picked up by Scoutman and moved from the bed to the bin. I didn't mind, they weren't kept or special—like the flower Chris (Cyprus) gave me.

The scrapbook begins the year with lots of Valentine cards, professing undying love and adoration, bloody men. It all started so well.
I had started smoking cannabis again, with a relaxed and happy mentality, on retrospect this was a selfish move going out with a non-smoker but I didn't entertain these thoughts.
I found that it helped me, not to get so frizzled and uptight with disappointing people and unpredictable situations, coping with the humdrums of routine and the chores of a disabled life. Maybe you are judging my choice, but that's what it was … a selection, since my options for escapism are limited, the alternative of an alcoholic fall is not always conducive to joyful times.

Then of course suffering the inevitable hangover in the morning, you all know what I mean, when it buggers up the whole day and you vow 'never again!'. What surprises me is that I will do it again.

But being in control of your options, is a marvelous thing, doesn't mean that you always make the right choice. But I'm not hurting anyone.

Scoutman said he was alright with this class C drug use, he even tried to smoke it himself, I would have liked him to enjoy the nicer side of this practice with me but not to start the nicotine habit.

By the bloody way being a smoker and suffering the consequences, whilst paying extortionate tax for the privilege, to be banned from a public house and shunned to the 'leper colony' is complete pants. By the bloody way.

It makes me sick that the ordinary person, with no criminal tendencies and no money, is continually singled out to change their lives and to pay for this thoughtfulness.
What will the government do and how will they recoup their losses if everybody in Britain stops smoking?

Incidentally one way of saving, the powers that be, a ton of money … whilst freeing up valuable prison space for criminals, is to bring back the death penalty. For those found guilty of murder, with planned intent. Why should the likes of Neilson, Jack the lad Ripper, Huntley and Maxine, the West couple, etc … live in a free and staffed hotel?
I ask you. (Have I said this already? On my stage)
With the opportunity of early release, to spend the money they won on the lottery!
What's right or fair about that?
If you have done the crime you pay the price, if you are stupid enough to get caught, one should be made to take responsibility for the chosen course of action. Real punishment and hardship must be reintroduced, acting as a deterrent, then just maybe ex convicts will not re offend.

Back to my personal bugbear of smoking.

The bingo hall where I go will suffer, it's struggling now and the new manager can only do so much.

If it's made to pay any more taxes the staff will have to work for free, then they will have to go outside with the others for a fag break, it's shocking that the 'little' people seem to be constantly penalised in this democratic life of privileged greed …

We have taken a huge leap backwards with all these changes in our lives, that were supposed to make our brief existence on this planet better. To all these well paid busy bodies—leave the ordinary public alone and deal with the idiots.

If it's not broken, as the time honoured adage dictates, don't fix it. All this meddling with fundamentals and the new confusing rules haven't made any, noteworthy, difference either.

They fuss about global warming, isn't it a bit late to be badgering the ordinary man to make amendments? Getting us to sift through our rubbish, sorting out all recyclable stuff, then take it in the car (?) to the local (sometimes) depot. Then after all that is it used and is it worth it?
Turn your thermostats down, don't flush the toilet, recycle paper so somebody can borrow your identity from a discarded bank letter, turn the thermostat on your washing machine down … blah blah. Wonder how many of the politicians do this.

I know what they should do—get some brain box to design a giant freezer to keep the North Pole at a constant temperature and frozen.

If anything these improvements have terminated with a negative equity.

What I mean is, maybe I'm just getting old and cynical, things are worse. Elements of society take and do what they want.

When everyone else is so thoughtless/advantaged/selfish/lazy/greedy/opportunist. I could go on …

There is a definite problem with no, as in none, discipline or respect anymore.

Arm the police with those, what are they called? Tazers?

Zap them all I say, I'm not into pain or power for the sake of it honestly. But if that's what it takes to get order in, for example, alcohol fuelled romps of a violent nature then use them.

The recent route of crime prevention is to supply **stab proof vests to nurses teachers and police.**

What?

Arm the police with something useful. When our law-enforcers are getting killed on duty … is that a good time?

Nobody's going to die and using such drastic measures will regain stability, control a situation, then our men on the job can do their work. You all must have seen the disgusting and disturbing incidents, in shocking colour on the television.

When I've had too much to drink I just fall over. Now I am completely useless,—worse than usual, with my legs and speech, so one doesn't bother getting into silly squabbles.

When I was younger I could drink more, hey couldn't we all? That's nothing to be proud of. But at the end of the night was just physically sick and speaking rainbows, to various toilets.

Reminded me of student days. I was being quite sick in a car park and my male friend was urinating against the same wall, he was also ratted but very encouraging, but he kept forgetting what he was doing as he turned to talk to me. My surprise visit boyfriend was rubbing my back and telling me to ignore the man who kept peeing on me.

Mm, those were the days eh?

Something else that's getting up my nose.

I did try to organise a group, concerning the legalization of euthanasia. Talking to people, regarding this issue. Only one person disagreed vocally, but my local MP (who managed to spend £100,000 on expenses last year—no wonder cigarettes are so expensive) wrote that he could not agree because pain management has improved vastly.

Yes, yes, but that wasn't my point Mr Thingy.

In a democratic society one certainly should be given the option? If beloved cats and dogs are spared, the excruciating inevitable outcome, why are human beings made to persevere and suffer? Maybe they don't want to go on and would choose to opt out, the only person who knows and has the right to this decision is you.

It's all mad and scary, nurses working on a terminal ward (I spoke to a few) do not share Mr Thingy's confidence. Those that have observed the worst of maladies in action, are quite unanimous with their vote, "Definitely, make euthanasia a legal choice".

Human rights, what a conundrum of doddering worms that is, who makes these guidelines up anyway?

Nobody likes change, that's human nature we are creatures of habit, be it drastic or otherwise.

But it's a fact of life that we all adapt to. Joining the leper colony, in the rain and cold outside, for a fix is not good, it's a frustrating pain in the bottom but you will get used to it.

Did you notice that?

I got disability in there but I didn't actually mention or name it. Oh bugger—I have now.

Let's get me off my high horse, Darlink, and go back to Egypt—I can waffle with my selective and stationary audience, if I want to, it's my book (2nd!).

I have kept the public information leaflet, we were given at the airport, about foot and mouth disease—do you remember that? 2001. Gone are those days, when you were warned that it was ILLEGAL to take fresh meat/ meat products/ fresh milk/ milk products into a foreign country.

Now they should give out warning leaflets telling you that it illegal to take dynamite or guns onto your flight. Also nail clippers, seriously we saw them in the confiscated pile, along with nail scissors, Swiss Army key rings (didn't actually see one … but they would have been seized) and of course extra lighters. I am always stopped, made to take my shoes off, then frisked. I usually have a forgotten lighter somewhere.

If you refuse to be searched, on any grounds, or have the possibility of concealment you must be refused permission to board the flight. Pretty simple. If you cannot prove your reliability and respect, then you deserve to be ostracised … so you shouldn't moan about it.

On the boat we were given a flyer advertising the extra trips available, as if our days weren't full enough, these additional excursions did cost money of course and since our funds were limited we had to be selective.

We had narrowed the choices down to two, Abu Simbel to see a very impressive temple or a hot air balloon ride.

All the passengers, on the entire cruise, had been divided into different groups. Each party had an individual tour guides. I can't remember the name of our chap—even though he was brilliant and informative—but he called us, "His Pharaohs". We asked his advice as to which excursion we should choose, "When you've seen one temple you've seen them all", he laughed with his advice.

The balloon ride it was. We watched it being inflated and smiled at our fat captain—who had the uniform with the adornments and everything!

As we floated over the ruins in the clear sunshine, soaking up a different perspective, it was peaceful still and quiet. The happy chatting people and hot air, literally refuelling the balloon, were the only noises until.
Our captain boomed the command.
We were all told to sit down, with our heads between our legs, in readiness for the landing.

The basket hit the sun baked land, with a heavy and crashing thud, when all was still we looked up.
It was then we saw that we were in the middle of a field. As we brushed bits of this meadow off our clothes, a screeching voice was heard, then we realised this wasn't just any open ground.
The angry tirade was the irate farmer, whose crops the basket had just ploughed into.
His living had been desecrated and he was beside himself, as he screamed at the man in stripes he was waving his arms about wildly, the passengers all watched with fascination as we climbed out of the basket. The now flat balloon had squashed a few more precious plants.
I think our pilot friend gave the distressed man some money.

Now, this spontaneous action of mine is at best questionable, I did a rather strange thing and I have no idea why? Our captain was standing on his own, he was a stocky chap fortunately, when I jumped up on him and wrapped my legs around his middle.

Scoutman shrugged in confusion at the others in answer, they too looked on bemused and in bewilderment, well my impulsiveness made the suited and official man smile.

Meanwhile the flight staff had noticed that I was having difficulty walking, the parched field was very uneven, so they got me a skinny and malnourished donkey from somewhere.

With one man either side holding my hands, there was no way I could fall off this bony animal, there was no blanket or saddle and I was straddling the donkey's spine.

Each step was grating on my coccyx, the fused bones at the tip of your backbone, it was very uncomfortable and it got worse.

When the dozy animal saw it's mates, on the same path, it got all giddy and started jogging with joy. What a nightmare. The two men, holding my hands, were running to keep up with this silly ass to make sure I stayed on.

Scoutman was walking behind and laughing his head off, when he caught up with us at the transfer vehicle he was still chuckling, ha bloody ha.

I was trying not to laugh, but was now walking like John Wayne, whilst moaning about and rubbing my bottom—which hurt.

It was a good choice and I'm glad that we did this. Relaxing back on the boat was a bit special too, there was a time for tea and cakes on deck, a bit of sunbathing by the tiny pool was in order.

But, it was too hot to sit or lie in.

I could not keep still and fidgeted madly, to get comfortable in the heat, eventually I gave up and joined Scoutman under cover. Then told our new friends that I had written a book. Managed to off load a few more copies of Gillian Mk 2, whilst flicking my hair back to disclose that this time next week I'd be appearing live on television

One woman had chosen to forego the daily outings, to stay on the boat and top up her tan, we watched the virtual stranger as she walked by. She had been out in the heat for far too long, her exposed flesh had roasted nicely, poor thing. Somebody should have told her, that emulating a fat tomato is not sexy, a bright red body is not a good look.

She made herself really ill, suffering from the symptoms of sunstroke, apparently there was no hint of protective sun cream. Silly woman was so sick that nobody saw her for days.

Fellow passengers were all very sympathetic, comments were made with disbelief, "What a waste of time" … "Missing the trips" … "She doesn't look good either" … "Serves herself right" …

Everybody was very understanding.

A few days later she was back in circulation, her skin wasn't a fiery red anymore, then blow me away she sat outside turned over and did exactly the same thing? Blimey … that's dedication to the cause.

She shouldn't have been on the cruise, I don't recall seeing her do anything else, it would have been easier and cheaper to cook herself on a sun bed at home.

In the meantime the rest of us were enjoying our journey down the Nile, going everywhere and doing everything on offer, we mostly sailed at night to reach various destinations. If we glided down the river in daylight hours it was interesting, drinking coffee on deck, to watch real life at the water's edge.

We had seen the landscape's configuration from the air, as our flight came to landing, the yellow of the sand bleeding into the green stripes of vegetation which came directly off and were on either side of the blue band of water. (can you picture that?)

We did visit an island, that homed a collection of trees. That's what to do when you own an island on a river, in a desert, fill it with big green things. As we got off the transfer boat we were accosted by women and children, selling trinkets and T-shirts …

They were also selling short sleeved Egyptian cotton shirts, with confident and forceful gestures, I succumbed and bought a white one. Scoutman shunned them, but later wished he'd got one too.

That night, at dinner, half the guests were wearing the same said shirts! Albeit different shades of pastel colour, but they were actually quite nice and cheap for us sucker holiday makers.

Wherever we were, seriously, the locals were trying to get your attention to sell you things. They were even good from the water, throwing merchandise up to the cruise ship.

They did have a lot of custom to choose from, on the waterway, there was a lot of floating holiday accommodation. When the ship stopped at an attraction we often had to walk over precarious 'bridges', then go through other stationary grand boats, to get to the riverside. There were too many big cruise ships for the limited docking points, walking through the foyers of other vessels was interesting and some were very flamboyant, we had passes for our floating hotel.

Having complete allegiance with fellow 'pharaohs' on our guided tours, they all took note of my walking difficulties and were very gracious, I tried to do everything with our new friends and wanted to see everything that I could.

All this trouble in the Middle East saddens me, the bombings and carnage in Israel in particular, they are such interesting and beautiful countries …

Anyway on one visit we had to be escorted, to the temple, by security representatives. Extraordinary. Note, that nobody protected us from the gaggle of children—all pushing their various goods for sale or simply asking for money.

After a few days you get used to it, then can manage to ignore them, bless.

The temples were awesome, the painstaking excavation and preservation of these buildings along with the artefacts took your breath away, seeing these treasures for real was an experience that cannot be forgotten.

A few columns in the temple in Karnak

If any of you have been on this adventure you surely stopped at Karnak, one of the most memorable excursions, we stood in the hyper styled hall of this temple. Amazing—we were surrounded by sturdy stone columns.

One hundred and thirty two of them, and as if this wasn't enough (blimey) they were completely covered with carved hieroglyphics. I mean the entire surface of this huge stone upright.

Then, gob smacked already, we were told that at the time of inhabitation (three THOUSAND years ago) every part would have been painted! Oh, my …

Fragments of colour, in the shaded extremes, could still be seen.

Truly remarkable, words are not enough here—I must find a good photograph for you.

Seeing the ancient life stories etched in stone, so clearly and hundreds of years after the event, is a privilege.

In the Valley of the Kings, another wonder awaited, you were able to go down into the unearthed tombs of various Pharaohs. Your modern mind boggles with question, using only manual labour a shrine was dug out of solid rock. I stumbled, mentally and physically with Scoutman, but got to see these chambers of brilliance. The dead kings were buried with their prized belongings, to take with them to the afterlife, many of these items were on show. At one temple is the mummy of a pet crocodile: being married to a Pharaoh must have lost its appeal when he died first.

In our group a married couple, they were fab, had a video camera and they sent us a copy of the tape they made.

We went with them to visit a posh hotel, Cataract, where Agatha Christy stayed when she wrote Death on the Nile. On this day we were dressed up, as we had been told not to wear holiday attire, and the first people we saw in this building were wearing shorts.

But the suite where Agatha Christy settled! It was huge!

The video shows us in the bathroom and I make comment, "I want you to know that this bathroom, is bigger than my whole flat!". But it was.

Then we had coffee and sat outside where I told the cameraman, "I've written a book and I'm going to be on television LIVE! Next week!".

Before we leave the cruise I have to tell you about the food. We were apprehensive about breakfast, after the disappointing first dinner of leather and chip with pea, well see that jaw drop.
We entered the dining room in the morning and every surface was laden with choice.
Fruits, yoghurts, cereals, juices, sausages, alternative bacon, croissants, bread raw and toasted, jams and a chef cooking eggs how you wanted …
We loaded our tray, well you had to try everything and we had paid for this privilege, this edible introduction to the day took us a long time. It was great and we were hungry.

Then it was morning coffee and cakes, followed by a buffet lunch. Again the choice of cold and cooked food was beyond expectations, with eyes bigger than belly syndrome we loaded up to test our eager gluttony and prowess.
More coffee and cakes were offered in the afternoon, then the waiter service dinner, to be topped up with an evening of alcohol.
I tell you this because as I packed my case, to come home, a few of items of clothing were clean—as in not worn. They were a little snug—ok tight and straining to be fastened then.
That's what you get for eating a ship! The only thing that was bothering me really was the thought of wearing a tent for my television debut, but I rationalised the sun kissed look was a good distraction so it was alright.

On the flight back a doctor's advice was called for, for when we landed, regarding the red sun worshipper from our cruise. The silly woman had made herself really ill, we only saw her once as we disembarked and she looked like a bloated and burnt sausage. The vain woman was visibly swollen and looked distressed, you could almost hear her hot skin crackling.

The sizzling woman was not that young either and, you would think, should have known better.

Most people have had a dose of sunburn in their lives, even the mildest case on your extremities is not pleasant, but self inflicted third degree burns all over your body is something else.

Then going back out for a second helping?

I don't know, vanity or masochism? Answers on a postcard please.

But I do know this much, she was in a bad way and for all her effort didn't look at all well or happy …

So back on dry land with a week to go, it blurred by, then it was time to tackle another new experience.

There were directions, to the television studio, but and Spruce Girl knew where she was going. Quite handy that, since Scoutman was rubbish at following maps, my partner just sat in the back with his brown head.

I was wearing an olive green silk dress, that looked good with a tan, though the buttons pulled a bit when I forgot to hold my stomach in.

We were greeted and then separated, I was sent to the make-up department even though I had a little on and thought I was looking good, my entourage were sent to the green room.

We had passed a familiar face from the Calendar news team, she had spoken to us with a smile, "Hello Darling".

I'm now thinking, my little mind was whirring, well here I am Darlinks. Wey hey. What happens next?

Make-up Sweety, I was getting excited now and kept forgetting to hold my midriff into the dress.

Sitting in front of the mirror I saw her pick up, what looked like, a big powder puff. She simply hit me in the face with it, and then got the mascara out. She finished and stood back, so I could see.

Ooer.
My eyelashe were long and sweeping, then there wasn't a hint of blemish or shadow on my face. Even my freckles had disappeared, cor, it was like an alabaster mask with eyes and lips. Very nice, I looked bloody good though, honestly, they had to pull me away from the mirror.

I was first on in the second half and so sat out of sight, in the background with the cameramen, to watch the first part of the show.

It was an exuberant male hairdresser who vowed to, " … make the models delicious, using only a can of hair lacquer!". The guinea pigs all looked indifferent, with straight and apparently boring hair.

The adverts came on, then I was helped to step up to centre stage. I wasn't nervous at all, which was surprising, but was bothered about the step up to the sofa. I was clutching a copy of my book and been told not to look at the camera, so I was thinking about that whilst trying to pose and remembering to hold my cruise filled stomach in.

The interview started and she acknowledged the book in my hand, she told me she'd read a bit of it and spilt her dinner of beans on the pages. Then it got silly.

My brain absorbed her questions, then got fuddled as I tried to answer her. I was trying so hard to get everything in, to make clever and discerning remarks, to remember things (?), not to swear and not to look at the camera. I ended up forgetting what the question was. It was a nightmare.

At one remark she accused me, "So you became an alcoholic!".
I snorted in response, making a glib and scornful reply, which made the cameramen snigger and I heard them . Ha: but I don't know what I said.
I do remember making the point, "Having your mum, dad and brother, around you is one thing but having someone who chooses to be with you regardless is another. My husband found somebody else and left me".
She groaned in horror and shortly after said, "Thanks very much Gillian, goodbye".
She got up then walked over to the effeminate hairdresser, and left me, just as I was getting into my stride!
Grr
Well the four youngsters had been transformed, the two of them went to speak to each of the models. As he was talking, explaining what he'd done, he kept spraying them just a little bit more stiffness from the can.
In conclusion she asked them what they thought of the makeover?

They all grinned and thought they looked better before. Now I should have jumped in.
Putting in my two penneth as it were, with the comment, "Yeah they all look like toilet brushes! He's rubbish come back to me!".

But I didn't and I regret this even now, damn, I missed another boat of opportunity, it would have made an immediate impact, being on live television.

Scoutman and Spruce Girl had watched the show in the green room, both smiled when they saw me and told me, "You were really good", my spontaneous comments had made them laugh.

I was mumbling and grumbling that I had forgotten to tell the audience, how to get a copy of the book.

All the way home I was moaning, about everything I'd omitted, nobody knew that the book was self-published and that I'd done it all on my own. So there wouldn't be the anticipated (bloody Darlink) flood of enquiries, because nobody knew where or how to get it!

Never bloomin' happy, you always imagine you could have done better, even the comments made by my escorts were scorned. They both tried to pacify me, smooth the ruffled peacock's feathers. Scoutman attempted, "You did really well, and just think of how many books have gone already!" Followed by Spruce Girl's wisdom, "I've never been on television". Now I had to smirk, as I looked in the mirror, well at least the make-up looked good.

When we got home and looked at the video, it was discovered that Scoutman had taped the wrong side … when I asked around most people had missed me.

"When were you on? ".

"Thought it was today? Did I get the wrong day?".

If you got up to make a cup of tea, in the adverts, the chances are—you missed me.

Fabulous.

My dad got it right, he's brilliant, so I got to watch my performance and was critical with regret at what I didn't say. It pleased me that you could hear the floor staff laughing but disappointed me—nay horrified me—when we timed my appearance and it was only FOUR minutes!

The finicky hair chap got ages! (and he was crap)

Oh well, it was another experience to add to my portfolio of life. But I'm still owed eleven minutes of that exposure, with four off the fifteen of fame.

Hey, call me vain.

I didn't wash my face until the mascara was making me look like a panda. Then I relinquished the thoughts of discovery and celebrity, reluctantly scraping off the remaining make-up. But what surprised me was that I did receive an order, or two, from intrepid and persistent viewers.

Back in the real world I had an inspired idea, but don't know what stimulated this, with memories of The Good Life floating in the background.

Scoutman and I could emulate Tom and Barbara!

Getting carried away with my imagination, I approached my motivation less man, "Let's get an allotment and be self-sufficient! Growing things, and playin' in the muck! Go on, we can have vegetables galore, lots of fresh and free green things!".

He stopped me from organising our lives and free time, mid flow, "No, it's too much work". But this negativity didn't dampen my enthusiasm, or deter me, "Go on! It'll be dirty fun, we can be Tom and Barbara".

He looked confused, bless him, so I reminded him of the classic comedy.

He smiled and shook his head, "Tom and Margo more like", I looked at my painted nails and laughed.

He was right, my knowledge of gardening in any form was limited to weeding, but I was convinced it would be good and challenging fun. "No. No. No, Gillian!", but he wasn't smiling now, "It's too much, they're hard work and you have absolutely no idea. You won't get one anyway".

I went alone to our local council and was given a choice of patches—from allotments available that were just across the road from where his mother lives. So I just went ahead and selected one.

When I told him what I'd done he shrugged with resignation, nodding his head and laughing at my stupidity. He probably knew I'd do what I wanted, regardless.

Unfortunately that's what I'm like, selfish and thoughtless, but it was in his comfort zone and he couldn't moan about that.

I went along to survey my plot, it was still an exciting new adventure, ever optimistic and keen. But standing at the end, looking over the expanse of land, I sighed.

Scoutman was not wrong it would be hard work, I couldn't imagine where to start, the entire space was a dense tangle of waist high grass and weeds.

But, I'd brought a flask with my cigarettes, I was armed and ready for battle with my trusty hand trowel. It was all I could carry and it represented my repertoire of gardening tools, which realistically was as much use as a single pronged plastic fork. The jungle was too treacherous and twisted to try walking, so I sat down.

To start prodding at the unyielding ground, with my trusty little tool. Hours later, when a micro-dot of this vastness had visible earth, I paused and looked up—to find that I had an audience.

Two men were standing and watching me, with their arms folded, both of them were smirking. One of them laughed aloud, then shook his head, as he enlightened me, "You don't want this one".

I stopped poking the couch grass and looked up to answer them, "Why not?". In the still silence they had laughed at my efforts.

Totally out of my depth, I looked around, it did cross my mind the enormity and impossibility of my chosen task. The men looked at each other, then down at little me, "It floods", they chuckled.

My imagined garden of Eden, with flowers water features and singing birds, crashed and plopped into the lake of weeds. I groaned, as it dawned on me, my afternoon of intensive labour had been a complete waste of time.

The men left me, sitting forlorn in the middle of my wilderness.
But I got up to go and join Scoutman, drinking coffee at his mother's.

I went to the people, that had taken my money, then insisted that a new plot was designated to my name. They did respond.

But on inspection I sighed, with déjà vu, the next site was also an overgrown mess.
This time I got Scoutman involved, he was better at digging than me and could use a big spade, with a lot of graphic encouragement and enthusiasm he too could envisage the larger picture.

I had started to do a gardening course at college, mainly because of the allotment but had coerced my mum onto joining me, with the hair brained idea that all these vegetables etc would flourish under my guidance. But I struggled and dithered with all the Latin words then got confused . At this point I lost interest and gave up then let my mum down, she was doing well and enjoying it. But I did get something from it, found out how to tackle the wasteland, the tutor told me to get some old carpets lay them over the jungle and just leave them.
To do their thing and starve the weeds of sunlight, thereby killing them—dead!

So, we got some old floor covering from the local tip (another charity shop basically, as in you have to pay to take the rubbish away). I had given up on the gardening education by then—it was too hard. My mum was pleased that I made her do this—not.

A day trip to the seaside provided this memory … Bridlington. (this was a reminder … I get round to it on page 153 …)

Yipee, it's camping time with our dwindling scout troop! Another cold weekend, of sleeping under the stars. This time we had two girls and a few inexperienced, though eager, boys. I was looking forward to it as we planned the time, making sure that all the equipment we needed was to hand and getting the food, then all we had to do was organise getting everybody and everything to the campsite.

Scoutman and I arrived to a smiling welcome, from the kids who were on an adventure weekend and the parents—who were also having a break. We set to task immediately, having an entire scout camp to construct.

The parents left and we only had one or two scouts that knew what they were doing—the rest of them needed time consuming instruction and guidance. Which wasn't the problem. In the chaos of sorting and unpacking, bits of tents and equipment, Divvy—the other assistant leader—told us, "I'm going home, to pack". Calm as a watery vegetable.

But I did not remain calm, nor did I keep quiet, stupid boy. I had to clarify this and asked him, "What do you mean?".

He smiled, as though I were being simple and unreasonable, but this was not funny. I kept on, "You've known about this for weeks, what do you mean you are going home! To pack?".

Scoutman was annoyed and under pressure, he has known this person for much longer—so expects this kind of dumb behaviour. This development was a shocking surprise to me and I screeched at him, "What are you doing here? Without your kit? Be prepared is the motto you Moron".

Our leader sent him away and was not at all happy with him, but we had to hurry up with the tents because it had started raining.

The older boys helped Scoutman and the zones were erected. It was still quite early but the rain made a campfire, or even thinking about one, impossible and just silly.

Only half the storage tent had been brought, we had laughed at the oversight but now this was a big problem. It was the only tent big enough for all of us to get out of the rain, we couldn't stand up in it, we all had to sit amongst the stores to avoid the precipitation. It had to be, it was the only way and it was better than getting the sleeping arrangements soggy.

Even though we were happily eating crisps and playing word games, you can only be squashed into the same inadequate tent for so long, we did our time and then sent all of the scouts to their beds.

Scoutman and I had the foresight to bring some alcohol, not that much we were responsible leaders, simply enough to congratulate ourselves for setting up the camp against all odds. Divvy didn't come back, I was pleased about that, he didn't cross my mind having been no help at all. We could only laugh about the whole camp sitting, eating crisps and playing games, in half a tent.

It was bed time, although dreading this part of the proceedings, I am an active and practising assistant leader—who has got this nonsense sussed. The camp bed was set up and keeping the hot water bottle off the cold ground. The extras were the foam mat on the bed and additional protection for me, mum had got me what was effectively an adult nappy, I was looking big bottomed and not at all sexy. Whatever!

Think I had the best nights sleep under canvas ever, the scouts could have held a rave outside and I think I would have slumbered through it, leave the cold and hard floor for the big boys I say.

Woke up the next morning in a good mood and needed to use our portable toilet, a bucket waiting in the fly of the tent, it was when I stood up that the weighted nappy dropped towards my knees and dragged my pyjamas down with it's weight.

Oh my goodness, looking down I sniggered in disbelief, the baby outfit had worked! I was obviously zonked … nice one. But on retrospect the sleeping bag was spotless, so had escaped dry cleaning, and I scrubbed up easily. Marvellous, not particularly attractive or becoming, absolutely brilliant, I was slightly mortified at the sad scenario but chuffed at the same time.

Scoutman didn't see this, thankfully, he had gone to sort the noisy scouts out and get the fires going for breakfast.

Divvy decided to grace us with his presence, strolling nonchalantly into the camp, after breakfast.

I was still sore that we'd set up the camp without his help. Idiot, but he wouldn't have fit in the half tent with us all anyway, idiot.

Often, when I'm not writing Darlink, I will dabble with arty things. I have a penchant for pencil work but have tried other mediums. I'm multi faceted Sweety, my level of success is not always outstanding— but hey, I didn't claim to be Van Gogh.

This time I was doing a watercolour of myself, funny that, where better to start? If you make a mess with the portrait of yourself you're not upsetting, or inadvertently insulting, anybody: by recording their features as abnormal or grotesque. I copied an old wedding photograph, they have their uses, similar to the picture used for the cover of Gillian Mk 2. Lost that photo too.

The finished painting was quite good, it looked like the photograph but not like me. It was proudly framed, then I got rid of it and gave it to my mum.

Next I was going to attempt a watercolour of Bro, he deserves that privilege, lucky boy.

I started a pencil drawing of Scoutman, it never got finished …

So at the end of this year I was floating on a whiff of recognition, it was good but I still was not as happy as … I wanted more.

The repetitive and reflective words from Scoutman should have been encouraging, "Look how well you have done already". But I scowled with impatience, "Have done, past tense!".

He couldn't and wouldn't disagree, he knew me too well now, besides he'd seen all the letters from readers and he'd heard people talking to me.

The page from The Daily Express was framed in the hall, he was right things had already gone beyond expectations, my folder of saved cuttings and letters had now become two folders.

They need sorting and ordering constantly, but I am pleased to do this, Darlink.

Still, to this day, I get letters and phone calls. Most recently a woman from Harrogate, suffering multiple sclerosis, positively gushed with admiration then she invited me to her home.

Harrogate Darlink for coffee and cakes (I hope!), how good is that?

September, I had forgotten about this—which is easily done—the scrapbooks were a good idea.

A late and cheap deal to Malta.

We flew on September the 11th, now I remember, how could one forget this date?

We got to Manchester and parked the car then took the transfer to the airport, so far so good, it was when we got to the terminal that events took a turn.

At the boarding terminal, every passenger was gawping at a large screen, big pictures were broadcasting the news in glorious colour.

Everyone was staring at images of an aeroplane flying straight into the Twin Towers.

We were confused, people were shaking their heads in disbelief, it was so ridiculous a notion that it looked like an epic movie trailer. The planned carnage was not real, it was bizarre, nobody would do that surely?

We were shocked and couldn't take this in, nobody knew what was going on, but it was a bit unnerving when you are due to catch a flight. Morbid fears that were not grounded by the transmission of a SECOND plane, doing the exact same thing, both of the towers were mutilated. What an unforgiving nightmare. Mumbles of disbelief were bouncing on deaf ears, nobody understood what had just happened but everybody was stunned with outraged confusion.

We flew to Malta, without any hitches or fuss, as though nothing had happened.

The hassle began when we got to the destination, and located our room in the hotel.

Room 660, yes on the sixth floor. Which wasn't a real problem, there were four lifts, but only one lift was working: now it's becoming a dilemma. We got to the room, it was overlooking a street full of bars. Now I'm becoming a Grumpy Old Woman. The street was already very noisy, it would get worse later, I'm pampered at home with a quiet ground floor flat don't forget.

We struggled with suitcases, well I did—mine was full of books, straight to reception where I explained my disability and sternly requested an alternative room. Being disadvantaged does have it's moments, this was thankfully one of them, we were awarded a ground floor room near to the main desk. Fabulous.

There was a television in the room, which was turned on almost immediately, so we could watch the news and find out what was happening. Whilst CNN was warbling in the background the coffee making facilities were utilized.

There was a loud bang, I jumped and looked at the television which now had a blank screen, the kettle had blown up and fused all the electrics in the room.
We were going out anyway—well we were now, to explore the immediate attractions and to find a café, so we left everything hoping it would all be fixed on our return.

I have a flyer and used tickets to the Blue Grotto, "The most beautiful spot in Malta DON'T MISS IT! Your once in a life time experience", sounds fab doesn't it? It really had to be done, bear in mind that we are gullible tourists, so we sat on the boat and travelled for twenty minutes to see this marvel of nature.
Apparently when you put your hand into the water it went, or appeared to be, blue.

"DON'T MISS IT.

I missed it. My hand just looked wet.

Although we were surrounded by magnificent views (water) I was eager to get back, for a coffee on dry land.

We sailed again, on a passenger ferry to the island of Gozo this time, it wasn't billed as an adventure not to be missed … take note? The journey was alright but the island was not. We got a taxi to the liveliest and most fascinating spot, good move it was far enough, it cost us sixteen pounds. But this had depleted our funds. So we had to find a cash point machine, in the fishing village, on this retarded island. But, surprise and shame on you, we found one and this was the highlight of the day—not the village finding a cash machine!

We got dressed up in our finest holiday attire, then walked down to the casino, looking very grand and swish, but we needed our passports which of course we hadn't got with us. Although we vowed to return, for this adventure, fully prepared. I wanted to do this, it would be fun.

I think Scoutman was secretly relieved, because we didn't go back, we found other things to do—drinking mainly.

I grumbled a lot on this holiday, just for a change. When you are in a new country you do a lot of walking and exploring. Well we did and all the pavements off the main streets were fraught with difficulty, they were a nightmare all potholed and broken or grossly uneven. My tired legs and bashed up feet would trouble me, after a few hours of tripping and stumbling.

Then we would have to stop, when I simply could not walk anymore, Scoutman was very understanding and we could always find a café to sit and drink milky coffee. Which is even nicer in the sun.

Back in our room the electrics were working, so more coffee and a dose of news on CNN was in order. This channel spoke of nothing but the events of September the 11th, there was absolutely no other news, naught else had happened in the whole world it seemed, it was like all other events had ceased.

They were interviewing everybody, and their dog, by the end of the week.

But they had no real, or conclusive, answers.

Time to go home and we had got another corkscrew, we never remembered or thought to pack this item, because it wasn't in our hand luggage it was safe and got back to join the collection.

At the airport it was scary, the staff were behaving with complete paranoia, the queues of passengers with open bags were long and everywhere. Strangely none of the inconvenienced passengers were complaining.

They were checking each and every item of hand luggage, for anything that posed danger in any conceivable way, there were a lot of items being confiscated. Nobody protested when their nail clippers, nail scissors, novelty corkscrews or spare lighters were taken. The bins of removed belongings was overflowing, they were very thorough, any items with sharp pointy bits were deemed dangerous. It really was on the verge of ridiculous, but we all shrugged off the intrusion.

This should have been the attitude before but, I predicted, it won't last. Things will slide back to normality, when the heat is off, the moment this routine becomes a boring pain in the bum.

At home there was a circus performing locally, I haven't been to a real live show for years, Scoutman was dragged along—literally forced to sit in the big tent. I made a fuss to go and see this childhood Fantasy, then we could eat candy floss down memory lane.

The Big Top was cold and the seating was rigid, kind of what you expect of a circus in November, but the show was bright and noisy. A lot of costumed people threw themselves about, in the air and on the ground, then some of the cast carried out tricks with sharp things.

What a disappointment, in this nanny/mollycoddling/spineless state of big brother, there were absolutely no animals to be seen— performing or otherwise.

With reminiscences of laughing clowns and jumping tigers we left, the general disenchantment was such that we were adamant never to return.

What on earth has happened? Grr, anyway.

We did go to the Lincoln Xmas Market mainly because, at the time, Scoutman's sister lived there.

Very nice, actually the day was quite good, we got into festive mode with ease as we were engulfed by all things Christmassy. There were two hundred and eighty stalls all decked with festive enticements, there was also entertainment with music and fairground rides, most of the day was spent walking and eating: as the food on offer was plentiful (yummy and fatty grub mostly).

The walk back to the car at the end of a tiring day was a hike, there were cars parked everywhere, they had provided a park and ride for disabled visitors but I couldn't really take advantage of this facility.

All too soon Xmas day came and couples have to designate their time: so a) you get fed and b) you keep everybody happy. By the way, from experience, I can say that Xmas as an adult is a pain in the bottom— everybody gets drunk and bickers about disappointments of the past year.

It's a nightmare of attitude and tinsel, with good intentions.

But my parents were cool, happy to go along with my plans, maintaining that we should come when we wanted. His mother was the one making a fuss and organising everybody, but that is one way of getting things done, leave this chore to somebody who wants to do it … you are not forced to agree.

But we got by, regardless, fuelled by alcohol no doubt.

My dad and I organised the Christmas bash, for the well known head injury charity, complete with buffet food, a disco and party poppers. With a valid reason to do mascara and posh frocks, with glittery bits, I was quite happy.

At monthly meetings ont committee the group's finances were disclosed, by the treasurer, all the raffles quizzes and activities that were instigated by my dad—mostly—were raking in the pennies.

We had oodles of cash to splash.

Just remembered one of my dad's money making activities, a chap came to a social night with a screen for an evening of betting on horse racing—have you ever done this?

It's a good night, funny.

But Xmas, we all ended up at his brother's—where I had to smoke with the rabbit, it was agreed that we would see my parents on Boxing Day. It was nice, we like Xmas lunch—especially when somebody else has cooked it. The food was fab and his sister in-law made it good, there was a lot of food and the bonus of thoughtful presents.

I like presents: not that I am spoilt and immature (December is my birth month too—9th) we love December. Child!

We happily went home, to drink too much in the flat, the others had to wait for mothers to leave or retire. His mother didn't drink, or had the occasional sherry (in a bucket ha ha).

You often have regrets, when assessing your past life in thoughtful mode, about the things you didn't do and the crass choices you made. At the time of my graduation I was numb, really not able to give it a thought. I was suffering, bloody men, from feelings of devastation and rejection.

The only thing on my mind and all I could think about, was the way a five year relationship had ended with a cruel and casual phone call. More confusing was the next day … blah blah …

Weasel.

My head doctor chap tells me that these episodes, of my brain dwelling on and singling out bad memories … that make positively ill with anger and disappointment, are medically termed Fugue attacks. Blimey, pronounced **FUG U**.

Anyway, the carpets are still doing their thing at the allotment. I can't wait for the result and I'm still excited, about transforming the wilderness, in my mad mind.

CHAPTER IV

Daddy Dearest. 2002

I've got to take time and plan this chapter, things are about to change, this allotment of a life is fraught with parasites and weeds. You have to dig deep to uncover the Passion flowers, inevitably being distracted by the sting of nettles and the creeping couch grass— then the weeds that are rooting to Australia and the baron brambles that draw blood and … this analogy could go on …

But with perseverance you do get there, eventually, with everything in life and this overgrown (understatement) plot is no exception.

I couldn't wait to see how much damage the carpets, we'd laid and left, had done. Now that Xmas was over, there was no excuse, I made Scoutman come with me to investigate.

I stood with my hands on my hips and gawped at the mess, then shook my head in disbelief as I moaned at Scoutman, "Somebody's nicked our carpets!".

Scoutman came to the rescue and laughed at me then spoke, "That's not your allotment".

Oh. I looked further down the allotments and I walked to my plot.

Then blinked with surprise and shook my head.

I was looking at a fence, the crops were in ordered and healthy beds, the chickens were making happy busy noises and there were a few sheds? A man smiled as he walked down the slabbed path (a bloody path) towards me.

I was confused and asked him, "Were there two carpets here when you got this patch?".

He nodded, "Yes", he was still grinning. At this point I growled and told him, "This was my allotment!". His face changed when he pointed out, quite succinctly, "Well you're not having it back!".

As I flounced off my parting words were, "We'll see about that". Honestly.

Those responsible were called, I was not very happy (another understatement) that they had just given my patch to somebody else! Having paid the monies I, again, insisted on another plot.

But, I was adamant: it has to be overgrown with lots of grass and big indestructible weeds.

I didn't really say this but, Oh joy, it was.

It's been a year now and I'm not quite so enthusiastic, with an allotment where all you can do is weed, though I do still have big visions and dreams.

This time we were in between two established plots, the men on either side were very dedicated and they had to go most days as they kept chickens. Did you know that these birds will eat anything?

If one of them dies the others eat it, apparently, so they are actually very fastidious as they clean up their home. One of the men said that I should see them eating long spaghetti, I told him to video this and send it to You've Been Framed for some money.

Scoutman had started to join me regularly now, I couldn't keep him away, he had mutated into Tom (Good Life) and was loving it.

Although we were enthused, until the flask was empty, we couldn't get on top of this overgrown nonsense. We'd be there for hours and at some point, having a caffeine filled bladder, you need the bathroom. Now it was either trek over to his mothers: by which time I would have wet myself having left it to the last possible moment (as you do). Or, the sensible option, water your weeds!

So I stumbled through the over growth to get into a corner, so I was at least a little less obvious, but still managed to wet my clothing as I struggled with layers and buttons then tried not to nettle my bottom.

We sometimes got so carried away, on the rare sunny weekend, we would take a picnic and refill the flask at his mum's.

Hours, of pointless and fruitless digging, later we'd go and get scrubbed up to have a well deserved drink.

Both of us were in this dream now, we were at least trying to make a visible difference, he had started getting wood from somewhere to begin making fences. I was still happy to sit weeding, with my trusty little trowel, though I did attempt to use the big spade—mm.

Scoutman was much better and faster with this tool. So I let him dig.

One day he was in pain and had managed to injure his back. I have been told that this can happen if you simply twist or turn sharply, must be bad—he was lying on the bedroom floor screaming. I was completely useless, in my panic, I didn't know what to do! He told me not to call an ambulance ... so what was all the noise about?

But, what do I know?

He was off work for a few days, being pretty useless, and the allotment was flourishing in our absence.

I still had time to join an art class, taking instruction from an established artist, it involved a lift (if Scoutman's shifts were right) or a taxi to the venue. It was in the conservatory of a public house, a gin and tonic or two encourages the creative juices—to be sure, there were some interesting people trying to express themselves and I told them about the book.

Well.

This event was covered by the local papers, so I was pictured again, a few members in the group didn't like or want their pictures taken: not me. I was holding a gin and tonic in one paper and a paintbrush, rather than a pen, in another.

The art-work I produced here was not display worthy, it was crap basically, maybe being in a pub was not Rembrandt inducing?

But my mum did get her watercolour of my brother (not sure when), it's up in her front room, my niece pointed at it and shrieked, "Daddy": so it can't be that bad.

Incidentally the a well known head injury charity group is ticking along nicely, my dad made a bagatelle and other wooden games for a fundraising event night. Then he spent a little of the money we'd made organising a ghost walk around York, we loved it and it was nice to have some of the cash spent on us for a change. My dad was quite vociferous as he maintained that the charity got more than enough from us, it was time we spent some of our earnings on the people that counted—the head injured members.

Gotta love him.

We were doing well and the little gang was happy, without any interference.

Things started to go wrong when we asked for help and then got outside intrusion, with a badge, telling us what to do and taking offence then getting nasty with me. It wasn't broken, so we didn't need fixing, but we did need a chairman to comply with the charity rules.

That's what she was supposed to do for us, well it's what we asked for.

But in the meantime Scoutman and I were getting a bit fed up of weeding, the ridiculously large unyielding space, so I demanded that our plot was rotivated. (pointing out that they were responsible for wasting a year of our time). We had been doing the same pretty pointless chore for much too long—well I had—and now we were getting impatient for results.

I wanted to grow things and live off the fat of the land! (George Orwell—Of Mice and Men)

Enough of this waffle, I'm sitting in the sun right now—in Ibiza with my pen in my hand (it's 2007). This is nice and it's been too long, I'm with my mum in the party capital—haven't been here before.

It's like a jinx.

What I mean is: when you have high hopes and are planning then looking forward to a good time!

It has rained every day since we got here, we had thunder and lightening this morning! The clouds are very thick and grey: if I wasn't optimistically wearing shorts (with blue legs suffering deja vous: Italy Gillian Mk 2) I'd swear I was back in Yorkshire.

Actually it's probably a good job it's so horrible: it will give my sunburn time to calm down. Being British, the whitest people here, I bared all for too long in the snatch of afternoon sun yesterday.

People are wearing jumpers, those that are only here for a week are crying.

Well not really—but they're not very happy and they're drinking a lot of beer.

We were allocated accommodation on arrival, but we had a vague idea where we would be from the brochure, mum and I were the last people on the transfer coach right to the other end of the island. We were miles from everything.
One resort had been described as having a lot of steps, it was deemed unsuitable for those less mobile.
I had laughed and predicted, "That's where we'll be!"

I was right and so were they, it has got a lot of steps, it isn't really ideal for anybody with walking difficulties and I haven't seen anybody else having trouble. I seem to be the only disabled holiday maker here, most of them probably think I am drunk. Well it will have to stay that way, I don't know 'disabled' in any other language. Anyway I'm not bothered, if they are talking about me and I overhear it, ignorance is bliss and I don't understand.

Even though I still have trouble with steps, if there is no handrail I would have to climb them on all fours and the descent would be on my bottom (ladylike), I am much smoother and faster than I was.
But I am saved: there is a lift.
Which you have to go up nearly twenty steps to get to. Bugger.

Anyway, I'm wandering, back to the year 2002.
You may have, unwittingly, been given a slight subconscious hint that things are about to start changing (again).

With numbers dwindling, in our scout troop, it was a matter of time before things became too difficult to continue. Well you cannot organise team activities with a handful of scouts, two of whom are girls and I'm not being sexist.

We had to be glad that at least one camp had gone ahead.

The a well known head injury charity group demanded a fair bit of our time, my dad and I gave it happily and freely, the old chairman offered my dad praise for his enthusiastic efforts. I smiled and then laughed, "It's all because of me!".

I meant because of my head injury—this was the reason we were all here—my dad smiled and nodded agreement. He knew where I was coming from.

Time for another cheap holiday with Scoutman, this time it was time to sample the bounties of Kos, my need to write copious instructions and lists was satisfied.

But before we went we had to look at our allotment, it had been done. It was weed free!

Basically they had pushed the upper layer of topsoil to the end of the plot, so it was cleared of all greenery, we left with buzzing thoughts of tackling this seriously and productively on our return.

Bit of a shock when we got to our self-catering digs, on the Greek island, the facilities were a little lacking: as in the apartment was not very well stocked. Unless of course the previous tenants had pinched all the pans bar one, along with all the cutlery, but we had one teaspoon and could make coffee so it wasn't a problem—boiling water in the pan as there wasn't a kettle.

We only attempted cooking once, that was enough to convince us that the set-up was rubbish. (this was our valid excuse to eat out all week)

Self-catering kit ... we ate out.

I still drop things all the time, when I am distracted by doing something else i.e.: two tasks at once, it's as though my brain forgets what it's doing. It doesn't remember, or tune in, until I hear the item I was holding hit the floor. It's rare that the said article is caught, I'll never play catch again I'm really rubbish—my young nephew told me this … "You're boring" … as he walked off to find something more interesting to do . It's quite funny, in a sad way, I don't bother trying anymore because I know I'll miss it. So I'll watch the thrown item hit the floor and then I'll pick it up.

My mum groans and rolls her eyes at me, then I shrug.

Back in Kos I am always pretty wary and concerned, when I see the bathing arrangements, if there is only a shower and no bath it worries me. Showers over a bath (with flimsy curtains that stick to your bottom) scare me, we throw a towel onto the floor to combat treacherous tile skating.

I'm all for eating feta cheese and joining the Romans but, being disabled, washing head to toe whilst standing on a skid pad with the hand-held shower really is another thing.

Told you it was cheap.

There was a flushing toilet though. I wonder if you become an expert shot with a hole in the floor …

I can tell you the highlights of this holiday in one paragraph. This is it …

We went to a circus, going back on my vow never to frequent a big top again, because in the adverts they boasted it had over a hundred different animals.

I know.

The mind boggles … over one hundred creatures. This had to be seen, we'd done everything else on this dot of land!

But the hippopotamus and the ostrich simply walked around the ring, then left, they didn't do any tricks. But still … a hundred animals …

They had numerous power cuts, on the island, almost daily. But in the restaurant it was just as we were served with the food, the waiters all ran around with the candles so they were ready and on hand. It was then we realised why our electric mosquito repellent wasn't working. We did venture a market on a nearby island, lots of stumbling around strange uneven streets, it took all day to decide which touristy rubbish to spend our meagre pocket money on.

So a week of sun and feta cheese and we were back, I was eager to look at the allotment and to get busy … woah … handbrake, stop. In one week, the churned up roots had not died, the conditions had obviously been ideal and the plot was a lush green overgrown mess again. Bloody hell …

We were very decisive and just went to the local garden centre, then spent loads of money on chemical weed killer. The act of dispersing the poison gave me a massive blister on my trigger finger (told you there were a lot of weeds).
Then we waited.

Meanwhile my parents and I prepared to go to London, for a well known head injury charity's AGM, we were looking forward to this event.
I planned this well and was ready and waiting for my dad, I was even stocked with two boxes of my latest print of Gillian Mk 2, allowing myself time for coffee and a smoke.
Dad arrived, looking quite relaxed, he was half an hour late. He came into the flat and scowled at me then growled, "You smoking that shit again?".

Then he buggered off, to the men's shop down the road, for a new jacket!
He was another half an hour, so I had another smoke.

We loaded the car to go and pick my mum up, we found her messing about with wet washing, then I realised and groaned that I had forgotten my new cardigan. That completed my outfit, it went with my new striped trousers and the new silk shirt.

"Borrow one of your mum's", dad had smiled helpfully. The offered items matched my outfit vaguely and I frowned like a spoilt kid. "It's alright", I said this petulantly with a big bottom lip, "I'll go without". My parents looked at each other and sighed, then dad announced, "We'd better go back".

We were back at my place, for the elusive jumper, when my dad laughed and shook his head.

"We've got to go back", he explained, "I've forgotten my tie".

So we had to make the same journey again, we'd been on the road for nearly an hour now and had got absolutely nowhere. We could only laugh.

Eventually we did hit the motorway, with a boot full of books and a change of clothes for a visit to the theatre.

An additional journey was planned, my parents had been invited too, to meet a family in Oxford. Contact had been made, with the mother, after she had seen the article on me in the Daily Express.

Having bought and read the book, the lady in Oxford had written to me, her words of praise prompted my reply and eventual telephone conversation. When I told her we would be in London, she passed on directions and we were invited to meet the family.

Their son had been a keen cyclist, he was the victim of a hit and run crime.

I knew that his circumstances were much worse than mine, he was wheelchair bound and had little or no speech—he uses a light writer.

This is an electronic keyboard, on which he types what he wants to say, and it speaks for him with an American accent.

On the morning of the AGM we couldn't take the car, we had to use a taxi, when I asked my dad to get the books for me he got all serious. "You can't take them", he told me in his sensible mode, "It's not about your book". He was being all level-headed, with his new jacket on. "Let her take some", my mum had shrugged and interjected to stop me sulking. So I was allowed to take ten.

The well known head injury charity headquarters was very impressive, there were a few floors too, we found the group and joined in with the friendly chat. Everyone was wearing a name badge and there were representatives from all over the country.

The first half of the day was about money, I don't think many people cared and probably less actually understood, then it was coffee break.

A selection of teas, coffee, drinking chocolate and biscuits was available. The venue was large, all the staff needed paying and all the guests expenses had to be covered.
Think on when you donate: that's all I am saying.
Without any advice or guidance I sold all the books I had with me, in the first coffee break, I'm too good at this and although happy I was left wishing that I had been allowed to bring more.

My parents were in the background, vouching for its popularity and relevance, love them, I was just nodding and grinning like a superstar.

The second half of the money talk started but, even though we had all the printed figures, I was taking no notice. My parents looked a little glazed, bored, too.

Grabbing my attention was a doctor, from Cornwall, who had just bought the book. He was reading it where he sat, I smiled and nudged my dad then pointed this out.

We saw this man's shoulders judder as he laughed, then he looked up to see if anybody had noticed, this single moment was a good bit to remember.

When he got in touch with words of commendation, a few weeks later, I smiled with his chuckling memory. He told me, "That was the best bit of the day". He ordered more books from me, as his was in demand and kept wandering, he subsequently asked me for quite a few—I should have appointed him as my agent or superstar salesperson.

Oh yeah my parents and I went to a West End theatre, we saw the production of Bombay Dreams, it was a good show and we enjoyed it. But I was fed up … because my black bra had not been packed.

I was wearing black and the white bra looked stupid through the top, wouldn't have minded so much had it been a nice bra that I hadn't washed.

We ate in a restaurant that night and the toilets were downstairs, my mum had to come with me because … a) I had left it till the last possible moment (as usual) b) I'd consumed too much of the falling down water (as you do) c) the stairs were steep and narrow (oops) and d) mum needed to use the facilities too (handy).

When we went back to my dad I was stunned, he was vocally challenging two men sitting at another table, he looked really exasperated and was a bit red in the face. He then explained that offensive remarks had been made, about me, and unfortunately they'd been overheard. I smiled because the chaps looked mortified, they were suitably embarrassed, no longer able to make eye contact and at a loss for words. They must have said something quite awful and ignorant for my dad to react, he wouldn't tell me what they'd said, I was secretly chuffed and hugged my placid yet fuming father He had dealt with it for me, brilliant.

At breakfast the landlady took a book from me, my parents now just smile, whilst chatting over the toast and coffee.

Dad drove to Oxford, where we were to meet the much anticipated family. Over coffee we heard the story: regarding their head injured son. We could only marvel at the brain's ability to cope with even the most strenuous of injuries.

I can only think back to those days … when the wheelchair was essential in my life. Not that I remember this time that well, but I do recall that it was a frustrating and generally miserable chapter of my life.

My mum was pleased, to meet another mother whose child had been so severely changed, my dad happily walked in the surrounding countryside with the head of their family.

Their son was able to walk a few steps, with a zimmer frame like walking aid, he had more difficulties to overcome than myself.

Just been stung with a memory regarding the wheelchair, my dad was stitched up by my ex husband when he had to buy a bigger car to accommodate the chariot (a pain in the bottom—quite literally), an annoyance that I remember .

Anyway.

My parents and I were taken to Oxford, for a day out, where we all split up as my mum took my dress back to Laura Ashley's. My dad had been given a mobile phone, so we could be in touch to join up later.

We looked around the Natural History Museum, pretty impressive as far as these venues go.

My friend in due course rang my parents, to establish their whereabouts, the call went to the answer phone.
She looked at me over her glasses and commented, "That's strange? I'll try again".

I shrugged as I answered her to explain the dilemma, "Dad doesn't know how to use a mobile phone".
She shook her head in denial, "He said he did …".

I laughed and shrugged again, "He would say that, but he doesn't know …"

She tried once more, then when it went to answer phone again she wailed, "We'll never find them!".

I remembered the dress and as we walked to Laura Ashley's we spied my parents, the sight made me laugh, my dad was staring at the phone in his hand and trying to work it out. My mum was being really helpful, she was just staring at it too.
"Told you", I laughed to my new friend, my dad grinned at me as we approached and we were all calm now.
What a lovely family, in a charming part of the country, we took photographs at a beauty spot they shared with us.

I told Scoutman all about it on our return: all positive but I was still moaning because I'd only been allowed to take ten books and that I'd not packed my black bra.

My partner and I had booked a brilliant holiday, taking us away for Christmas and it was exciting as neither of us had done this before. It was a week long cruise, followed by a week at a hotel in Tenerife.

Eager to expand my repertoire I had just started an introduction to counselling course, at the local college, with some mad and hair brained idea that I could use my new skill to counsel others like myself. Those suffering the frustrations and limitations caused by a TBI.
Mm—that was the theory anyway—what a jolly good idea.

Actually I was doing quite well with the basic theories, but became unstuck when trying to remember the learned and associated names. I bought the relevant course book and had to give myself a codename, Gillian was known as Galloping during class (I wish I'd said Gorgeous or Glamorous—bloody Galloping!).
Our tutor was Starfish which was nice.
We were all invited to talk about ourselves, cue, so of course Gillian Mk 2 was mentioned—I was asked to bring books with me to the next class.

A few sessions had gone by and I was getting confident, being nosey with clever probing questions was fascinating, but you had to listen to the responses (there be my downfall).

The monthly meeting of the survivors had been the night before, it had been the usual bumbling of familiar faces with the obligatory raffle of rubbish and knick knacks. It's good for just that.
Scoutman was working so my dad and I went.

I had stood at my front door and turned to wave goodbye, to my smiling dad, he was leaning forward on the steering wheel to see me before he drove home.

The next night was the counselling session.

For this exercise the tutor had us all seated and relaxed, we were thinking about a deserted beach silent in the moonlight.
We were all calmly beach combing and a bloody mobile phone went off! It was mine.

By the time I had realised it was me, then scrabbled for the phone in my bag, the call had been missed. I blushed with annoyance and apologised to the silent class—who were now all looking at me.
We went back to the beach and listened to the gently lapping waves, this time interrupted by a mobile phone as it sounded a text.
I groaned, it was mine again. Starfish smiled sweetly but was probably, understandably, miffed.

In the coffee break I discovered that my mum had been trying to contact me, bare in mind that mummy is quite new at all this mobile phone stuff, I called her back and told her I was at college.
It wasn't a mistake.
Something was wrong, but she wouldn't tell me what, she sounded too calm and told me she was coming to pick me up.

It was bad news, my thoughts were racing with the unknown, my brother or my dad that was it but my dad was fine last night?
Mum called again and told me to get a taxi home, still not telling me why, saying she'd join me.
I went to tell Starfish I had to go home, I didn't know why but knew it wasn't good.

Back at the flat I boiled the kettle and lit up, five minutes later the kettle was boiling again and another cigarette was lit.

Scoutman was doing a shift at work, I was creating a sauna in the kitchen. Eventually I had lost it and had to call my mum, "Where are you?", I felt awful.

"We are coming now". I was shocked and questioned her, "We?", she was still too calm.

"We?", my question was ignored.

I was still boiling the kettle, I kept forgetting to make the coffee, whilst chain smoking, my mind was now numb with thoughts.

The intercom announced their arrival, I let them in and went into the kitchen to put the poor overheating kettle on.

I turned as my mum walked into the small room, followed by my stricken and pale brother.

"Dad", I whispered.

My mum nodded, "This afternoon".

I wailed a loud and painful release.

My dad had smiled and waved goodbye … last night.

Then the three of us just held each other tightly, in mutual grief. The kettle clicked off unnoticed.

The evening from hereon was just so strange: we chatted about nothing and laughed inanely, then broke down with sickened sobs.

He'd gone swimming after work, his body was taken out of the water, he was probably racing a younger man but I'll bet he won … at a cost.

Then we all laughed hard, to cry again, the mood was repetitive and intense.

Scoutman called by and he smiled with surprise, "Hello", then he looked at the three of us and had a furrowed brow of question.

I was sitting on the floor and looked up at him, to explain. "Dad's dead".

There was no other way to put it. His face suddenly changed, he was startled and looked at us waiting for the joke, then he shook his head with realisation. Without speaking he turned and went into the next room. We all heard his shock and pain as he cried. Which set us all off again. It was an awful night.

When a distant relative dies it's sad, when someone so close dies it's devastating: I have cried whilst writing this.
I still miss him: Derek John Firth 21.4.41—6.11.02. (the same day as Betty Boop's birthday)
He was sixty one had stopped smoking and was fit. Go figure.

Shortly after Richard Whitely died, aged sixty one too, I cried for a week. Seriously, I didn't cry for Princess Diana (shame on me, but she had the rest of the world shedding tears for her) but the Countdown King's death floored me.

Friends that I called, with news of my dad, all gasped shock … "But he was such a nice guy". The charity work was put aside for a while, the group missed him almost as much as we did.

When sorting out his things we found a pile of questions, all hand written, for the group quizzes.
There were hundreds of questions, on lots of paper, they were kept as one of those emotive things that you can't bear to part with. You know like your favourite, out of fashion, tie-dyed suit (that I did myself) that doesn't fit anymore. It's a one-off so it's fabulous and it'll come back into fashion one day … then I'll miraculously fit into it. I will keep it.

These things should hit the bin or a charity shop, but you keep them … just in case … cos ya just never know.

I have let the suit go, it was a wrench but I simply have no room and it will never fit me again, it took a long time. Ah.

The anticipated cruise had been booked for a while, we really had to go. It was good in one way, we avoided the painful family get together, but at the same time I wanted to be with them.

But we had already bought and wrapped all the gifts.

Each family, his and mine, had a large Xmas box. Big wrapped and decorated boxes that contained everyone's gifts. It was a treasure trove complete with inclusive tinsel, party poppers, sweets and a bottle of bubbly alcohol.

My niece and nephew loved it, the slippers (Sex God) meant for my dad were claimed by my brother.

Scoutman and I had an utterly miserable time, before we even got out of England.

We had already made the trip to the airport, to time the journey, in readiness. Best laid plans …

So on the day we left with time to spare, more than enough, even though I had to have the last smoke and coffee, we set off quite happily.

The point where the M18 and the M1 converge, to become one motorway, wasn't a problem—until the traffic just stopped? I shook my head, "What's going on here?". The whole motorway just became a disturbing crawl, we looked at each other then the clock, "We are still alright … plenty of time". We watched other drivers switch lanes to try and get ahead, it took us an hour to do one junction, we were silently clock watching now.

We laughed with empty eyes and spoke positively to pacify the panic, "We'll be a bit late, the flight will be delayed …".
Suddenly it became real, we could kid ourselves no longer, "We have missed the flight!".

A crane had caught fire, it was announced on the radio, as we crept past the inferno we could see that it was indeed huge and motorway stopping.
When we were at the airport we rushed around and tried desperately to get another flight, we were there for hours, but it was not to be. No flights were available to us, that could catch up with the big boat, a lot of people wanted to be away for Xmas.
Eventually we had to leave and admit defeat. The journey home was sombre.

The worst thing, wasn't family and friends groaning in sympathy, was passing packed suitcases stashed in the bathroom—giving it 'We're ready come on let's go! Look we've got sun cream and everything!'

A flight was booked to Tenerife, to go four days later, which was good but we were gutted that we had to forget the cruise altogether.
We had to discount that we had missed out, on the all inclusive and festive bonanza, and be happy that at least we got the second week in.

We managed to get there with no problem, we were happier now but for the days we should have been on the cruise we had no accommodation, we found and went along to the big posh and clever hotel where we were booked for the second week.
They could put us up for these extra days, at this point we were still happy and relieved, but it was when we were sat in this fabulous bedroom that I started crying.

I had just realised, with a sickening thought, to pay for this time here would deplete nearly all of our spending money.

"We have to leave", I was upset that it all seemed to be going wrong again, it simply could not be done. We dragged our suitcases across the huge lobby, to get our money back, then out of the front door past the security guard—feeling disappointed, stupid and cheap.

Then we had to traipse around unfamiliar territory, searching for a cheap room, dragging full suitcases and carrying bulky hand luggage. All the hotels in this vicinity—within our price range—were fully booked. I was getting whiney, my knees were hurting and my walking had deteriorated, I was getting rudely gawped at as well.
Scoutman was getting wound up too—most probably by me. This was not good.

I had stopped to rest when we fortunately happened upon an office, that advertised accommodation. We went in and I promptly burst into tears (really useful), but I couldn't stop myself, I was getting myself into a right pickle.
This situation was an utter nightmare, I blurted the whole story and was inconsolable. I told this complete stranger about the flaming crane on the motorway, my difficulty with walking and then broke down inconsolably when I spoke of my dad.
The man patted my hand and smiled then said, "Don't worry".

In a nearby resort a self-catering alternative was located, it wasn't as plush nor was it coordinated, it was a fraction of the price we nearly paid so it would suffice and the sheets were clean.
It was alright, comparatively cheap and cheerful, thankfully, but we had no choice.

We spent four days there, then went to honour our waiting deluxe digs.

The Xmas tree in the lobby was massive, worthy of mention, the reception itself was a big space so a normal tree would have looked lost and silly. They had left no detail to chance and the staff seemed to be cleaning, something, all the time.

The Yuletide decorations were tasteful, we took photos of the lobby in our excitement!

Xmas away from home was now looking good.

I even took a photograph of the toilet in our suite, a touch flusher, it was amazing and you would think I'd never seen a toilet before— simple things do please uncomplicated minds.

Xmas day itself was greeted with a mixture of emotions, it was sunny outside but I cried for my dad.

My mum was staying at Bro's and I really missed them, now more than ever. I remembered that their Xmas box contained all my dad's gifts. They would be feeling quite numb I imagined.

It had been just over a month now, though it felt like yesterday, I had to speak to them.

This reminds me of a poem I wrote, it's in the first book, called Maybe written in 1994.

The first line is: It seems like only yesterday …

We all cried, but life goes on and doesn't stop for grief, it wasn't real yet it takes time to accept and get accustomed to the loss.

At the moment I am going through the finished book, final check, I keep crying. It is 2008 and I miss my dad. Bro couldn't finish reading this chapter aloud either …

Change the subject …

Incidentally I am still shocked and surprised by the comments, nay healthy and flattering feedback, that the first book has encouraged. I fear that this time people will say: "Yes, yes, you've made your point. Disabled life is a pain in the backside—shut up now".
If any of you are thinking that … please don't go out of your way to tell me. Ignorance, after all, is bliss! When I get to Gillian Firth 'She's Still Talking' Volume X—you can say this then

Anyway it was Xmas day in Tenerife, it was warm and sun drenched, we had to go out, so we went to the beach. Here we had something fizzy and alcoholic, along with the towels we took along Eddy our blow up snowman. The photo's were funny and we left Eddy in Tenerife, I wish we hadn't now, ironically he was sitting in the sun on the balcony.

Eddy still on holiday.

One thing I did notice, it would most likely have missed my attention in the previous life, Tenerife catered well for their disabled visitors. With ramps in the hotels and on walkways, the lifts in the buildings are always beneficial.

So another twelve months over and this was an emotional mixture of a year, bringing to mind the thoughts that you never know what you've got … until it's gone.

Time does flieth—it's true—this year put my disabled existence into perspective and makes you think.

Before this chapter ends let me share with you the final event of this year, the writer's class that's a drive away had an evening planned. Where us would be Darlinks read our work aloud, to a paying audience, worth a mention and a good conclusion to this year.

I went down well, the laughter was with me and felt genuine, faces were smiling.

I needed this.

CHAPTER V

But Seriously 2003

Y ou will not believe how annoyed we still were, about missing the cruise. (maybe going straight in there at the beginning of a chapter is a bit of a giveaway)

Fellow holiday makers, that we were supposed to have been with, all told us, "You should have been there it was fabulous!".

I'm sure they weren't being thoughtless, much, we just had to smile and say we were glad that they had a nice time. We were glad, but eventually stopped smiling if they offered more and went on.

The descriptions and information was given readily with enthusiasm, about the food and dress code at the captain's dinner, but it got a bit irritating on the second or third hearing.

At least we saved our waistlines in the first week, see every cloud does have a silver lining, but made up for it in the second. Oh boy did we? Question for you. Why is it that all caution is abandoned, silly if you're sitting in a swimming costume all day, when you are presented with an array of garnished food?

You argue that it's already been paid for—and cooked for you, an excuse to be greedy really, you are on holiday and you have to get your monies worth.

(It's okay I didn't really want to wear that slinky and rather too skinny dress anyway!)

Well, you have to try everything!

Well you do don't you? That's what it's there for after all. The summer gear looks okay, if you wear long or distracting tops then remember to suck your gluttonous stomach in.

I'm getting good at this now.

I know now that the two weeks, of indulgent overkill, will not be remedied on my return … I will not get organised and do loads of sit-ups. Back to your routine, a disorganised life rich with good intentions, the wobble preventing regime won't happen. This is where being disciplined and bothered helps.

Some of the people that we met were fabulous, most of them either took one of the books I'd got or (when I ran out! (Oh yeah)) ordered a copy when they got home.

My friends and family were absolutely disgusted (not by the few extra pounds—I was wearing baggy jumpers).

I had written to the holiday insurers and explained the dilemma (that's a calm way of putting it). It was a comprehensive explanation of events, including all the receipts we had painstakingly collected of all the additional expenses.

We had high hopes that our situation would be recognised and accordingly compensated.

This was a genuine claim, not a bogus scam for money.

They wrote back with a lot of words and said, "No … erm … it's not going to happen!".

We were shocked and wrote again, to contest this decision.

They replied and told us … "It's still no. Now go away, leave us alone, because you're not going to get anything unless it is a fraudulent claim? Ok?".

But I am not resentful or bitter in any way.

Apparently if the car had overheated, then died a death in the traffic jam, we would have been covered. (If we had we known this eh?)
So we paid extra money for gold (more like yellow plastic) holiday insurance cover, for nothing! Worse still I have no doubt that a few of you have been in a similar situation.
It makes me mad, that some people are able to scam the insurance companies out of thousands of pounds with fabricated claims. Then get away with it ... grr!

On this point it is ghastly that there are some people that profess to be disabled, ripping off the system, deceptively claiming benefits and getting big insurance pay outs.
When and if the truth is uncovered (the video footage of them being able bodied) their shabby behaviour should be made public. Name and shame the lazy liars!
Then make them pay back all the money they've scammed, with interest.
God I'm hard eh?
Lastly break both their legs so they can try disability for real. It will only be for a few weeks, not permanent, so a taste of disability can be experienced. (I'd break their kneecaps—with a hammer—then get arrested! But it would get Gillian Mk 2 and Typically Gillian ont' telly)
Blimey ... rebel ...

Just looked at the scrapbook for guidance, 2003 was another full on year, now I don't know where to start.
I will tell you what I've been up to: but first let me share some information.

It was all gathered from the internet and these figures are quite alarming.

Mr Arty Farty, a local businessman, is enraptured with Gillian Mk 2 and pretty taken aback with me—he told me so. He is amazed at the progress I have made and impressed that I wrote a book, like other readers he only had a vague idea of how devastating a head injury can be. He found the book both informative and humorous, then he bombarded me with relative questions.

He was trying to put himself in a life changing situation, you cannot possibly contemplate the negative and rippling effects to you or your family.

But Mr Arty Farty couldn't, then he gave up trying and made me coffee.

He has become a friend, yet another acquaintance due to the book, through Gillian Mk 2 I am collecting a diverse array of friendships.

Incidentally the Wee Lassie and her partner (My number one and two Gillian Mk 2 fans! Who am I to argue?) came from Scotland to meet me. They brought a box of shortbread with them and they were both lovely—not because they gave me shortbread.

Though it was very nice and didn't last very long. How good is that? The Wee Lassie (Number One) suffered a TBI and her girlfriend (Number Two) married her. They had a posh civil ceremony, I have seen the photographs. Brilliant.

Anyway Mr Arty Farty made me think, as he questioned and wondered aloud, "How much did it cost the tax payer to get you where you are today (here) via intensive rehabilitation".

Even though I do know that it's very costly, the exact figures escape me, also it can often be a lifetime expense.

So, curiosity aroused, I set to the challenge on a path of discovery.

The occurrence of head injuries is quite prolific, ranging from mild abrasions to serious brain trauma, the damage can be sustained in a variety of ways: accident at work, road accident, public place, assault/attack also clinical negligence and illness.
Then they can be categorised as external—usually scalp injuries, or internal—this concerns head injuries that may involve the skull, the blood vessels within the skull, or the brain.
Blah blah …

The internet is an invaluable tool nowadays, very complex and detailed, you don't realise how comprehensive it is until you are looking for something specific. A good example I can give you, that has nothing to do with head injuries but is nevertheless traumatic, is looking for an item on ebay.

I was dabbling on tinternet and decided that I needed … so would look for … a watch. Simple.
Well, it gave me pages and pages of choice, everybody is trying to sell their redundant watch!

To limit the numbers one has to be more specific, so I entered 'lady's watch', but still there were hundreds to choose from. Hours later, having been distracted and blinded by the selection, it gets boring and you just start looking at the sheer junk some people are trying to sell. Has somebody tried to sell a rubber chicken yet … from the advert. My dad's old fishing rods found a new home, nearly, but they couldn't be posted.
Bro had spent a lot of time wrapping the large pole, he ended up driving the rod to its new home.

It seems that everybody is trying to make a fast buck, by selling surplus bric a brac from their lives, maybe I should try selling signed copies of Gillian Mk 2.

Anyway, getting back to the point, presenting head injuries to the search engine creates the same quandary. I had to limit, then change, my request to severe and serious head injuries.

Still you get a minefield of information, that you have to laboriously sift through, it all roughly says the same thing. Sustaining a serious head injury is a bloody nightmare, honestly between the lines of medical text and amongst the Latin, this is what it says. Brackets: it is basically a testing time for all involved.

The figures, although they vary from site to site, are consistent with the facts.
That injuries involving a blow to the head—loss of consciousness for any amount of time is taken seriously—this injury takes up a large amount of medical time.

Two examples that I found give numbers that are quite saddening. 700,000 people in North America suffer serious head injuries each year and 70,000—90,000 are left permanently disabled.
Whilst here in Britain a million patients present hospitals each year with a head injury.
Further statistics were revealing and disturbing, head injuries account for 1% of all deaths and 15-20% of these are children.
About half of traumatic deaths are associated with the result of a head injury.
So how lucky am I?

Am I blurring you with figures yet? Sorry but I have to share a few more, they make valuable reading.

Cos ya just never know

After moderate head injuries 63% of patients remain disabled, one year after their accident, this figure rises to 85% after a severe brain trauma.

Even with less severe injuries the patient should be observed, for several hours after impact. So the person's state of consciousness, orientation to time and place and immediate memory function can be evaluated. Any deterioration of these factors may be a sign of the delayed effects of brain injury, due to swelling or internal bleeding.

The way the severity, of these injuries, is described and graded is by using what is known as the Glasgow Coma Scale. The figures concluded predict the person's likelihood of recovery. If the score is quite low, then the damage to the brain is more extensive, the probability of improvement is lessened.

I'll show you what it is because it's quite scary, as in my initial score was not good.

I wonder if this technique is used worldwide? I did see it mentioned often, whilst doing my research for this chapter. (Cor research … that sounds good eh? It must mean I'm a proper writer! Darlink.)

There are a lot of words and lots of people have something to say, I found a whole site dedicated to children's head injuries. This is of course to be expected, as more people are aware of the implications of a head injury, as a sign of the times (hustle and impatience) there are more incidents both happening and being covered by the media.

For example most people know of the television presenter David Hammond, he had a high speed car accident and is lucky to be alive, he seems to have escaped with minimum damage and even remained with his partner. Unfortunately this is a rarity, not surviving—marital or committed partners sticking around to support during the bumpy and uncertain ride. Bloody men.

Anyway the figures, associated with the occurrence of such a relatively straight forward injury, are quite shocking and a bit of a wake-up call. More serious injuries can be avoided taking simple measures, safety belts and helmets for example reduce brain damage, or you can like cover yourself with bubble wrap and never go out.

Do you recall that I wrote a letter to our government? Outlining my thoughts on the drink driving laws and pointing out, quite succinctly, what a pile of rubbish our current system is? The reply was an insulting waste of my time and effort, written in bad English by a name that couldn't be pronounced.

But they have managed to devise a law whereby you can be fined for eating or smoking whilst driving.

So if you are driving and you have been drinking, you are more likely to be caught if you get munchies or need a nicotine fix and then take a mobile telephone call.

Judging from the survivors I have met, no disrespect intended, Gillian Mk 2 has been extremely fortunate—I must be made of rubber. So at some point in your lives you or someone close will be affected by these statistics, how disturbing is that.

AS PROMISED.

Glasgow Coma Scale

<u>Response Score</u>
EYES OPEN
Spontaneous
To speech
To pain
Absent

VERBAL
Converses/oriented
Converses/disorientated
Inappropriate
Incomprehensible
Absent

MOTOR
Obeys
Localises pain
Withdraws (flexion)
Decorticate (flexion) — not sure what these mean—something
rigidity   to do with
Decerebrate   — movement or lack of. I'll check with my
(extension) rigidity   doctor.
Absent   (It's basically abnormal posturing i.e.:
                            hands turned in/out with severe brain
                            injury in response to painful stimulus)
                            There you go … clear mud.

Mild 13-15 points
Moderate 9-12   "
Severe 3-8   "
Less than 8 = coma

So now you know what a Glasgow Coma Scale is.

I have to stop reading through this, to an audience or otherwise, because I am really critical and it sounds rubbish—it's now important to satisfy my reader's. Darlink.
Blimey, maybe I should start wearing pink and change my name to Babs.
So back in Gillian's little world:

My mum needed to get away and have a break, she asked me if I would go with her?
I thought hard for a split second. What two weeks in the sun and away from here?
Would I …
Two weeks were booked in Tenerife and Scoutman wasn't invited, but he was a bit too happy to take us to the airport. He was going to visit the flat to sort Joey out and then vocally twitch at his Play station uninterrupted.
Well that's what he said anyway.

He had tried numerous times to get me interested and involved with Tomb Raider, making Lara Croft run then jump and shoot things. But I kept forgetting the route and which controls did what, so was pretty rubbish. After being killed for ten minutes I was usually bored and didn't see the point, of playing a game where you just run then jump to your death or get shot.

So I was more than happy to pack my case and leave him to his games.

It was late evening when we arrived and we all chatted on the transfer coach, we stopped at a few hotels and saw the open shops with lots of lights. Only mum and I were left on the coach now, as we drove past and through all the noise with movement.

Our home for two weeks was quite a walk away from the beach and everything else, it was on the outskirts.

So we sat around the pool a lot, it was easier, but they did cater for this and they provided daily entertainment. Not really worth mentioning, other than to say, the usual package holiday stuff.

Things that seem to be more fun if they are done in a multitude of languages, especially when you have sunburn and an alcoholic drink (or two).

Quizzes: you sit there for ages and have actually only been asked a few questions. But you're usually in the bar, drinking foreign measures, so you don't really notice or care.

One thing I do remember: we went to a theatre to see a dance performance, the costumes and choreography were pretty extreme so the show was a good one.

The troupe executed a variety of dances, which I could tell you about because the programme is in my scrapbook, but what sticks out in my mind is that my toe was pulsing and throbbing with pain the whole evening. I was fidgeting to relieve the ache, all through the show, so I couldn't concentrate to do it justice. The venue had been a fair walk into the centre and being dressed up, my sandals would have looked silly with a linen dress, duh … I was wearing appropriate (stupid but classy) footwear, with heels.

Yeah … I know.

I literally hobbled back to the hotel, clutching desperately onto my poor mum, knowing that if I took the shoe off it wouldn't go back on my now fat and deformed foot.

My mum was reprimanding me all the way back, since I was hanging onto her there was no escape, making the situation much more bearable. I was trying hard not to listen, she was telling me, "You should have known better. Being so vain was stupid, when you have difficulty with mobility".

Bugger.

But she was right, of course, the next time I shall wear my Laura Ashley dress (i.e.: posh frock) with slippers.

Imagine, if you will, me seated and looking my bestest then struggling to stand up.

You may be distracted briefly, by the general appearance, but then will notice the furry boots of my slippers. How ironically attractive.

At the hotel's bar mum and I were partaking of refreshments, I was smoking, when a man came and stood near us. Mum told me later that I was grabbing attention, he was sidling along the bar to join me, I didn't notice him until he moved my ashtray, a pleasant chap who chatted easily and had been here for a while. He was due to be back in Britain, if I did know why … ? … I cannot tell you, we saw him every day because he kept finding us. I called him Olga, that's what it said on his arm, he was posted a book to his brother's house.

Shoes … I rather think I will be seen suffering in pain (you can't tell if I don't move,) for fashion.

Cos I can …

Though I know it's silly and it does cause more difficulty, with an already dodgy situation, but … Truffle does it!

She wears her strapped skinny sandals in the winter … well they go with her outfit … they're the kind of footwear that I can't walk in (specially with frostbite).

It is fun to notice some of the exhibits around the drinking holes, on a Saturday night, it makes me laugh and I comment, "Freezing", to Truffle. As shivering goose pimples go by.

Don't know why I'm being smug, in trousers with my coat and umbrella, I probably did the same thing when I was their age. Now I'm warm, with my older and nesh head, but I keep losing my gloves.

I have saved a flyer from an antiques fair, written next to it is my reaction to this outing:
'Rubbish—don't do this again'.
But later on there is another fair visited and this is where I bought a teapot, Scoutman bought some whiskey memorabilia selecting one jug from many. I rarely drink tea now, a complete turnaround as in I didn't drink much coffee before my accident. So it was not that I needed a dust collecting and space stealing teapot.
But it is an unusual pot, in that I haven't seen one like it before, well I had to buy something so I hadn't hobbled around all day for nowt.

I do collect and buy coloured and decorative glass bottles, there are approximately sixty of them now, I have tried to count them … but get muddled.
With which bottles have been calculated? Then forget what number I'm on?
After a few attempts I get a rough figure, then give up.

When you collect anything you become an easy present option, for example: Teeny used to collect frogs … I gave her a big (big) green pottery frog for her eighteenth birthday.

I had to tell friends to stop buying me bottles, explaining that my flat is full, Teeny doesn't do frogs anymore either but I think she still has her eighteenth birthday present .

I say full as in there is no space left! Anywhere!

I must get rid of some stuff, but throwing things away is scarey. Or is it just me?

Sometimes my space just gets too cluttered, with nonsense, so I have to do something. "Not often enough", my mum chunters.

This is usually after I've been wandering around from room to room, where I will kick things and stub my toes, trying to find something essential and important. Scanning the same arrangement of untidiness, but now hoping this task will provide a clue. As to what it is that I'm actually looking for. Inevitably I will have forgotten, I then get distracted by something (anything), so it means having to retrace my steps … again.

Which in turn means that, theoretically, I should know where everything is and shouldn't get sidetracked.

But I do and ages later, the item may or may not have been found, the importance of routine and organisation becomes screamingly obvious to me. It's pointless beating myself up about it because with hindsight, a marvellous thing, I know that I do this and will probably continue to.

But, always think I'll remember (stoopid) as I'm much better now

"Write it down!".

I can hear you yelling at me and this has been tried, imagine this scenario, locating the essential tools for the job takes time. Then, with the pen and paper in hand, I'll doodle for a while until I remember what I had to write down. Then! Either forgetting to take the list with me, when I go out, or simply ignoring the crumpled paper in my pocket. Blimey.

So this pointless exercise will, no doubt, become papier mache in my washing machine later as the forgotten list goes through a cycle (in a dark wash probably).

Hey I can walk much further and for longer now, on straight even ground anyway, this is a bit jerky and rubbish if it's not flat or paved or if there are steps.
People still ask me, "How far can you walk?", but I dunno never walked and measured the distance. Anyway there are good days and bad days, so it varies.

Still not very good in crowds, with lots of distracted people, I don't side step well or in time to avoid collisions. After being barged and knocked off-balance for a while it gets painful, then tiring. Mum says, "You should use a stick on these occasions to show people that you need space". But I can't walk with an aide anymore. How strange is that?
From once not being able to walk any distance, at all, without one.

Mum means use it as a visual reinforcement, so it can be seen that I have got a genuine problem and I'm not drunk. You should see me if I am, actually no you shouldn't, it's not a pretty sight and it's not at all clever. Honestly, you would think I'd have more sense.
Or some anyway …

I really did fall down last night, but nobody saw me as there are no cameras in this particular area yet, I didn't hurt myself but buggered up another pair of tights. Damn!

Elvis hasn't got back to me yet, about the classroom talk, I'm disappointed with my redundant teaching head. Although I did see him a few weeks ago.

My mum had to come, she insisted on taking me and going into his office, I'm pleased that I recognised him immediately though he's grey haired now. The distinguished man (get me Sir) took us on a tour around my old sixth form, it's changed drastically and has it's own coffee bar now. Happy memories flooded back and it was strange. Odd going back to past haunts, after so many years, I wasn't expecting it to be the same but wasn't prepared for it being so different. Blimey.

Annoying that I remembered running late, through the corridors and up the stairs, to get to various classrooms. That was many years ago. Now I had my old teacher and my mum, waiting for me at the bottom of the short flight of steps, watching on with attentive and concerned faces.

Tell you what was the nicest peculiarity, on this trip down memory lane, at my old school: I hugged and kissed Elvis goodbye.
Now that couldn't have happened when I knew him before, in my previous life, he'd have been arrested.
Curious that I haven't forgotten him, or his recent request for my insight and new expertise on disabled life.

Joey died.
Ahh. My cute and vicious little bird, Scoutman found him and called me. I just knew what it was from his voice, subconsciously I hadn't heard Joey attack his bell when we came in, my pretty bird was taken to and buried in the allotment with a half eaten honey bar. Nah.

At the allotment Scoutman, who is now infatuated with the green dream, thanked me again for getting him involved, he was busy nurturing and cosseting his pumpkins. Obsessive!

The trusted advice was taken from our gardening bible, Mr Percy Thrower ... the mentor, we were following his instructions with precision. Well Scoutman did.

His fixation worked and the pumpkins got so big they couldn't be carried, we had to roll them to the car!

There is a disabled ramp outside this house, leading to the front door, so the biggest one got into my bathroom. He took the giant pumpkin to work to weigh it, an industrial weighing machine had to be used, it would have crushed my puny bathroom scales.

It was 89kg—the biggest Halloween lantern ever!
The rest of our enormous candle holders were gladly given away. Whole in their entirety: as in we didn't bother to scoop out the flesh, we had more than enough of our own. (I'll say)

I had got impatiently curious, wanting to know what this monster looked like on the inside, so sawed the top off it to have a peek.
On scrutiny we discovered that in, all three of, my cookbooks there were no recipes for pumpkin anything. So we looked on the internet. Found pumpkin soup, looking at our specimen, we would have enough flesh for soup every day for three months.

It was a daunting prospect and, I'm embarrassed about this, having walked past the monster for a few weeks it was eventually rolled back to the allotment—to feed our compost bin.
So all that for nothing!

We should have taken a photographs of them, you'd have been impressed, they were mean pumpkins.
Scoutman was like a proud father, but he didn't fuss or cry as the big daddy hit the pile of rotting matter.

We were now reaping the rewards of our experimental labour, we were enthusiastic but didn't really know what we were doing, having just bunged seeds and bulbs in the ground then left them. Just waiting and hoping for the best. We had listened to advice from other knowledgeable allotmenteers, proficient and dedicated, who knew much more than we did and had lots of leafy green things on their plots.

Scoutman got very carried away and wanted to try allsorts of things, I was generally weeding on my hands and knees in the background and helping when I could, it was all pretty idyllic in a clueless and industrious kind of way.

I had been given a shed that was quite big, so we would sit and drink coffee with biscuits and everything, it even had a toilet (bucket) so I didn't have to water the plants anymore.

Our parsnips were wizened and rubbish, shame as I love them roasted, but our carrots!

Fabulous and spoilt, they had their own bath—to avoid carrot fly in fact. They were of differing sizes and shapes but edible.

The cauliflowers, we vowed to try them again, were gangly and had a will of their own.

Something (?) had gone drastically wrong with them, being inedible and unattractive, they just took up space.

The beetroot was brilliant, there is a certain joy of surprise when you unearth a root vegetable, they were easy to grow too so this would happen again. Success! How exciting.

Scoutman was in his element and we had lots of pickled beetroot!

I had to buy a new freezer to accommodate our produce, the tiny box at the top of my small fridge was just silly, we had a production line of blanching and bagging numerous vegetables.

It was a boring task, having to clean peel then chop everything in preparation, but ultimately when you have a freezer full self sufficiency it's very satisfying.

Purple sprouting broccoli, this has to be the penultimate rendition on the good life.
What can I say?

It was purple and it was sprouting, it's looking good so far, therefore ready to be eagerly harvested, to be used with dinner that evening.
Blimey, from the ground to the plate within an hour! Go on how good is that?
Scoutman has graduated from crispy, black and crunchy, bacon over a camp fire!
With a bit of instruction: he's getting good at following orders when stirring and chopping things.
He can cook broccoli too … this is a desperately weak link but anyway.

It wasn't until we got the broccoli into the kitchen that we discovered it was riddled, swarming and alive, with mayflies. Infested with the tiny black dots, "Extra protein", argued Tom aka Scoutman—bless him. But when I looked at the crawling café blind at the window, then had to clear and clean the window sill a few times, I insisted that the broccoli was binned. Ugh.

Soft and tender green beans are fab, we grew far too many, hard and woody leather is not.
You can have a pile of them tossed in butter, yum, but eating one undetected cheat is enough. It is so horrible a sensation in your mouth that you have to spit it out, then you look at the beans left on your plate in dismay. But, it's not worth the risk, they are pushed aside ah … all those uneaten green things!

Scoutman visibly grimaces as he tells me, unconvincingly, "They're not all bad! Some are ok".

But you know … there's a whole traitor of a tough bean in there somewhere.

The freezer was emptied of our time consuming beans then we went to Iceland, much easier.

Which reminds me that since the catering course I have never made bread. Without looking through my books … I have no idea how to anymore. But I do know it takes ages and I know I'll probably never do it again.
I hope I never sleep in a zipped up bag, on the hard and cold ground, again either. By the way.

Overall the allotment has manufactured a real sense of pride and achievement, we have both worked very hard for the results, to have actual crops that could be eaten and given away was just worth all the aggro. I was beyond pleased and still had ideas for the end of our plot, that we hadn't managed to get to, it was covered with old carpets and waiting weed free (kinda) for attention.

How annoying: weeds find all the holes in the covering!

Thinking along these lines, with my dream allotment, I bought some reduced price fruit trees for our orchard. Five different fruits: apple, pear, peach, plum and erm something else. They were dormant twigs in a plastic bag, with a bit of muck, in need of growing space. We followed the instructions meticulously, Scoutman dug the holes deep and filled them with lots of healthy manure, then planted our trees with high hopes and expectations.

The bench and flowers would come next!

I had already planted honeysuckle, to climb and disguise the boring shed, then Scoutman had bought me two rose bushes and they were blooming beautifully nearby.
Other than one bad fall, tripped over then fell onto a big thick plank with sharp bits, my feet didn't move quick enough to avoid or prevent the inevitable . I bashed up my knee quite badly, I can feel a loose bit of floating bone now (I hope that's what it is), which had me limping around and walking terribly for a few days.

There have been few personal injuries, having attempted to use the petrol fuelled strimmer once—only to give up with premonitions of blood and pain.
I had to go to the hospital to find out why my wrist was creaking, it's the weirdest thing: you could feel it and it was creepy, it was a repetitive strain injury. Told you there were a lot of weeds, on a big plot. I had to wear a Velcro fastened splint for a while. Which was only a real problem in the bathroom, on top of everything else.
Fortunately the earth and weeds provide a soft landing, when clumsy feet get tangled in the undergrowth and throw me onto the floor .
"Pick your feet up!", Scoutman advises.
Thanks. I'll try that.

My fingernails were awful, they were ragged and always looked dirty, no matter what I did and how hard I scrubbed them. I had a selection of gardening gloves and I was even following advice to put soap under my nails. Which is a jolly good idea! In theory.
In reality I'd take them off, to have coffee and biscuits, then forget to put them back on and get carried away with the task in hand (usually industrious weeding) .

Then with a shrug I'd just carry on, thinking, I'll be careful and only pull the big weeds!
Yeah right.

Before long I'd have forgotten about this and be down there, on my hands and poor knees, weeding relentlessly.

Deserving and needing time out, away from our dirty routine, we planned a holiday. This time with a difference, it was with two disabled friends of mine.
We had organised the first week as a group, then Scoutman and I planned a further week on our own, half board in Benidorm. He deserves a lot of praise for this, for coping and putting up with the peculiarities of three disabled travellers.
So the intrepid quartet were bound for some sun and fun.
Truffle, who I met when she bought Gillian Mk 2, Rigid, who I met through the structure of rehabilitation, and me with Scoutman … the lucky boy.

This situation, between Scoutman and I, is a pain in the bum. He still lives at home and pays his mum rent. He just stays here with me sometimes, the amount of his junk that has crept into my space though does make you wonder. I'm telling you because getting everything together for trips away is just silly, it would of course be easier if we officially lived together but: that's too complicated.
Nor can I be bothered to mess about with the system, the authorities know everything about me and what I do—they basically control my sad little life.
I often feel like an easy target, however headstrong and independent I think I am, being physically vulnerable and reliant on the system.

My circumstances now dictate the existence that I have and lead, I do try my best to get on with it and not grumble—erm too much. But I'm happy, more than, to have Scoutman around me basking in my glory. He is a good audience and genuinely applauds my achievements, he too is amazed by the correspondence and feedback that I get.

Actually I am not an unknown enigma to y'all now am I? (You all know that my favourite meal is spaghetti Bolognese, thought I'd tell you again)

A friend was reading the book on a bus, he told me, "It was as though you were sitting next to me and talking the text". It's written as I speak because: I'm not a writer nor am I that clever. Dippy maybe … I did get a letter from Nomad once addressed to, "Gilly Shakespeare". (cool—I liked that)

So in Benidorm Scoutman was lumbered with three of us bumbling around, but he wasn't bothered, it was us that had the problem of feeling and being different.

Truffle and Rigid shared a room, because it made financial sense and they were able to look out for each other.

Which did make me happy but, of course, they fell out and squabbled like big kids … Each having a tolerance level of none, inevitable really, they were not being very kind about each other.

Bet the flight home was a laugh though.

To be expected in hindsight, with good intentions and verbal commitments of harmony, jolly good times don't always happen as planned. Especially when coping with a brain injury, making you a tad more selfish and guilty of tunnel vision concentration. When you can only contemplate and deal with what's going on now, you think you are being fair—open minded and grown up, but in fact you are probably being egotistical and metaphorically throwing your toys out of the pram. Usually when this syndrome is pointed out you will argue your point, with venom and aptitude, until you have convinced yourself that you were right to throw a wobbler.

Even with evidence, to prove the sequence of events, in front of my very eyes I will still not quite believe that my short term memory is indeed rubbish .

Then I will look sideways sheepishly and say, "Are you sure?". When they sigh, "Yes!".

Then I can't argue my point anymore. Gotta laugh.

Anyway having four brains of varying aptitude, drenched with sun and alcohol, served us well most of the time.

But it was highly unlikely that we would have let our differences spoil the holiday. Well completely anyway.

This night Truffle and Rigid had bickered, or disagreed to disagree again, but we all went out regardless. We were tipsy tourists and trawled the hotspots, looking for adventure, we were searching for Sticky Vicky! People that had been to Benidorm told us, "You have to seek her out … seeing is believing", we were intrigued. Those that said this usually laughed slyly, with a nudge and a wink!
Say no more.

So we found her, it wasn't difficult the adverts are everywhere, by all accounts she is one of the Benidorm attractions.
Well … who needs to go snorkelling!

Well, seeing is believing, the woman is not young and has been perfecting her art for a number of years, we did not have a ringside view but got the gist. She pulls a multitude of items from her vagina, not all at once, a vast array of objects and some items are more shocking than others. The bottle of beer was a surprise, but a baby will fit in there—so a bar would have been more impressive, but a string of razor blades was frightening. If I'd done that there would have been a lot of blood, then my leg would have fallen off!

Worth a gander but we didn't go out of our way to seek her out again. If any of you go on holiday here, if she's not available I believe she has understudies, her daughters are taking over the fannily business. So you can go and watch the antics of Messy Molly or Tacky Tracey! (These names are a fabrication of my tainted mind!)

On this night our two friends were not really speaking to each other, they had verbally fallen out of room buddies again but were not budging, both of them were fraught with obstinacy.

Scoutman came and kissed me, "I won't be long", then he disappeared and so did Rigid?

We were alright and there was an act on, but we questioned Scoutman on his return without our friend, apparently Rigid was not well and so they had walked back to the hotel.

"Why didn't you tell us? ", was the first thing I said in the morning. Rigid looked over his breakfast and shook his head, "Because you would have said something".

What an outrage, "No I wouldn't", I had laughed.

Scoutman and Truffle looked up and both of them snorted in unison, "Yes you would …".

Well if he'd been that ill he would have got a taxi … instead of walking and surely we'd have noticed?

We all went to Benidorm Island so we could experience the underwater world, travelling on an AQUASCOPE, the short journey was made in a glass bottomed boat basically.

We stumbled aboard and our expectations were heightened by the pictures on the advertisement, the opportunity to see marine life from a different angle was exciting, well what a disappointment.

The Red Sea it wasn't.

We saw a few, very difficult to spot until they moved, small silver fish. They were the same colour as the seabed and there wasn't even any seaweed to add interest!

The captain generously told us, "You can stay on the boat and watch the marine life if you want to". But we'd seen the three silver fish already and they were rubbish . So we got off.

There was a hill on the island, with a designated walkway, it was perhaps too difficult for Truffle who stayed at the bottom chatting to Scoutman. Rigid and I went ahead and tackled this challenge head on. We eventually made it to the top but it wasn't easy, then we looked downhill to see how far it was, we were both chuffed and giggling like silly children. It was invigorating, we had made it to the top unassisted! Truffle and Scoutman waved up at us, then we started the descent.

Here we stopped laughing and had to concentrate, it was much more demanding. It takes longer to go downhill, as your balance is essential. To prevent yourself from tumbling head first, for a long time, onto the sun hardened dirt and hurting things. (whilst looking a bit silly) The view was good too … well it was better than the ridiculous boat ride. First one to spot a fish wins.

The four of us went on an organised evening out, a night of entertainment with a meal and copious amounts of cheap wine, it was a chance for us all to get dressed up in our glad rags for a special occasion.

A photograph was taken of us all before we left the hotel, whilst we were primed and still looked good, then we got a taxi and left. We arrived at the venue much too early and it wasn't open, a pretty good excuse to go to the bar we'd passed down the road.

When we did wobble back at the right time the queue was massive, and I, Miss Impatient Knickers, grumbled with hindsight.

Well, "We should have been at the front, first in, almost sitting on the stage!".

The others just shrugged at me and laughed.

Inside there were lots of tables (if there was space it had a table in it) all in front of and facing a large stage, it was noisy and bustling—brilliant.

We had to catch our waiter's attention, for refills to the glasses of alcoholic vinegar I mean wine, which sounds ideal. But everybody in here is doing the same thing!

We were ready and had a secret weapon, we were told to tip our man for guaranteed and prompt service.

So we did, a good idea, but everybody else had been given the same privileged advice.

Bet one of the waiters started the rumour, nice one.

They were catering for a lot of people and delivering three courses, the food was edible but nothing special unfortunately. But we didn't care and we were happy, it was different and we were getting our monies worth in cheap wine.

Truffle is cringing now and psychologically begging me not to tell you, but I have to because it's so funny.

The stage was alive with music and dance, three of us were drinking whilst clapping and cheering, it was hard not to get involved.

Truffle was not watching the performance, she was not with us anymore …

She was bent over the table with her head on her arms, not joining in, we had all tried to speak to her to make sure she was alright. But eventually we gave up and left her alone.

She was still breathing and the three of us had a show to watch, with alcoholic paint stripper to drink.

Rigid had leaned over to confide, he was grinning as he told us, "Truffle's been sick under the table!".

He was too pleased.

We looked at him with raised eyes of question, he was nodding conferment and stifling surprised laughter.

Oh my, that was sneaky, but nobody had seen and she wasn't making any ill noises.

So we all just shrugged and just left her alone, then carried on partying.

When four waiting staff came to our table and stopped, we were startled, they were in uniform and each of them was armed with a mop and bucket.

Truffle was stirred and made to stand up, so somebody had seen her apart from Rigid, the crowd near to us were not watching the show anymore they were fascinated by the cleaning crew.

We all sat back down and Truffle moaned, with her head back on her arms, "I'm so embarrassed".

It's a good job that the photo was taken at the beginning of the evening.

On another night we found a bar that played bingo, only three languages were used and Rigid won!
He didn't even buy us a drink. Tight Arse!

This night it was Truffle's turn to sulk, I think it was the same squabble with a new twist to keep it alive, I'm still sure that they would have been worse off if they'd had separate rooms.
She was stropping off on a mission to do her own thing, because nobody wanted to go to the bar she'd seen the cute guy in, we couldn't stop her. After a few minutes I followed and caught up, then told her off, "That was silly and annoying behaviour, like a tetchy child not getting their own way, so behave yourself".
I don't do this much now, strop off, Oh I remember some of the times that I've set off to walk home from my mum's.
I have yet to tackle the seven miles: alone, on a notorious B road with no pavements. I'll probably be drunk, at night and there are no street lights, where the ground is lethal underfoot and every so often you have to go around the commemorative bouquets . It's that bad.
A search party, of upset family, will be sent to find and rescue me. Thank you. I told her about this.

Truffle grinned and knew she was being out of order, she came back to the party and apologised to the boys. Sometimes you need to catch that runaway train, before it is totally out of control and you have crashed on your own. She does listen to me, because I understand.
I may recognise and observe others in this situation then react … but can't see myself when I'm in the act of losing it.
Sometimes I should just think about things more … maybe … I should put my own advice into practice eh?

We caused underlying ripples, when we were all out, generally there were a few cowardly mumbles that were almost overheard. But one time it was both directed at us and offensive. We were called a bunch of names and ridiculed cruelly, it was very disheartening and quite sad, they were drunk young men. The reaction from the three of us was noticeably different.

Rigid was silent as the immediate male target, but shook his head and mumbled under his breath, making no eye contact.

Truffle launched into explanatory mode, she tried talking sense to these people.

I was a bit fearful and encouraged my friends to move on, to get away from these ugly men, "LOSERS!". I looked over my shoulder as I said this. Scoutman was, sensibly, observant and calm.

I was a bit shocked and disturbed that neither of our friends wanted to buy holiday gifts, token or otherwise, for their mates and families. I have noticed that, people with claims are very cautious (stingy), the more money you have the meaner you become. This may be true of all walks in life.

But, on the other hand, I suppose there is only room for a certain amount of well meaning holiday rubbish in your life.

Reminds me: Scoutman's mum bought me an ornamental pottery dolphin, it was cheap looking and had nasty glittery bits on it. But it was in my bathroom, for long enough, before it swam off to the sea of charity shop.

Scoutman and I bought things from a cheerful tourist trap market, I will not be upset when I see these items in the same shop at home, when you haggle with foreign money and walk away thinking you just got a bargain.

In a clearing, away from the bustle, we were bewitched by the human statues. Have you seen these?

People dress up, this man was entirely dressed and painted silver, then pose and just stand perfectly still for ages. We were amazed, more than most, everyone else in the market seemed to just walk by taking little notice. Three of us were standing and watching, absorbed in fascination, he really did not move anything at all. Having virtually no sense of balance and little coordination really does put a different slant on things.

We all played crazy golf.

Which sounds simple, if you are able bodied and in control of all your faculties it is. The people behind us were patient and didn't laugh at our endeavours—probably because standing around in the warm sun isn't a bad thing. Truffle was not as bad as I thought she'd be, only having the use of one arm, we all had the odd good shot—by chance rather than skill.

Of course Scoutman won overall, how rubbish would he be if beaten by three disabled goofers. Actually I was trying really hard—he only beat me by two points on both games.

Back on British soil things quickly got back to normal, as the tans faded. Incidentally, to add variety hence spice, my extra curricular smoking was becoming routine and I wasn't at all unhappy about it. It made me feel better and I argued that it made me more creative, remember that I think I'm a writer now Darlink. I had even started to write a story that had nothing to do with me. (This is on the backburner—as it were—to be completed. One day)

It was a real test to my imagination, I became totally transfixed with it and the idea of world domination. (Again) The words poured from my fingers and I was reading it to anybody at any given opportunity. (Again) Although the feedback was good, which was of course what I wanted to hear, the sentiments were different as it wasn't what was expected from me.

It was nothing like Gillian Mk 2.

A real test of memory too, the words had to keep being reread to remind myself where I was and where it was going, in chapter ten I happily weave a story about a character … that was killed and written off in chapter three. It's not easy.
Anyway, it's going nowhere, Typically Gillian has taken over.

I know how lucky I have been …
My mum is brilliant, she is my backbone and I couldn't cope without her, she still gets cross and upset by rude and ignorant people—that feel they should point out my disability. (In case I'm a bit slow to catch on and hadn't realised? Or do I just need reminding in case it had been forgotten?)
I am only disturbed by crass comments, but stunned by downright offensive and thoughtless observations:. Spacker and cripple are the worst that come to mind.
The most recent is "Retard". (?) She must have a CSE in Stoopidology.

I'm going to start carrying a mirror on my person. Then will scrabble in my bag for it as I say, "Hang on I've got something for you", putting the offending (or offended) article in view. Then smile sweetly, "What did you say again?". They will see their ugly mugs … and I'll probably get a smack for being smart. My friends say she is jealous of me, they have their reasons why this might be.
I think it's her BIG backside to be honest. (so there)

Music Man is a friend that I have gained through the pages of the first tome, he was looking at books in the charity shop and I tried to sell him mine. As you do.

Unbeknown to me he had read the copy in the library, which was stolen (blimey), he was looking at me sideways.

Then he questioned me.

"Is it you? ", he grinned and then answered himself. "It is you isn't it …", he was shaking his head.

Now I was confused and smiled as he went on. I looked at him again, quizzically. Oh no, did I know him?

No he's not familiar, or I didn't recognise him, I shrugged then answered.

"It might be …", I joked not wanting to offend …

He told me how he knew me, "I've read your book already, I recognised you through the words".

He laughed, "I've noticed you before getting around and about … just now I realised that it couldn't be anybody else".

Then he dropped to his knees and started fanning me … no he didn't, but he was chatting for a while and we parted agreeing a day to meet again.

He now owns a signed copy of Gillian Mk 2 and is one of my favourite people.

Music Man is sound and able bodied … most of the time. He sings whilst playing the guitar and collects old toilets. (I attract them all) He often makes me feel guilty and stupid, though I'm sure he means well, he asks me, "How's the writing going then eh?", with raised eyebrows. Then answers his own question, "You've done nothing have you? Eh?". (He says this a lot eh?—I think it's a dialect thing—he's not from around here)

He goes on and continues, "Well get on with it girl. People are waiting! Eh".

He tells me, "Your words are well received and meaningful, they made me laugh and cry".

I told him to write a song about me and clapped ! "Cos I is brilliant".

He has met Truffle and she smiled, telling him, "I bought her book! That's how we met".

Gillian Mk 2 has already made a significant difference, to my alternative life, maybe I should get on with Typically Gillian.

When you are first injured it is beyond your control, you can do nothing, everything has to be done for you. The trouble begins when you start trying to do things, like ... anything, unaided.

Similar to a big, clumsy and lanky, toddler ... with a drinking problem.

The walking and talking skills were there in my grey matter somewhere, scattered amongst all the other adult achievements, just a matter of finding them and then putting all the bruised elements into some order. But there are still chinks in this chain, meaning that it isn't smooth and orderly in connection.

If it physically feels wrong I consciously try to correct it, my right arm automatically hugs me sometimes and my bum still sticks out, relentlessly without concession.

But I would say that although there have been painful episodes, I'll remind you: the broken and subsequently right angled little toe, then tearing my chin on the bedroom carpet ... Oh yeah not forgetting my kidney going into overdrive and making bricks, then my creaking wrist and bashed up knees ...

The numerous falls have hurt but not incurred any permanent damage ... yet.

Anyway the biggest grievance, causing the most anxiety (resulting in propulsion ... that's my theory), is:

FRUSTRATION!!

I remember that I could jump and I can recall doing it, but now the connection between the two goes as far as ... one laboured bounce.

Do you remember my analogy? The computer keyboard and the brain?

Well my keyboard (brain) has excelled, in repair, and has created me. Da da ...

My brain has rewired itself, although it has taken me a long time to decode these jumbled messages, but the changed route of instruction and action is not totally reliable. Some cables are still a bit loose and if the orders are too complicated (i.e.: more than one demand), we have a crash situation as the wires get into a tangle and progress stops. Sometimes this is literal, there is nothing more to offer, at other times I just stumble and stammer until I catch up with myself. It's now an annoying part of the course, but it's not a huge deal anymore, the disability doesn't stop me it just hampers progress, I will simply apologise for nothing then smile.

However fab I am, it is obvious that there is something wrong, but helpful people still tell me that I am different and disabled. I can't hide it under a baggy jumper and it won't go away.

Getting dressed ... a simple task.

No. It is a chore, let me attempt to describe the tedium, that of course has to be mastered.

To put trousers on is a skill, hopping about on one foot whilst tugging at your waistband, *think about it.* This notion and speed of reaction escapes me completely.

So, necessity breeds something, I have had to adapt and change my attack to achieve this task.

Now the waistband is held open at my feet, so I am bending over like a lady, then I lift the toes of the left (always) foot enough to pull the material under them. Still with me?

I then pull them up the left leg, some of the way. So now there is half a leg in one side, but I have to hold onto something to repeat the action with the other leg. Imagine putting trousers on with one hand. Because, if something isn't grabbed, I fall down. Just keel over.

Onto the bed usually, which is where I should have started in the first place … seated and in control.

The worst thing is ripping the flimsy summer trousers, in the moment I forgot that I can't do anything complicated on one leg.

Gradually, many bruises later, you realise that you can't take anything for granted anymore. Now I have to think about the mechanics of movement, its like having an imaginary robotic sketch in my head. Like a cartoon drawing, it goes through the steps it takes to bring about an action, be it walking or one concentrated and flat footed baby bounce. Then we have stepping over things. One of our new do good finable offences, somebody made money out of poop scoopers, is beneficial as I no longer have to scan the walkways to see the dog doings that I'm going to attempt missing.

Anyway if the action is too complicated, requiring speed and precision, my robot can't keep up and doesn't know what it's doing … because the instructions are rubbish!

So it falls over ... and whirrs in whitewash. The cartoon sticks, mid-action, moving no further.

Then I know that this feat of accomplishment isn't going to happen, it's too hard, and I put the gymnastics off to another day.

When I was at the rehabilitation unit the physiotherapist had asked, "Do you think about your walking?".

At the time I leant on my walking sticks and looked at her then slurred, "No", I explained with too much attitude, "This comes naturally".

I cringe at the thought, of me doing what came spontaneously and moving away ... smooth as peanut brittle.

Nothing comes to me naturally anymore, this is not the problem, forgetting that this is the case and trying to be clever is.

What I mean is you can't just throw your legs about and hope for the best, I've tried it and it's not good, there has to be an element of control or you would never get anywhere.

So the answer is now:

"Yes, I have to think about my balance movement and mobility all the goddamn time".

Prompting myself every walking moment: Bend knees, swing arms, big toes down, bum in, lean back, stand tall, heel first and roll off toes, stop looking at the floor.

Gadget Boy, an invaluable part of Gillian Mk 2, comes to mind as he started these messages of retraining. I still have to, continually, remind myself of these fundamentals to mobility.

So a belated thank you to the man x ... better late than never eh?

I hereby challenge you to try and think about how you walk, then try to explain it to somebody.

If you have heard this already … I'm not bovered. (My little brother used to announce, "I'm not bollered" … ah … back in those sherbet pip days when a packet of tomato Snaps cost two and a half pence). Anyway I digress …

Truffle and I brave a Saturday night out in the throng and I can dance now!

I do try not to take any notice of ignorance, or actually listen to snide comments, easily done in Gillian's world as the tipsy wobble takes over and I don't care.

I like to describe my expression as interesting.

The only time my weighted feet, it's feels like my legs were filled with lead when I was in the coma, leave the floor is when I overbalance and stumble. Blimey. I'm such a lady.

In my bathroom there is a trellis on the wall, on which there hangs one pair of pointed and dressy shoes, the footwear displayed is a reminder of days past. When I was a student I wore these, I can wear them now but can't walk anywhere, I'm now resigned to sensible and comfortable shoes that old ladies shuffle in.

I will be wearing a jacket too, exposing copious amounts of flesh in the winter is not sexy, I suffer the cold more than most though as the thermostat function in my brain is a bit broken.

Mum bought me a bag full of grains, this is placed in the microwave for a few minutes, it is a no messing hot water bottle and I use it for most of the year.

Just thought about doing some toast, do you know anybody who doesn't like toast?

It reminded me: I was queuing in a local baker's as a woman, with a lot of bags, fumbled about with her purse for loose change. The chap in front lowered his head and looked at me sideways, then he grinned in confidence and was shaking his head, "There's always one".

I smiled as I nodded, "Yeah … it's usually me".
He laughed but looked a bit bewildered, he didn't know, ah, that I wasn't kidding and was being quite serious.
He was lucky that I wasn't in front of him too.

Back to the point: I will round this chapter off with an anecdote about a well known head injury charity. (The charity for head injury victims and their families—just reminding myself)

It was time for the AGM in London two of us went, to represent our thriving group in York.
We went on the train, because I don't drive and Scoutman wasn't at all excited with the prospect of London traffic. So he refused to drive, convincing himself and happily arguing that this mode of transport was a much better idea.

Yeah … for him.
I couldn't smoke at all—not even within a hundred yards of the open air station!

Just reminded me of an irksome train experience: the delays and already full to bulging replacement train was bad enough but, goddamn bloody hell!, being told to stub out my anticipated fix was beyond. I had looked at the coordinated uniform, pause, then taken a maximum lungful and snapped:
"Are you serious?".
He was.

This is madness, which body of jumped up importance decided that smoking on an open ended train platform was bad for public health? But blimey a cigarette butt might get onto the lines and derail the train, or maybe one of the staff injured themselves sweeping up and emptying the ashtrays. Smokers are picking up the work injury compensation tab.

Incidentally those that pick up and utilise discarded cigarette-ends were fighting, outside the station, for rich pickings.

They weren't really, they probably had their own patches. Like outside any building where there might be people! I almost squirm, with patriotism, when I think of the stupid mess our country is in.

Gingerbread PEOPLE?

Bet they, the grey persons, eventually ban Dr Doolittle on a cruelty to animals spin and chocolate white mice will be a distant memory. We will all be micro chipped soon, there will be no escape, it's a sad world when the law enforcers have cameras strapped to their helmets.

But it's sadder that they show all this footage, many times over, on our magical television box things.

The latest news that our fire service is under attack? What's going on here?

When one of these families needs the fire brigade, because their pile of tat is not insured, then the fire engine being damaged and the men being injured will make a big difference. It's appalling that everyone suffers the effects of this behaviour, what are the parents doing?

Wouldn't you be mortified if one of these kids, that the whole country is watching, showing such a blatant disrespect for life savers, can be linked to you.

Is living under your roof?

But the use of stocks would become a status symbol, it's too mad. Then why do they blank out the faces of these scallywags? (That's a good all encompassing word isn't it? I'm sure victims of heinous crimes could think of something much better) .

But if they didn't the suing mad compensation crowd would ooze from the woodwork, making it ultimately worthwhile being a retard especially with a greedy or violent twist.

Then you can write books in jail ... or get on Big Brother?

Anyway ... no I haven't finished yet ...

The smoking ban! What a pile of pants that is! Oh my god ... don't get me started.
Seriously.

At this moment in time if you go to China with forty pounds you could buy **five cartons** (two hundred in each).
At home, here in the good old United Kingdom of Old (well is it united?), you will get **eight packets**.
That is a thousand verses ONE hundred and sixty. Let me spell that out to you:

£40 = **China 1,000 cigarettes V 160 cigarettes United Kingdom**
    = **0. 04** each smoke = **twenty five** each ... 25 whole pence!

Blimey!
So take a holiday in China, where you start out with a suitcase full of clothes, but only take shabby attire with you, wear the item once, then bin it! Voila!

An empty case to fill with cheap fags. Also with the money you just saved—splash out and buy yourself a new wardrobe when you get home.

Brilliant and you could eat battered testicles and the like whilst you're at it.

How good is that?

Bet somebody's done it …

Us: smokers:

For bailing out the system, by paying so much tax, we are penalised? Being an outcast wouldn't be so bad, if it was pleasant, if the climatic conditions were not so unpredictably rubbish.

My local bingo hall has provided large umbrellas to combat the negative aspects, wind / rain / hail / sleet / snow. But they're not very good, most of them are broken now and bare ravaged prongs.

At break time the smokers run, well move a bit faster then, to get outside into the smoker's room.

So about twenty people will be happy to get wrapped up, then exit, all on a mission to make a grab for the least broken brolly. Which I usually get, being at the end of the queue

Then try to light up, in the wind, with gloved hands and a temperamental cheap lighter. Whilst realising that the umbrella is a waste of time and the exposed spikes are dangerous in a gale. There is now a real danger of impaling a fellow leper.

Now holding a cigarette in your car, on which you pay tax, is a finable offence. Outrageous. Public places are a no no and penalties are fixed, then as if the money making and reliable scheme isn't bad enough you are a criminal (asking for an on-the-spot fine) if you toss a butt into the giant ashtray of open air.

Soon there will be a designated and inoffensive field on the Outer Hebrides, if they can't get the moon, where you will be allowed to smoke as much as you can afford. But then, some do gooding, politically correct nonsense will call for a ban. Because the birds and insects are suffering!

All the slugs will get cancer, we don't want that it's cruel and they have got rights ... to be a slug

Might as well be a class A drug, a nicotine habit carries more penalties and costs enough.

If money was no object I would open a big pub, complete with extractor fans and windows that open, refurbish it to make it really swish and then call it Choice.

Look around you, there are worse things to be judgemental about, it is truly sickening to see. The police must be armed with Tazers (?), no muckin' about waiting for an episode. Nip it in the bud.

Disrespect, discipline, disability ... dissing ... got a bit stuck there.

But you get my drift, bring it on, it's like having a classroom full of kids and the session is interrupted and paused by one. So, the other children lose out as the lesson stops, control and discipline are vital, such behaviour should not be tolerated and is a waste of time.

I reiterate ... outrageous. What happened?

I interrupt this grumpy old woman, getting on my high horse, rambling with an anecdote. Phew.

Me doing my make-up! Or me trying to make things look better. Was that a bit Freudian?

Anyway. When I'm going out an effort is made ... and it takes me ages!

Having to lean on the sink for balance is one thing, being faced with a blank canvas and a basket FULL of cosmetics is another.

I am spoilt with an assortment of colour, with various uses, a few of the containers are lidless others items are broken and grubby. So like a birdbrain I get distracted from the task in hand.

Then wonder where the blue eye shadow came from, I don't use blue? Why is it still there?

Then I remember what I'm supposed to be doing and search for … mascara.

Why are there three black and one brown to choose from?

Liquid eyeliner? That's a wicked concept, to do a photo shoot finish of lined eyes, a broody femme fatal with alabaster features. Well that's the general idea.

But I cannot do a straight line, with precision or speed, and then I blink. Usually when the loaded wand is touching my eye-lid, which waters in reaction, which of course means a big black mess. The set smudge of black is very difficult to get off, it just ends up everywhere, then looking at my watch I won't have time to try doing this again. So the image of a vamp disappears from my thoughts, as I look in the mirror and face reality, where do I start?

Then we have to find the mascara. Blue eye shadow?

One day I'll get round to sorting it out … I only need one mascara and my niece needs some blue eye shadow. Yeah.

I got smartened up for the charity's meeting in London, we were looking forward to it.

I knew what to expect, having been with my mum and dad last year, so getting straight to the coffee then heading outside to join the fellow lepers was easy. We spotted our area manager, Fat Badge, who was loving herself and flouncing, in the broadest sense of the word, with big smiles and showy gestures.

She didn't speak to us, a plastic smile of acknowledgement was thrown our way—we returned it with the same nonchalance, but we weren't bothered as we were fact finding for our group.

In the break I stormed ahead on a mission, it was an action taken on my own decision ... so I didn't think about it much, with fanciful notions of recognition. I went straight to the top dog, a titled patron of the charity, then put a copy of Gillian Mk 2 down in front of him. In my outburst I explained the progress with the book, the touching and relevant responses from readers were disclosed, finishing with a request for their help to publicise my work in their literature.

The man shook his head, when I explained that all of this had been instigated by me.
"We'll see about that", were the parting words from my knight.
Scoutman gave me the coffee and asked me what had been said, I was grinning when I told him—note **was** positively buzzing.
A few months later I was itching to know what was going on, so I called the head office in London.
I didn't expect to speak to the big man himself, at all, so was happy with anybody. That knew something.

Firstly I spoke to the chief executive's secretary, then was passed onto his personal assistant, but got through to him eventually and was assertively excited.
He asked me, "What do you want?", think that it was at this point I mutated into a Darlink (it doesn't take me long). "I've written a book", I told him, the anticipation is killing me and subconsciously I'm clapping my hands in wait for the reaction. Maybe I should have told him who I was ... but he didn't ask.

"Everybody's written a book". His tone was flat with disinterest and I imagined him, sitting back in his leather chair, looking at his manicured nails.

He had delivered the first slap to my eggshell ego but, although this bothered me, I carried on and described my conversation with his colleague. Concluding that Gillian Mk 2 really should be promoted in their literature, sand to the Arabs, they advertise a lot of books and one or two of them were written by people like me (injured). I knew that.

"They usually offer donations", I did hear him drone in monochrome but was still rattling on about the bloody book.
He audibly sighed then offered his penultimate insult, "What makes you so special?".

That stopped me in my tracks with a sickening lurch, I was mortified in insult and confused, that wasn't supposed to happen? I blame you lot, telling me the book is poignant and funny, because I thought he'd be impressed too and might even compliment me or something? Didn't expect that though, Sir you surprise me, so didn't know how to react.

I shook my head and apologised for any misunderstanding, I was numb with shock and couldn't think on my feet, he sighed again and pointed out, "We've been going round in circles for twenty minutes now".
Then he put the phone down on me. Woah, can you believe?

Completely flattened in spirit, my bubble of confidence had been shattered, I wondered if the man that made me cry had heard anything that I'd said. Was he even in the right job? I was in a real state, sitting on my own in tears and shocked with the attitude of my charity, I had to talk to someone and had started shaking.

I wailed to Scoutman at work, he insisted that I gave him the name and number of this autocrat.

"Don't swear at him". I offered weakly, "I'm not gonna swear at him, just give me the number", he was serious.

He entertained the secretary and the personal assistant then spoke to the man, who said seeing pound signs, "If you are trying to sell something call back later we are very busy".

Can you believe the audacity of the number cruncher?

Scoutman asked him, "Why has my girlfriend just called me, at work, in tears after speaking to you?".

I was overwhelmed with feelings of outrage and disappointment, a letter of complaint was drafted and sent, I firmly believed my reader's comments and couldn't understand why they wouldn't help.

The reply was what my friends and family expected, they had all warned me not to get my hopes up, it delayed a reaction until internal investigations were completed.

"They're playing for time and they're not interested in you", those around cautioned and calmed me down again, I was still convinced they would see the potential.

The finale left me in no doubt, the letter informed that all the chums had got together, it was decided:

I was not worthy of their time.

They even arranged an appointment to chat with Scoutman, not sure why, but I was banned nobody wanted to know my thoughts. I saw the write-up of the meeting and it was pulled apart, basically it was a load of twaddle, Scoutman nodded and agreed.

So I grilled him, "Why didn't you say something? You should have told them everything".

Like a rabid dog, I would not let go, incensed beyond distraction I was making myself ill and alienating people.

Good good.

Truffle and I were out when I bumped into a friend, Ed, that works on the local newspaper. It's been a while and he asked me how things were going with the book. With a drink in my hand I told him. 'Charity Snub' was documented, they used an old picture of me holding a copy of Gillian Mk 2.

The next time that I saw this article was at the monthly committee meeting, when Fat Badge demanded an explanation, "What's this?", as she produced the paper and was glaring at me. (no idea where she got it from)

Nobody knew what she was talking about, the offence was being passed around, they all smiled and commented, "Nice picture". But I couldn't smile.

Fat Badge was verbally attacking me and the viciousness was upsetting, I felt like a stupid child, this was quite awful, each time I tried to defend myself she spoke over me. This was not right.

In here nobody knew, or cared, it was old news anyway now and the article had made no difference. To anybody? Except me. It was probably wrapping her chips ... ah ... that's how it was seen and where it came from!

I was still fulfilling my role and making them money, nothing said was not true and nobody was bothered or affected by it anyway ... until now. She was being really nasty and had metaphorically stabbed me, repeatedly, with the pin on her badge.

By this time I was a bloody mess. Well done, you represent the charity with malice.

Frustrated at the unfairness of free-speech and angry with this goading woman, I am rubbish and I started crying. Then one of my friends took me out of the room.
I did go back in, but offered the group nothing more of me, then we went home.

We did keep going to both the committee meetings and the socials, the only person now bothered by these episodes was me, even though Scoutman was aware of the situation he didn't do anything else, but it has to be said that nonsense like this is soon forgotten .

Everything carried on as normal, routine, then I got all excited about an event in York.
It was a day for various charities to make money on a market stall, ours was booked and we requested a big name banner to put on our pitch.

Nothing came (erm quelle surprise) so I drew and coloured a big poster, then everybody knew who we were representing.
Things had to be organised and I got Spruce Girl involved. With a trip down to the old scout venue we rescued then cleaned bric a brac, leftovers from the last jumble sale, there were loads of tom bola items too.
We were there for hours, but had a car full of stuff to put on our stall, the tom bola prizes were ticketed too.

The date came and we travelled to York to set-up our enticements, nobody came to us that we knew all day—to say hello or to help, but it was good way to kill time and we let them pay for our coffees.

We had a good day and it was fun, our endeavours were praised and thanked at the next committee meeting. No they weren't.

Fat Badge was present and she had brought two allies with her? Shuffling her important papers, she lowered her eyes as she began, "Something has been brought to my attention, it is my duty to inform you and to sort out this dilemma".

Sounded serious and we all looked at each other but nobody spoke, we were all waiting, she looked at Scoutman and I then dropped the bomb.

"Somebody told me that we were seen stealing at the charity event".

Woah ... we looked at each other and both replied, "What? ".

We shook our heads and laughed at this ridiculous accusation, "How was that then? And from where? Our own stall?". Scoutman was taking this on as the insult that it was, "I have done twenty years as a scout leader and how dare you ... who said that and what are they TALKING about?".

I was furious too, "We took some cash ... for refreshments ... because we were there ALL day ON OUR OWN! Making money for you!".

This all went unheard as the meeting was just a shambles now, the collaborators were taking notes for more vital paperwork, a few of the volunteers were shaking their heads and knew this fiasco was a farce. But I reacted.

Oh my Gawd, I so wish that I hadn't done this now.

We had counted all the money, taken on that day, and it was with me now. The money was firmly slammed, bag by bag, on the table in front of me.

Aha! So there ... Fat Badge!

I should have put two out and kept the rest, then she would have been right and we wouldn't have been ON OUR OWN ALL DAY for nothing.

But I have been brought up well … and wish that I hadn't.
I felt sick and Scoutman was outraged, he wanted to know who had been talking out of their backside, this was nothing but clumsy and malicious slander. In their paperwork we were smeared and there was nothing we could do, the drive home was heated with a multitude of unanswered questions, "What had just happened there?".
I blamed myself and regretted the day I woke up, then decided to write and self-publish a book, I still did not understand why this charity were not applauding my efforts and encouraging others with my example. Poor Scoutman had been rubbished by the charity too, for his efforts, I must have really p'ed them off.
Fat Badge told me off, again, "You took the book to the AGM and you didn't have permission". Oops … but I didn't know and neither did anybody else, anyway that was months ago, bit late now.
Was that why?
My thoughts on and about this bitter rejection, were making me ill.

But that was the final straw, the group collapsed, all the funds that we had given our time for were taken by the charity. I wished that my dad was here, he could have asked why the money donated at his funeral wasn't even acknowledged, my mum had her 'I told you so' T-shirt on again.
She was gob smacked and told me, "Do not to bother with them anymore, all charities are the same, they help those that make them look good and don't know anything else? ". Good point. Fat Badge's son is going to write a book, she told me once then was creepy when smiled and said, "But it won't be as good as yours". How would she know?

"It's a shame", mum concluded, "But you are too clever for them and look how well you have done on your own". (I hate this statement)

So the rude dismissal, pointless beetle drive, the nastiness, no help with the silver jubilee celebrations, no support with the charity stall, accusation of theft, the unkindness that came with it, this was all ignored and the little people suffered. As usual.

What a hateful chapter this turned out to be ... I was gutted. The FUG U attacks were haunting and took very little provocation, the headaches came with the frustration.
I was told to stop thinking about it, easier said than done, in fact it's annoying me now and I am still bristled by the injustice.
But Rommi Smith, the writer, did a brilliant appraisal of GM2 ... so there ...

This is a long chapter, I do waffle, but I have a lot to share with you ... said the actress ... anyway it's your own fault you asked me to do this. Paulos must be mentioned, he is one of you but is chariot bound ... so he is in my gang too. I met him at the rehabilitation unit when we were both inmates. His base is in Chester now and occasionally his support worker drives him here for a visit, he usually takes me for lunch, Paulos is funny and he is one of my fave people.

CHAPTER VI

Now we are talking. 2004

When I said never going to the circus again, ever …

This time it was a Chinese Circus, viewed from comfy chairs in a theatre, the picture on the flyer shows a woman so bent that her feet are flat on the floor … either side of her head.

Mum, Scoutman and I went, it gets a bit same same but the dedication and skill was amazing.

On one chair, wooden with four legs, they balanced nine other wooden seats. This is with the seven acrobats, all doing handstands, on the balancing chairs, imagine if one of them sneezed.

Blimey.

But I was nearly that flexible once, when I was a child, in a gymnastics competition at middle school, I plucked up courage and started my programme with a back flip.

Then landed heavily on my knees, the rest of my time was an uncoordinated mess with a few cartwheels and twirley bits. Beverley, with stringy long blond hair, won … and her routine was rubbish.

There is a photograph of me doing a handstand, aged twenty seven, in Gillian Mk 2.

But, not any more.

At the moment I am mastering putting trousers on and challenging my dancing skills, contortionism will wait, it's quite funny really how simple things become such a chore. You now spend time working out the quickest way of putting trousers on, in a mad jolt of trying to walk and hold the bladder in before you get to the toilet, then fumble to undo the said trousers before you wee on them.

My laundry basket is often a bit damp.

Music Man told me about a coach trip he'd been on, "At the toilet stop I sprinted to relieve himself, the older folk stayed seated and drank flasks of tea. The same thing happened at the next stop?".

At the destination he discovered they were all wearing the equivalent to nappies, what a brilliant idea.

I remembered me wearing one on a camping trip, thankfully nobody saw, full of wet weight it hit my knees when I stood up the next morning. So asked, "Didn't you notice that they were dragging their pants behind them?".

He said, "No, I recognised the smell".

I think this might be a joke, just realised, I'm not very quick.

Saw a fridge magnet, that had a woman with crossed arms saying, 'If God had meant you to touch your toes he would have put chocolate on the floor'.

I was going to buy it for Truffle, should have bought it for myself … I'm not very fit or flexible.

Basically the Chinese balancing show was worth going to see, it was impressive.

I had to go to the hospital, a growth had appeared on my nose … obvious and in the middle of my face!

Because I thought it was a spot it was squeezed, they say you shouldn't pick but everybody does …

Well this wasn't a blemish and bled for ages, making it even more noticeable.

It was annoying me and so this was tried again, the same thing happened, it was then decided that this course of action … not really a good idea. It started itching so I went to see my doctor, he referred me to the local minor injuries department.

Scoutman came in with me and the nurse told me what she was going to do, the anaesthetic was injected into my nose. My eyes squirted water and I yelped, Scoutman's hand was crushed, it hurt a lot and surprised me. Then, with a medical hole puncher, the growth and surrounding skin were cut out of my nose. One single stitch held the small wound together, I was trying to be careful but the suture ended it's usefulness on the towel. It wasn't bleeding so I left it alone, it healed nicely, but it was now a big unsightly hole. Scoutman had laughed, "Bet you wish you hadn't had it done now", he is so funny with his observations but I didn't see the funny side of it myself.

This was a busy weekend to blast-off the year, talking of launches Dara Obrian came to do his stand up comedy sketch at our small theatre.

I didn't realize who he was but recognised his poster, a picture of him in his children's television role. If I identified with this image, he had hair then, it must have been taken a while ago.

We were late, mm that'd be me again, so stood in the aisle and tried to be low profile.

Yer man was on the small stage, he's bigger now and apparently has got huge feet, he stopped talking and looked at me then pointed to the empty seats on the front row.

"Come and sit yourselves here …", Irish accent, " … why don't you?".
As we sat down I laughed at him, "Everybody in here hates us now!".
He smiled at me, "Because you are on the front row?".
I nodded, he's very quick.
Chatting to him, outside in the smoker's and drinker's break, I told
him my latest joke and mentioned the book. Should have taken one
with me to give to him … it would have saved me the postage. Not
really sure why I did this, maybe I thought it would make a difference.
But the theatre is small and has a serving hatch acting as a, miniature,
bar. So not really the make a difference venue, it's nice but small.

A day trip to Flamingo land was organised for the charity group, the
area manager was uncannily available then … and so was the rest of
her family, who all joined us with the dog.
A lot of the park was closed but we had a packed lunch, made and
bagged by one of the parents.

Ah bless, she did well with funds of twenty five pence per head, we
had a packet of crisps each and that was over half the budget. The
flat white rolls had something equally plastic and tasteless inside,
I'm such an ingrate, the baby with us liked them though. The area
manager's grandchild.
It killed time but I'm not sure I'd rush to go again, off season anyway,
all the animals were still hibernating.
Like my dad, who wouldn't have said anything about the packed
lunch either.
When she reads this: sorry but the boring lunch was horrid.

Mind you there were fun times, when all is said and done, there were
some really lovely people there that I was sad to leave behind. I've
known some of them for years. The charity had big ideas with plenty

of money, but in my opinion expanded into everything vaguely head related, then got completely lost. So they have to employ more people, issue more badges, to sift through the minefield of paperwork and literature.

I still find wasted paper with their logo on it, not read by anybody that I know, bet you Fat Badge doesn't read all the stuff that they print. It had to be expensive to produce and send, full-colour documents, to the numerous members country-wide.

Anyway it was left as an unfortunate experience, for which I held myself responsible. They, after all, know about and help people that have survived a serious head injury. They understood that I suffered a TBI and had asked for their help, to publicise my work, I understood that they wanted nothing to do with me.

But my questions were left unanswered … that may be why I'm still harping on about it!

Well it's not fair … I worked hard.

Look at the television coverage you get, if you help yourself. Yeah, to other people's belongings or even to their life.

It's coffee time.

Just reminded me, an odd thing that I always do, the canisters containing tea, coffee and sugar are always turned to face the right way. They are not grubby and caffeine splashed for long, if I notice any coffee spills and get a cloth in my hand … that's it. I will then look around, at all my white goods then doors, skirting boards, floor and sides. Everything. Firstly I am amazed how I manage to spill coffee on so many things then wonder how I didn't notice before.

The cup is not filled to the top, theoretically to reduce the spills. It's faint at the moment, but you can definitely see it. There is a trail on the carpet, from the kettle in the kitchen, to my usual pew in the front room.

Music Man always looks at the drinks then at me he and raises his eyebrows:
"Is the water on rations? Eh?", pause, " Is the kettle empty? Eh?", pause, " Has the council pop ran out? Eh?", pause (there's more), "Do you pay twice as much? Eh?".

I always do the same thing, he always goes on. I explain, "If it's not full I have less chance of slopping it everywhere", then shrug at the normality. He scowls, "I can carry it!", but I simply forget that he's a big boy and can manage full cups.

In my scrap book there are four Valentine's cards and one of them is from Posh Boy.

A reader had suggested that I give talks, about the implications of a head injury. What a brilliant idea.
So I had called the Women's Institute (WI) and followed their instructions, an advert written by me was placed in a local newsletter. Three responded to the advert and I just exploded in preparation, a rainbow of felt-tips hit the paper as I drew sketches of my life.

Pictorial anecdotes from a normal childhood, into teenage years, up to the coma and onto the new life.
Then my tact changed and the audience were encouraged to participate, disability affects more people in more ways than you realise, then finally to conclude the video made with the BBC Telling Lives team (OAR) was to be shown.
www.bbc.co.uk/tellinglives

Humber Region: Gillian Mk 2 This was the plan anyway.

Then I imagined answering questions and trying to part with a book or two, whilst eating home-made cake filled with jam made from a harvest of garden fruits and drinking coffee.

I was ready and this was exciting.

The journey to the first venue at Eskmoor was harrowing, the meeting hall really was in the middle of nowhere, we had absolutely no idea where it was.

We were going in the right direction ... and then we were lost. Completely surrounded by open fields, with the odd house and a lone sign post which made no difference, we didn't know where we were.

We were going backwards and forwards, in the same area, past the same things. It was now winding up my clockwork coping mechanism. I am not good at being lost, it eventually just irritates me, also my patience is rubbish. The journey was just getting into intolerant and unreasonable mode, but he was saved when we spotted a blue woman (it was cold and she'd been stood there for ages) waving her arms to attract our attention.

I grinned at Scoutman, then sincerely hope that I apologised.

The women were ready for me.

After my chat I was generally pleased with myself, they had all laughed in the right places and I was buzzing with achievement.

There were smiles all round and one lady came over to speak to me. She told me that her godson had suffered a TBI. Don't forget that I am giddy with recognition and brilliance now, "Get him a book ... he will love it". I was full of myself.

The book was signed to Posh Boy.

At coffee time I scanned the room, greedy with anticipation and expecting a cake, but no chocolate fudge or butter cream anywhere! Not one cake … or jar …

I did a few and the talks went down well, each time they were different and never to plan.
But always finished with the BBC video, then I always cringed, everybody saw my attempt at running.

A few weeks later there was a letter in my PO box, it was the woman's godson who had read my work.
He wrote, "The book made sense to me … it was identifiable", then, "I gained tremendously from your words and couldn't stop himself from responding".
I had to reply because he knew the score and I liked the tone of his letter, this was somebody that had literally been there, he had convinced my Darlink ego.

Almost immediately a letter hit my home address, it opened with, "I can't believe you replied".

The correspondance became intense, he was smart and funny, but it wasn't until I had spoken to him that I had any idea. His speech was a giveaway, it was such that repetitions for comprehension were frequent, it was like mine used to be but I was clearer now. He reminded me of a few friends that are in my life.
He was the passenger in a mini, in a coma for many more weeks than me, goodness he was very lucky. Though he knows this I'll bet he doesn't feel so fortunate sometimes.

We were standing on the steps outside, I had stopped to listen, "What's that noise?", Scoutman shrugged and I answered myself, "It's a cat".

It was a constant mewing and we followed the pitiful noise to the church, the grill was unlocked by a convenient key holding chap, it was a tiny kitten shivering with wide eyes.

I tried to lift the heavy wooden ramp on my own and struggled, then the two men helped me, I scooped the kitten up and was completely hooked.

It was gorgeous, trembling and mewing, in frightened confusion.

"Food", got a tin of tuna out, "Litter tray", sacrificed a large metal cooking dish. I knew what to do, I love cats.

"We don't know if it's been weaned?", I ignored Scoutman's advice, "Yeah yeah, we'll soon find out", then I put the food on the floor.

The reaction was so funny, it would have made money if we'd had a vidoe camera, it made an excited growling noise with each mouthful. He did exactly the same with the second dish, I looked … it was a boy and I called him Tom.

Scoutman came back with kitten milk, ah milk for the baby, he was smitten too.

Tom was picked up and dumped in the tray until he used it, sorted, he was just perfect.

One seriously cute tabby.

But I had noticed that he was getting a bit too preoccupied with Joey, I had a water spray handy. I didn't see him do this, so have no clue how, sneaky little cat! I blinked when I saw him, suddenly Joey was flapping with alarm and squawking, Tom was standing on top of the radiator looking into Joey's eyes.

He was always with his stuff in the kitchen when I went out, I knew he was alright and the old bird was safe, all my throws had pulls in them made by tiny claws. Ah … but he's so pretty!

Although it was unsaid, Tom couldn't stay, but I so desperately wanted to keep him and wish that I had. The kitten was with me for a week, I couldn't stop myself and bought him toys. Hoping to distract him from Joey and lessen the damage to my furniture, it worked sometimes.

I took him to a cattery and on the phone they had asked, "How old is he?", the woman sounded happy when I described him, "He's a furry dot". Then I sighed as Tom bounced past me, "He is so cute and I love him!".

Tears came the day after he had gone, I was sitting at the computer looking for the bouncing dot of fur, it was a surprise to me that I missed him that much.
A few days later, in the heat of the moment, I got a taxi to go and see him. It was quite a distance and the driver told me, "It will be about twenty pounds". Oops. It was further than I thought, blimey, or didn't think!

He came immediately to sit on me, when I was inside the pen, this made me too happy.
The money I had left was donated to the cause, he purred on my lap for a while and then went to play with his new mates.
Scoutman came to pick me up, as arranged, but as I neared the car I remembered how far it was. Going back into the house, it was a good idea to use the bathroom, I saw Tom in the front room. He was looking all settled and fit well into his surroundings, so she had fallen for him too.
I didn't do this again.

Just found this:

A little game that has a funny and creepy outcome. Don't read ahead, just do it in order. It takes about three minutes and it's worth it. When you are asked to write a name, make sure it's people that you ACTUALLY KNOW, then go with your first instincts.

Are you ready?

1. Write the numbers 1 to 11 in a column.
2. Then, beside numbers 1 and 2, write any two numbers you want.
3. Beside the 3 and 7, write down the names of members of the opposite sex (same if gay).
4. Write down anyone's name (like friends or family) in the 4th 5th and 6th spots.
5. Write down four song titles in 8, 9, 10 and 11.
6. Finally make a wish.

The key.

1. You must tell (the number in space 2) people about this game in (number in space 1) days, for your wish to come true
2. The person in space 3 is the person that you love.
3. The person in 7 is the one you like but can't work out.
4. You care most about the person you put in 4.
5. The person you name in 5 is the person who knows you very well.
6. The person in 6 is your lucky star.
7. The song in 8 matches with the person in 3.
8. The title in 9 is the song for the person 7.
9. The tenth space is the song that tells you about your mind.
10. And 11 is the song telling you how you feel about life.

I have another routine.

When a lost memory comes crashing back, into my slow recall centre, I will visibly jump. This can happen at any time, in mixed company usually, I will have already been trying to remember something and eventually given up. Then suddenly I will be taken by surprise, with wide eyes will exclaim, "Oo". Followed by, "Ah". Then I generally interrupt, whatever, to disclose my memory before it's lost again.

But it's now irrelevant and I'm just waffling, my startled company are now looking at me and expecting brilliance. Then will shake their heads with disappointment, "Is that all?".

I have to shrug and laugh at the spilt coffee, which inevitably will have been a full cup in my hand, when my call back pounced, thrown everywhere when my surprise recollection made me jump.

We went to see The Beautiful South at the Hallam arena, in Sheffield, the ticket stubb says rear standing. It also says: 'Plus special guests' ?

I've got a few of the band's albums so knew some of the songs, but the only thing I really remember is getting the T-shirt.

Inbetween all of this fun stuff we are still grafting at the allotment, but dry and spare weekends are sometimes better spent doing other things. The large patch opposite was commandeered by a group, with good intentions, hoping to motivate naughty teenagers. It was very overgrown and abandoned, shortly after it was started, on our plot we are getting there: with fences, sheds, and a greenhouse. Well a cheap plastic house.

We couldn't choose a variety of tomato, so we planted them all, ultimately there was no room for anything else in the small space … except one cucumber plant.

It was all ticking along quite nicely, we plodded on and had coffee with biscuits in the shed, though we were never really on top of anything it was good wholesome fun.

I felt sorry for the vegetarian woman (Turnip), somebody in her family had just died, so I invited her to kill time at my allotment and then she could take some of the produce.

Well I thought it was a good and thoughtful proposal, but she was completely useless and arrived in full make-up with her thin hair all styled.

But, she always looked the same (never seen her any different) so I wasn't surprised, my shock came when I suggested jobs for her to do, things needed action and she was supposed to be helping that was the idea.

"Weeding is easy, it always needs doing and uses up a lot of time", Turnip had looked at her nails, "No I can't do that" …

I was busy and looked up, I suggested something else for her to do, "I can't do that, I don't know how", Turnip was a bit stupid.

I was getting fed up of the Prima Donna and I had things to do, so sighed and shrugged then looked around. "The pumpkins, greedy things, need to be watered. Can you do that?".

Hey Turnips are able to hold and use a watering can. That was it though.

Scoutman was explaining, he'd read it in our Percy Thrower bible, the finer points of growing the vegetable he was showing Turnip. I shook my head and carried on, then was astonished by her reaction. Turnip simpered and blinked her made-up eyes, then smiled, "Tell me again Scoutman".

He was in his element and started to give details for a second time!

Blimey, I wouldn't have noticed if they'd been busy, nothing was getting done, but he was trying to be clever and was getting boring. We were standing by our plastic house, that was suffering in the wind, I interrupted them with a brilliant idea for him to implement. I'd found a piece of thin metal, shaped like a giant staple, going into detail and explaining, "If this was hammered into the ground, over the metal bar of greenhouse, it would effectively secure the structure". Can you imagine this? Even without seeing the twist of metal or greenhouse? Scoutman looked at me as though I was talking a foreign language, out of my bottom, then I noticed him glance at Turnip and shake his head. He was smiling like a simpleton and he shook his fat head, "No idea what you are talking about". Then he shrugged at Turnip again, I noticed but didn't think anything except 'stupido', I explained what I meant for the second time but could have been talking to myself. He still looked confused, Oh my God! .

Eventually I lost it and crawled into the greenhouse, to put the giant staple in position, when I started to hammer it into place myself … Scoutman woke up, with half a brain, then took over.

Turnip did nowt all the time she was there and then Scoutman drove her home, I was busy so didn't really notice how long it took him. I don't think she liked the idea of messing herself up, there were no facilities to check and reapply her face, mind you she would have looked dull without foundation and eye shadow etc … honestly, I'm not telling lies. I simply embellish the facts.

About this time there was a high school reunion planned, I was notified by post, I was intrigued and rang an old friend to sort out details of sleeping arrangements. Then transport—it was in Doncaster. My girlfriend, Vidal, has stuck by me since the accident and was a good mate at school.

She trained to be a hairdresser, whilst I was in the sixth form, I let her practice on me, she cut my hair and did a good job … well it looked alright and I was happy. It was the 80's and big shoulder pads with massive hair was the trend, being a teenager and having a personal hairdresser was cool, I let her perm my hair.

Oops.

The curls were very tight and my brother commented, "You can see all the spots on your forehead now!". Not the right observation to make to a teenager with corkscrew hair, he has still got the mark on his leg, I hit him with the hairbrush.

Reminds me of being Bonged, disastrous perm by a Philippine chap in Gillian Mk 2.

Vidal cut my hair again, but this time to lessen the madness, she didn't persue this career—by the way. She was sensible.

Her birthday is two days after mine, we were in her front room sampling her mother's Xmas stash to celebrate, it was our sixteenth.

Her mum's keys were heard at the front door, Vidal had looked at me in all seriousness and warned me. "Pretend not to be drunk!".

Yeah yeah. I pretend not to be disabled all the time, then I get up. I still see people (usually men) look away quickly, so it isn't obvious and rude gawping, then they won't have to try to talk to me.

But it doesn't bother me anymore.

The first time I went to a nightclub was with her, we were seventeen and as we queued I was mumbling an incorrect birth date so if anybody asked I was ready. The doorman, I've pulled already, was staring at me and giddily I followed his gaze.

Vidal was more developed than me and I had stuffed my bra with cotton wool, when I looked down there was one boob in the middle of my chest, it had all fallen out of the inadequate support and was a Cyclops of bosom! I remember pushing Vidal up the stairs and to the toilets, where I flushed all my chesty evidence away, muttering, "Oh my God … don't you dare tell anybody about this!".

She told everbody at school and my mum had asked, "Where's all my cotton wool gone? Have you seen it?".
She knows where it all went now.

I was really happy to see a man at this reunion, he had lived next door but one, but hadn't recognised him until he said who he was. Apparently he was really stuck on me, wish I'd known, but I remember him fondly and he still has a space in my head. He has a daughter now called Molly … nice name.

Blimey a lot had changed for all of us, one of my friends had about ten kids and she said she would get the book but didn't, locked eyes with a woman who I fell out with in the sixth form (attention-seeker) but had no wish to forcibly communicate with her.

My first love was there, he hasn't changed and I still adore him, but the night was short and Vidal's husband picked us up. The others went into town to carry on partying. We left early, not sure why, but I was gutted not to be carrying on until the wee hours.
A few knew what had happened to me, one or two asked, but generally the party was an ego trip going back into teenage mode.

Some have lived in the same area all their lives, so are still in touch with and see old school chums, I came to this place when I was thirteen. We moved from Wakefield on my birthday.

When I came here in 1998 I didn't know anybody, fortunately I stand out (use your imagination) and can talk. Along the way I have gained some strong friends and lots of pleasant acquaintances, I am lucky. Most of them have a copy of Gillian Mk 2. Some have orders in for TG and are always asking, "Have you finished it yet?". Kebab and Orchid, my bingo friends, are both fab. Kebab bought me a slice of the home-made cake for my birthday, she is one of the people that I have to answer to—Orchid is another.

"Mm, more or less …", I smile when I tell them, " … well I'm nearer to completion than I was".

We got a bread making machine, it was a free gift from a cigarette company, selected from a catalogue, it was an easy choice as the only thing that was any use to us. Don't need a camera or a suitcase and I'm not ripping up a load of packets for one lighter.

When I say free … we spent hours dismantling duty free cartons and then packets, which I'd paid for. There were loose cigarettes everywhere.

Then after all that, they messed up the delivery, I spent hours on the phone tracing the order and talking to receptionists who generally had no idea what was going on. The phone bill had to be paid.

When it eventually arrived a space was cleared in my kitchen and we were like kids, couldn't wait to play with the new toy, it went nicely with the idea of self sufficiency. Now we just needed to rear a cow and get some chickens.

The first loaf smelt fab, we were ready with butter and jam, but the heavy and solid dough was binned. Not beaten we tried again, the second loaf was better as in edible, a book with different recipes and ideas for the machine was bought.

It was opened a few times, we were simply overwhelmed with the choices, but it was never used. The machine was put to use once more, before it started to collect dust and home spiders. My brother took it and has used it once, it's either collecting dust at his house or he's sold it and he won't tell me.

It will go to the car boot sale—along with the redundant sandwich maker.

Actually Music Man has just bought a sandwich toaster, from a charity shop, maybe they'll make a come back. I wonder if my mum has still got one … at the back of a cupboard somewhere with the soda stream and all the microwave dishes (the ones you make rubber omelettes in). They are all good ideas, in theory, until you get fed up of cleaning them. Think on, the shops do nice bread.

Donning the coat and grabbing the umbrella, it's almost definitely raining or about to, then wobbling to the supermarket is actually less of a bind.

Blimey and it was really only a few years ago, on the large scale of things, that this staple was produced at home—people actually hand made their own bread daily.

Back in the days when they made their own cakes and jam, the WI don't even do this anymore.

Bought some new shoes, that's not a big deal … just go to a shoe shop. But I have just noticed that my footwear collection is all starting to look the same. Apart from the patterned Wellingtons and the furry boot slippers. They are now sensible. Flat. Practical.

But there are still times that I choose a pair of risqué footwear, if my mum is with me she will shake her head and say, "I don't think so".

But sometimes I persevere and if I can stand in them, that's a good start and I'm almost convinced, I will then totter around the carpeted floor of the shop a few times to bring on a purchase.

Mum just shakes her head, muttering, "Stupido", under her breath, because she knows.

Then I get them home, put the shoes with an outfit, to venture beyond the carpet.

I couldn't walk in the low heeled black shoes, they kept slipping off and would not stay on my feet, the black boots were too high and I couldn't stand too long in them. The charity shop keeps getting nearly worn shoes and boots, not that many (sounds like I do this all the time …). The other boots had a small stiletto heel, but I couldn't balance to walk in them and would have eventually broken an ankle. Stupido! Mum was right, I should listen eh?

Meanwhile I was still disappointed and upset, outraged and sickened, by the head injury charity's reaction to me and the book. I had gone to the citizens advice bureau to find out if anything else could be done, on my box again, unable to cope with what I interpreted as a personal slur. The chap was very understanding, he sympathised with my dilemma but pointed out that I am little and they are big … which translated in my mind as: you are wasting your time. I left this meeting with a personal invite, to a disability event in York Minster. It's not what you know … it's who.

I told Scoutman and mum excitedly, with notions of recognition pretty much intact, "The Pageant of the Donkey, in York Minster, Her Royal Highness Princess Anne is going to be there!". I remembered the same feeling in 1977, the Queen's Silver Jubilee, I saw her Majesty at Elland Road (football ground at Leeds) with my classmates.

Scoutman bought me a classy and special frock, to go with the new dusky headress, the high heeled shoes that are new would go perfectly.

I had spoken to a super sounding lady about this event, to ask, "Could I take a copy of Gillian Mk 2 to be forwarded to the royal guest.? Please".

She was going to meet me to take the book, "I will arrange to pass it onto the Lady in Waiting".
She paused, "What will you be wearing? To be recognised then I'll find you!".
"I'll be the tall one …", the shoes were vain and much too high, " … with a pink flower on her head".

We parked nearby and watched the hundreds of children, filing into the huge church, then holding onto Scoutman we went inside. It was a very impressive set-up.

A small woman, the shoes were making me very tall and I felt like I was on tiptoe, held out her hands and laughed up at me when she introduced herself as the lady on the phone. She was a bubbly and happy woman, as suspected and I was pleased to meet her, the book was passed onto the right person as she had said.

When Princess Anne arrived and walked to her seat, I am patriotic but was surprised by my reaction, I started crying and felt so happy to be there. I smiled a lot during the entertainment, a lot of disabled children did things and the hours flew by.
Princess Anne got up to leave and everybody was clapping, bloomin' eck, that was good.
I was crying again.

We sensibly decided not to traipse around York, on foot, then I admitted defeat and the mindful heels of stilts left my shoe rack.

My brother, Mr State the Obvious chiropotist, suggests quite seriously, "You should only wear decent and comfortable shoes". Does that mean SLIPPERS? Or sensible and boring stuff?

I don't care, you can't wear dead flat day shoes with a dress. Male readers … you simply cannot.
You have to wear high-heals. End of.

Even if: you do not walk well in them (even when sober), they keep slipping off, then they rub your heels and make the balls of your feet ache … it's unavoidable. C'est la vie …

It's taken a lot of practice, but I'll still slip up occasionally and get beyond myself … no doubt, to fathom out the appropriate footwear. As a vain teenager I wore fashionable shoes, to school, that bashed up my heals so badly that the back of my knees swelled up to pain in sympathy and required a course of antibiotics.
Limping home at about two am from a nightclub, with my first love, with cheap heals on that were crippling me so much that I remember it over twenty (woah) years later.
Am I still trying to be a teenager? Being vain and silly?

Anyway. The holiday in the sun this year, I'm sure one was taken, is not in my scrap book so I have no idea where we went. Mm … no can't remember. It will have been good though. When I dig through some photographs for you I might be reminded.
Was it Turkey???
Yep.

This was the year, the horriday … the holiday, a break in the sun that everybody involved has tried to forget. (until now)

I cannot think who's stupid idea this was, but it seemed like a good one at the time, four of us were going to be abroad together for TWO weeks.

Scoutman with his mum (Sourpuss) and me with mine … who doesn't suffer fools gladly either. The parents would be company for each other and were sharing accommodation, Turkey sounded great, new faces with sun and alcohol, there you have it best laid plans … what could go wrong?

The people that I told all laughed and questioned my sanity, "Why? Are you sure?", as they shook their heads with disbelief. I was still convinced it would be brilliant. Spruce Girl offered helpful advice, "Well make sure you have a good time. Don't fall out with anybody". That was a strange thing to say? Why would I do that?

It didn't even start well, Sourpuss made a fuss about the taxi to the airport and made sure she got in first … as if we'd leave her. But the mood disappeared, as we travelled and spoke in clipped sunshine tones. Then we got to the departure lounge, Sourpuss needed help choosing a purchase for a grandchild. Scoutman was there to assist her, so I was left struggling on my own and my mum had wandered off to do her own thing … thinking that I was alright.

Eventually I caught up with him at the check-out, I was a bit cross but didn't need to say anything because I was alright at the end of the day.

At the resort we all sat by the pool, me in the sun with my writing stuff and cigarettes, Scoutman at the other side in the shade talking to his mum and my mum chatting to anybody at the bar.

She wasn't drinking alcohol, that came later in the happy hour. We discovered the big and clever, all singin' n dancin', cocktails. We were lining them up and taking full advantage of the offer, somebody should have stopped us but we were all adults ... so they couldn't but they should have. Sourpuss, who never drinks ... yeah right, it's only cocktails then, was making up for lost time and seemed quite happy but only really spoke to her son.

She wasn't being mean or anything like that.

This wasn't annoying the first few times, but every day ... come on, Sourpuss would tell Scoutman, "I've got to take my tablets". Then she would ask him, "Remind me to take my tablets", fair enough. Then getting up she would tell him, "I'm going to take my tablets"
On her return she reported to her attentive son, "I have taken my tablets", he would nod.
Good, good, clever girl ... I can take mine in public and I don't tell anyone ... nobody at all. Though I am often reminded when it's time to take them.

Being at the bar so long makes you talk to anybody, about anything. One chap had asked, "What's wrong with you?". My mum responded, it was getting late and she was on a role, I could only shrug as she told these people about me. "Yeah yeah ... she's had EVERYTHING! Fleas, ringworm, threadworms (we lived in Singapore when I was little), scabbies (scabies) ...", she went on.
Bloody 'ell! But it's a change from talking about comas and disability I suppose.

One evening there was a sexy and young belly dancer, ironically she had a flat stomach, she grabbed Scoutman and pulled him up he was a happy boy.

So we became divided and a gallon of blended alcohol (each), with umbrellas and straws, did not enhance the mood. I felt a bit put out, sitting on my own was not part of my holiday plan, but as usual I wanted to explore and dragged everybody into the exertion.

Weird dynamics were happening: I wanted to be happy on holiday, with my man, but also wanted the mums to be smiling. Sourpuss did speak to me, but not very much, the mums were being polite and there was Scoutman trying hard to keep his mum cheerful.

We were at one stall and I spied the perfect present for my nephew, I pointed it out to Scoutman, in the pause Sourpuss grabbed the toy for her grandson.

Again, I was exasperated, but said nothing. I'd get something else. But niggles like this intensify, just add a few cocktails, to reach an annoyingly ridiculous fall out. Between me and Scoutman.

They were loud, oops, and verbal. The mums were upstairs and so heard everything, I was drunk and unpleasant and didn't hold back my feelings, mummy's boy got a whole load of abuse.

I am not proud, in fact I'm embarrassed now, but he had a visible scratch on his manhood and I had a chipped tooth.

I had left the apartment and gone to the shop, because I could, even though I was really too smashed. Brilliant, the young chap there poured me a drink, he then offered me some cannabis.

I said NO? (???)

Scoutman was going completely mental and had no idea where I was, I feel seriously crap about this incident now (selfish ***), but gave it no thought at the time. The young man had to leave the shop to walk me back, I was in a dreadful state and would not have made it on my own. But, seriously, I was really bad.

I was the catalyst, apparently, being the thoughtless drunk trying to induce fun times (that was the idea). But being literally legless is not easy and the others weren't laughing.

This misunderstanding happened for two weeks, two, it could and should have been good times in the sun.
But at the end of the fortnight none of us were taking to each other. At all … about anything.
It was pretty bad … sickening and ridiculous, I felt awful, it was unexpected and unpleasant.

The taxi driver had greeted us with smiles and as expected asked, "Did you have a good time?".
He didn't ask again. The journey home was almost silent.

Back in the greyness and Scoutman stayed with his mum, so they were talking, my mum went home and I was alone here.
Those around me shrugged, "Well … saw that happening". Spruce Girl was horrified that it had all gone so wrong, "What on earth happened?".

The bad taste lingered for a while and then Scoutman came to the flat, he was crying, "I miss you, let's forget the horriday and go back to normal". But it was never the same, it still wound me up when Sourpuss called and asked him to get her some milk or bread. I am disabled and don't ask anybody to stop what they're doing to go to the shop for me. If at the end of the day you have no milk … use powdered or do without. I do, nor will you fade and die without bread for a day. Blimey.
But he always went, even if it was inconvenient, when she called, I loved him because his attitude was good and he could see no problem. Bless.

Scoutman and I had some photos taken, in Turkey, by a local man with a big camera who did this for a living. He had me hugging trees and looking seductively over my shoulder, they were really good and were the only pictures taken … even though we all had cameras.

Scoutman told me that the best bit of his holiday was, "The wet shave and haircut". He'd paid pence for the pampering, but they did a good job and were very thorough, when they had finished he looked fab. It made me sad though, that this bit of fuss was his highlight.
I collected all the cocktail paraphernalia, I've still go some of the large straws, the sparkly bits and the paper umbrellas. How sad is that?

Started doing pottery at college, it was so brilliant I was gutted that it hadn't been done before, the tutor is one of the nicest people that I know and the other students were all great.
To start this course the basics had to be learnt, so you begin with thumb pots move onto coil pots and then master slabbing. I was taking all my efforts home, there were so many at one point I had to give these, obviously hand crafted, creations away.
My mum has still got my first attempt at the slab technique, it's a house, that I did at school aged ten.
But she's now got a large plant holder made with coils of clay, that's quite good and she uses it, not sure what happened to all the other experiments she ended up with.

None of them are particularly brilliant, but you get the gist and you can see that I'm having fun with creativity. I absolutely loved it and the tutor, with her chatty smiles, this made the two hours a week too short.

The year span by and I now had a flat dotted with hand-made pottery items, square boxes, patterned vases and a tall green thing (my first attempt with coloured glaze).
But I did bin the really rubbish ones.

CHAPTER VII

Plodding on 2005

Hey from where I am sitting, right now, I can see out of my bedroom window.

Just noticed a pigeon (they are a pest at the allotment—Scoutman grumbles, " flying rats") it was flapping on a roof. Then realised he was dancing and swaying, trying to impress the ladies.

It worked he's standing on her now, I can see him keeping his balance but she is out of view.

Oh, that was quick … he's on his own now eyeing up the next one. Bloody men.

Spruce Girl has left me, she has been an exceptional part of my life for a lot of years. I chose not to have a replacement. Having been there before, I couldn't be bothered to train another support worker, they all come with different ideas … on what's best for the head injured client. Anyway I knew that if I ran into trouble there were people around that would help me, if Scoutman couldn't. My mum still comes here once a week to sort me out, I am easily distracted and a bloody good procrastinator.

But at first it was strange, as I realised what a mess I make without even trying, I had to find things myself and pick stuff up, washing dishes, I was responsible for everything. Spruce Girl was not appreciated as an addition to my life, my second mum … the same age as me. But because of her, years later, I no longer buy cheap toilet paper … you should see it now! It's like sheets of soft card and it's gently scented! Then I had to retrain myself to iron.

I'm much better at this task now, there are the odd scorch marks on me and the clothes, but I still will not do the sheets. They're well hard and take a lot of coordination, my mum does them for me … when she visits and does the rest of the ironing.
I do it, sometimes, when I need to.
Now I often buy clothes that don't need ironing, especially trousers, no longer am I seen with tramlines on a shiny background.
Actually and physically setting up this procedure is the difficult bit, then putting it away, the ironing board can be erect in my kitchen for days. It's ready and in the way, I just move it around or lean over it to get to the sink, it will be waiting for me to finish off the pile of ironing. The board, used as a temporary dumping space, will have to be cleared of stuff to be utilised or collapsed then put away.

I really missed her, I would have to encourage Scoutman to get involved with a "blitz" of the flat. This in turn motivated me and I too would get off my bum, the flat wasn't dirty but very disorganised and untidy with abandoned items just hanging around. As usual these episodes were triggered by something that HAD to be located, a case of needs must. Blimey, it would be easier to get myself organised, I do file things eventually. I think that I've always been scatty, for example I have just noticed a spider dangling in my window … it's building a web … I want to catch it a fly and find my magnifying glass. I'm not super-keen on spiders, per se, but they are fascinating and it's in my eye-line.

The documents were found, to travel, then we flew to Schiphol the airport in Holland.

This was the start, of our test to navigation as it's a massive space, the airport is huge.

It's got trains that go directly to Amsterdam! How good is that?

But we had to find the station and then the platform, get me and our luggage onto the train, then we had to track the booked lodgings down at the other end.

The comfortable boots I had on were to be abandoned, when we got to our hotel, they were killing me. I didn't think they would be trouble, but hadn't thought we would be walking for so long.

I didn't think basically, full stop, they looked good though … when I was sitting on the aeroplane.

This time the hotel was much better, the wallpaper was still stuck to the walls here, it was en-suite too so I didn't have to urinate in the waste paper basket. The walk-in shower was brilliant, there was nothing to fall over or slip on, it was big enough and Scoutman held onto me when I washed my hair.

Breakfast was lots of things in sachets to go with bread, the coffee was nice and you could have dry cake with it, so it was easy to fuel up for the ensuing trek. We were on the outskirts again and just knew we were going to spend most of the day finding things by chance, my sense of direction is rubbish and we had Scoutman reading the map in a foreign country.

But this is all good, again I didn't hear or see anything untoward directed at me, but I am looking back and it wasn't all peachy. Mainly because of that disabled woman called Gillian.

Being lost drives me mad, more so if a map is implicated, Scoutman knows that my patience is like a fly with one wing (brother, naughty boy, not me) or a daddy long legs with two limbs left (again bro). Exasperating and pointless … literally going round in circles, poor man would get the brunt of it, when those long dangly bits bellow my bottom with shoes on started to trouble me. It was getting too painful to walk, this just tips me over into frustration mode, it's exasperating when I simply cannot do what I want comfortably and with controlled ease

The sad hindsight is that: when I was growling at him it made my mobility worse, as I lost concentration, which would transpire into painful discomfort. Sometimes we had to stop and find a coffee shop to sit for a while, I would calm down and he would eat cake, so we were happy when we found a fair with a big wheel.

We did see a lot of things, I loved looking at all the buildings, it was good talking to the lady with a child in the trolley on her bike.
It was on this trip that I planned to gather information about euthanasia, but had no idea where the clinic was. There was a language problem, at the hotel reception the staff smiled blankly when I asked, "Where is the clinic concerning euthanasia?".

Eventually they smiled and sent us on our way, so we set off armed, with a map a pen and paper.
We found it, blimey, but were a bit surprised to see young people walking past us.
This time there was no misunderstanding, we smiled at the youngsters, we were going to ask questions about euthanasia at the reception of the sexually transmitted disease clinic.
What had the hotel staff been thinking!

We gave up and went to the nearest art gallery, there are quite a few— Amsterdam is very inspirational, then found a good spot for coffee.

I am still involved, obsessed and on a creative high, with the challenge of writing a book that isn't autobiographical. It fascinates me … how your choice of language can evoke such differing emotions.

At first I was surprised and stunned, when people started to tell me what effect my chapters in Gillian Mk 2 were having.
I didn't really know how or why, many reasons of appeal were given, but it made me giddy to be producing a spark of light, with understanding for so many different people.

This wasn't happening with the second attempt at discovery, the shock to my audience was sometimes audible, my theories of brilliance were going squiffy as I presented an alternative to my usual patter.
A vicious and mean writer controlled this pen, I was killing people all the time and in the most imaginative scenarios possible, exposing the dirt under my nails beneath the coloured varnish.
It was really gruesome and awful, but good, it was getting the reaction that I intended. Genuine shock with wide eyes.

Now I want to dig it out and read it, to remind myself.

"Your readers don't want that, get on with your own life story", this was mum's response.

I was trying all sorts of things, reading some of my scribbles at the writing classes, poor Scoutman and previously Spruce Girl were a captive audience. Therefore, somebody stop me the quill is smokin', they were subject to my waffling, about everything and nothing.
It was a powerful feeling, like a hot sun on bared skin, being able to make people laugh and cry at the same time.

One writing class was fortnightly, homework was set by a tutor here (hello to the fab cat lady), the other was local and weekly, here you chose what you wanted to read (hi to a happy group) and whatever I had written was received well. Apart from my attempt at fiction, nobody really liked that, but it wasn't the writing style it was the content.

Another book idea was played with, I was going to do drawings too— to compliment my observations. Something else I've just found.

YOU KNOW ...

... it's time to wash up, when all your tea-spoons are dirty and you're onto the camping mugs.

... you're getting on when your kids are forty.

... you're advancing in years when you tried to pluck an eyebrow for five minutes. Then turned the light on and blamed failing eyesight, to realise it's a wrinkle. (bugger)

... you're getting old when you could have given birth to all your new classmates ... and the teacher.

... there's a problem when you order bite-size or mushy food at the restaurant, instead of corn on the cob or juicy steak that you really want.

... you're getting fat and lazy when you select a high trolley at the supermarket, so you don't have to bend at the check-out to unload.

... you've got a pampered life when the young man upstairs takes your wheely bin back into the yard for you ... and somebody else took it out.

… you've lost it when your best clothes look like they came from a charity shop … and, probably did.

… you've put on a few pounds when your bikini top explodes in your foolishly grinning boyfriend's face. The horror comes when you look down and notice the extra curves … that the bigger boobs were hiding.

… you have to stop pulling out grey hairs or you will start to look silly … dye it all black and look scary and stupid instead.

… you are changing when you make a supreme effort with the Laura Ashley dress and still only attract idiots, the problem comes when you can't get rid of them.

… you are getting old when It's Xmas again … but the last one has just gone and you have no idea what anybody bought you.

… the only bloke you fancy is young enough to be your son, you look closer and you are probably older than his mum.

… you are going to be a fatty when you buy big cakes and you live alone, you know it's a problem when you'd rather stay in to eat it.

… you have got a bad memory when you decide to buy that necklace but have no idea where you saw it … there are only a few streets of shops too! I'm sure I'll pass it again, one day.
(found it accidentally—it wasn't even near where I thought it was)

I had another sheet of them but I can't find it, as disorganised as a panic and distracted easily like an animal in mating season (I can see the pigeons again … bloody men), it's a wonder I get anything done.

Even got as far as packing my bag, for a writing adventure, with the big flask full of sweet coffee and all the necessary writing stuff. Remembering the keys, thank goodness, to trundle along to my big shed at the allotment.

This was massive in my mind, I dreamt of peering through the window with pen in hand and watching the birds through a wisp of smoke.

In reality I sat there and firstly, the window is covered with chicken-wire, then secondly behind this wire the fat spiders spin lots of traps and eat big bugs. So the view is obscured.

But I was happy sitting alone in my shed, I could ignore my mobile phone if I wanted to, this was a good idea until I had to get home. All the coffee had gone, so the flask was lighter, and my pen had worked but. Having to empty and clean the toilet, then walk home, wasn't that brilliant.

At the flat my writing den is cluttered, coffee cups ashtrays and scraps of paper with good intention scribbles on them, I lose and find things all the time so it's interesting … hence off-putting.
I'm getting better at putting things away where they're supposed to be, not always, but there are only four rooms here so whatever it is it will turn up eventually. I'm not at all worried.

It was my mum's sixtieth birthday and something had to be done, other than the vertical 60 I had made at pottery. We decorated the pub for my dad's and I had made a big banner of announcement to hang over the bar, my brother and I put our heads together. It was organised so that friends and family met at the pub and waited, then mum was brought to the venue, she squealed with delight when she came through the door and saw her brother.

Betty Boop and her mum came from Portsmouth, Spruce Girl was there and my mum held back tears, with an overdose of emotion, my dad would have completed this day.

There was one boy there, don't know who he belonged to, who was standing out. Not because he was eating everything, or because he was generally behaving like a nerd, or even because he was being loud for nothing, but he pulled ALL of the large party poppers that I bought and nobody was looking.
Stupid boy.
But other than that … we all got some of the decorated cake and mum was happy.

I had graduated from thumb pots in pottery and was now onto another part of the course, so had a more interesting abundance of creations to give away, some of the fellow potters are the same as last year.
Suddenly a lot of coiled creations were produced, then square and lidded boxes took over, but at last it was my turn to have a go with the potter's wheel. The lady that had been using it, before me, was making a dinner service and it was really impressive. My first and only attempt looked nothing like this, but it did stand up. I had decided against my idea, it looked silly, to paint a metallic design right in the middle. But it wouldn't come off, so I have a small dish with a black (I thought that would make it better … der) and copper smudge as decoration.
I can't actually give it away, it's rubbish really.

My old tutors from the catering course are still seen occasionally, my favourite instructor (not because of this … though it helps) was the first person to praise my literary effort unreservedly.

A special person because she wasn't obliged to make any comment, she laughed again with recall then hugged me and said it made her cry, she asked me a lot of questions and thought about her children. I am a firm advocator of helmets being worn, by children on their bicycles, they could reduce the damage if not prevent it.

Able bodied people, especially if they are parents, should visit a TBI rehabilitation centre and see for themselves how badly a blow to the head can affect you. Although there will be improvement, my own has been short of miraculous, the brain damage will be a lifelong complication.

Some victims of this affliction will never walk, eat alone, go to the toilet on their own, speak or live independently … ever again. That's as bad as it can be, if not worse.

My niece and nephew are made to wear head protection when they ride their bikes.

Incidentally I wish I could mention and thank all the people that have written to me, I still have all the letters, it's my book so … mm the folders are big and they're in the front room but I am not … maybe I'll do something at the end as a finale?

At the allotment we have new neighbours on one side, an industrious man who's lovely wife visits occasionally but she does the pretty gardening at home, he often observes our lack of experience and offers helpful tips. I like this feeling of togetherness, a single mind, allotments are a good analogy of life.

We are often given surplus crops by our friends who know what they're doing, all big and clever, which is good because we were still learning and some of our efforts went straight to the compost heap. But hey, this pile of waste vegetable matter is impressive and healthy.

Do you know what I've noticed, you cannot give people compliments if they are unprompted, on a night out recently I told a young woman, "You have got lovely eyes.".

Was she pleased? Was she flattered?

She stepped back in shock, she was not very tall, so she could look down her nose at me as though I had just offended her. I shook my head in wonder and assured her, "That was it. No hidden agenda", should have kept my stupid mouth shut, maybe she thought I was trying to hit on her?

"That was it", I shrugged, the scornful look I saw was the last time I bothered to look at her.

Don't think I'll go out of my way to do this again, next time I'll say something about her dress sense or her hair. No, thinking about it now, there really was nothing else to say or make a nice comment about …

Oh my goodness … I am mutating into a grumpy old woman.

Anyway.

Maybe nobody ever said nice things to her or about her, but then again I'm not really surprised (ha), I must have looked like an aging odd ball.

A cheap holiday was required and this meant a booking to Zakynthos (Zante) in Greece, I took the second book of science fiction with me on reams of paper, two weeks of continental breakfasts with good coffee.

I learnt something valuable on this break, one of the holiday-makers, sitting by the pool in the sun, was a nurse and she had asked, "What are you doing?".

On reading to her I was detailing a death, no stone was left unturned as it were, or so I thought. The nurse told me, "You cannot eat insulin because your stomach acid breaks it down and renders it useless. It has to be injected". I hope I never get diabetes, must be a real pain.

They had taken a wide photograph, of the one street, but we managed to cover it in a day. There wasn't very much to do, or look at, but we enjoyed what there was, on exploring we discovered a restaurant tucked away up the hill. Going back down is when we had stopped and had coffee, have you noticed that I drink a lot of caffeine … everywhere?

We were tourists and fell for the glossy pictures again, or were persuaded by the fat Greek with the moustache. He was selling the excursion to us, but was looking over our shoulders all the time, he was ready to pounce on the next tourist who paused to look at the advertisement.

Hey, we didn't need any coercion, we needed things to do and this did look good, the coach to the boat was packed so the big guy was onto a good thing.

We weren't, on a good thing, the coach had stopped everywhere, it was too hot to be sitting in this cramped space for too long. Kids were starting to make unpleasant and bored noises, people were beginning to glare at the parents, by the time we arrived at the boat. Or where it should have been, we had gone around the whole island twice and we were still too early, it hadn't come back from the last outing yet. We had to stand in the sun and wait for it, then, when it came back we had to watch whilst it was cleaned and restocked.

Just another float, with food and alcohol, no dolphins or castles … well there wasn't anything of interest really that sticks in my mind. But I do know that the brochure, in my hand, was showing pictures that must have been taken … somewhere else in another country!

It was pleasant enough there was the obligatory stop, this is usually when you see the effects of alcohol and sun, namely dehydration to the brain, on young men mostly. When they start hurling themselves off the boat, making loud noises from ridiculous heights, in an interesting variety of ways at first … but it gets boring.

The last time I did that, threw myself into the sea off a boat, I nearly drowned. I forgot what I was doing, when I surfaced, then kept getting lashed then knocked off kilt by the waves, a young girl saw I was in trouble and rescued me. Thanks to her! I would find and use the toilet now.

At the end of the trip back, on dry land, we had to hang around for the coach to pick us up. Blimey this chap will own the island soon, but they were still stripping the boat when the next lot arrived.

We were grabbing them and pulling them off the coach … well we should have.

Everybody was getting fed up of the children now, annoying little brats, even the tipsy parents

In small areas one quickly learns where the best places are, for toilet accessibility the food etc comes second, thereby avoiding any accidents. But we really should have just gone to Cyprus again, then I could have tried to find Chris.

Scoutman did listen to my work, this was helpful, it was all that I had done to date and I had been messing with the bones of this fiction for a while.

But I couldn't keep up with it, it was too intense and required skills that I haven't mastered yet, if I repeat myself and get lost with this it doesn't matter. As much, you will hang in there, no problem, I'm sure … if only to see what your code name is.

We travelled to go to the party, it was Betty Boop's fortieth birthday, my mum was with us and it was going to be a good weekend. Which would have been better if it hadn't rained, all the time.

It was a weekend that is remembered for two main reasons: the brilliant party isn't one of them and doesn't count:

Firstly. Mum ended up in hospital, after the family dog jumped up and bit her in the face, she was doing, "Coochy coo", it was a temperamental and scarred rescue dog.

Betty Boop cried and whisked my shaking mother to the hospital, then took the dog to the local vet.

The dog was put down, mum shook her head, "Oh no", she felt truly horrible but you could see the teeth marks on her face. Betty Boop explained, "It had done it before, I vowed that if it happened again the dog would be dealt with".

Well yeah … but you don't want that do you? On your Birthday.

Secondly. Scoutman was behaving strangely, but I didn't know why. Something had been left in the car and there was a path of steps, with no handrail, to get to it. I asked Scoutman, "Will you go and get it for me, please". He had growled something under his breath and indicated no, I was surprised and could have waited I suppose … but of course I didn't.

When I was at the door, to go myself, he was getting audible glances of disapproval all round. My hand was snatched from the door handle as he muttered, "I'll get it", then barged past me. I was startled by this outburst, of uncalled for nastiness, but just thanked him profusely when he came back.

We were all out having food in a pub and my man wasn't really talking to me, or anybody else, in fact I would go as far as saying he was being really boring and incredibly rude. Of course it was noticed … but nobody paid that much attention, it was obvious he didn't want to be there. I was not sure if it was me, had I done something or said something? Had I been more annoying than usual?

We bickered for no reason, silly, about nothing that important. His behaviour was bothering me and I was upset with embarrassed confusion, but he had to be largely ignored because I was with friends trying to have fun.

My old friend Betty Boop has known me from childhood, we have always written even when I was abroad, so she is aware of just about every crucial event in my life.

In a quiet moment, we were washing the dishes and funnily nobody else was around, she had looked at me then asked outright, "Are things with you and Scoutman ok?".

She had noticed his unpleasantness, he hadn't tried to hide his mood, there was nothing to say because I had no idea what his problem was. With a shrug I had laughed, "Whatever it is, it's probably my fault", but it wasn't funny.

All he had to do was say what was bothering him, maybe that would have helped?

These two scenarios marred the weekend, yet at the same made it more memorable, mum's face was alright and didn't scar, but I felt betrayed and let down by my partner.

Onwards.

My thoughts regarding euthanasia were still unheard and my questions were unanswered, so the meeting was arranged, in a pub on the edge of town, the local paper covered it giving the time and date.

There were a few people there, nothing happened but we all did a lot of talking

I wasn't enthused enough to pursue this, one lady was herself ill and had no sympathy from those in charge of her destiny. She indicated that, "It is a losing battle, nobody cares. I have paid my taxes and have no children …", then she went quiet.

Why isn't this action of choice available and legal? It's ridiculous, Mr Thingy was the only person that disagreed with me.

We had a party for my fortieth, Oh my … 40 … what a rubbish number.

I have been disabled for over a quarter of my life now, which is pants! The room was booked with a disco and karaoke, buffet food was also put on because: I could and everybody loves nibbly finger food … well my nephew did, he was never far from the grub.

Nomad turned up, a complete surprise!

How brilliant, I hugged him, quite a few friends from my previous life were there. It wasn't as buzzing and hectic as I'd planned, or hoped, but it wasn't my eighteenth (by a long shot!). It was, nevertheless, a good night and I drank too much … nothing new there then.

Betty Boop chose a song to perform, she dragged me and my mum up to join her with her mum, I was on all fours to get onto the stage, then I stood to complete the quartet and the music started.

That was when it all fell apart. None of us knew the song!

Two of us vaguely knew the chorus, the video camera shows me shrugging with a drink in my hand then trying (unsuccessfully) to join in, the mum's follow the words for a bit then look at each other and giggle. It's funny, poor Betty Boop is, in all seriousness, trying to keep it together … but she doesn't know the new modern version either. We were are all too old …

As I was helped off the stage my friends clapped, note when I was climbing down, then somebody (sounded like my funny brother) shouted, "Yeah gerroff! Yer rubbish!".

Insulting … but true.

Being me … I thanked people for my presents and put them aside, to save for later thereby dragging this birthday out until the end.
I opened everything when back at home, if they had labels they were amongst the discarded wrapping paper and quickly forgotten. Nice one, so I had no idea who bought what.

One present was a chunky necklace, which I liked, but when it was tried on I broke it. It was moved so many times that it could be anywhere, when found I might actually get it fixed? Then it will be out of fashion … to end up at the charity shop with my shoes and boots. Life can get very complicated.

There is only one regret that I have, with hindsight, I didn't throw a drink in Turnip's made-up face and smudged her mascara to reveal the ugliness. Got nothing to say 'Happy Birthday', from the make-up counter either.

This was the first Xmas ever spent alone, by choice. My family thought I had plans and so were quite happy. Scoutman, having failed to persuade me otherwise, went to his family.
I didn't feel anything at all, no childish excitement or burning desire to overindulge with everything, but knew what I did want. To be on my own.

Xmas day 2005 was spent right here, in this spot, doing exactly this. But I was still plodding on and writing, or correcting it again, the best selling and on the back burner sci-fi!

It must be good eh?

If coffee, toast and solitude, replaced bland turkey and noisy kids with tipsy adults.

I just didn't want to be with anyone, usually December is my favourite month too, nobody except Scoutman knew.

I didn't think about it, just another day, though my mum and brother were called and they reminded me of what I was missing out on. Boring turkey and fuss decorated with tinsel.

I had thought that tearful regret might creep into the day at some point, when I was stumbling around on my own and then eating toast, whilst watching the Queen's speech.

But, although I missed my mum dad and brother, the day was ... the 25th of December.

The only disappointing part of the day was Scoutman coming back, I'm kidding, no I'm jesting.

He'd had fun and been fed so he was happy ...

I had done what was intended, watched predictive twaddle on the television that was on in the background, drunk too much coffee and concocted a few paragraphs in an unhappy mind.

CHAPTER VIII

Sheikh it off 2006

The year began in the sun, away from here (obviously), two weeks of all-inclusive at Sharm El Sheikh in Egypt. A holiday that had been booked for a group of us, my mum and brother with his partner's family, Scoutman and I were roomed away from them. Actually the complex was sprawling so we were all spread about, we would meet each other in the restaurant, by the pool (somewhere) or in the bar. There was no need to go anywhere! Just about everything was built-in, that's why it's called all inclusive, this was the first time that I had been on this type of holiday. Can you tell?

You eat ice-cream every day, because you can, each day begins with a cooked breakfast and snacks were offered in-between.
You should go on the diet before you go away, on deals like this in particular, because you will not resist or be sensible. Why should you? Holiday … inclusive ie: paid for already … shame not to … it's cold at home now so baggy jumpers are in … and … why not? I'm very predictable and this argument is not needed, being greedy n all, but I do wonder what happens to the waste. There must be a load of food left over, bet the staff don't take it home. Especially the deserts, that always look fabulous but are generally sweet and colourful with synthetic cream.

We made it to a casino this time, it was off-camp, only Scoutman and I went dressed in our glad rags.

It was brilliant, but they wouldn't accept their own money. So we had to get it exchanged back to sterling, effectively we were on a losing streak before we even got there.

I expected it to be seedy, with television images as my reference, but it was simply a glorified and adult arcade with a lot of big money slot machines. The tables offered card games and roulette, the staff provided coffee, there was live entertainment, it was a good way to lose money. We, I, had a few goes on the roulette and then wanted to try the pontoon. When we only had enough money for the taxi home we left, I don't think we were there for that long,

The next morning I told everybody that we lost all our money, detailing how I had got carried away and lost all control in the moment, I had got us into debt. Scoutman sighed then nodded and cursed me, "You should have seen her … stupid woman!", as rehearsed. They all shook their heads and rolled their eyes. When they asked, "How much did you lose?", we started laughing and gave it away. I shook my head in wonder, none of them had expressed surprise, they had all believed the story.

At the bar the nights were good, apart from ridiculous amounts of alcohol … no, actually, that was good too. Entertainment completed the package and I didn't care why people clapped for me, when the karaoke was utilised. There was a dancing competition and I was annoyed, that I didn't get up for it, especially when it was noticed that the staff searching for volunteers had actively looked over me and avoided my eyes.

On the small beach there was a walkway into the sea, which I needed help to get onto to, but the water was so clear. You could see the brightly coloured fish from where you were standing, on the swaying platform, it was definitely worth the effort.

There was a group of Lion Fish in view, incredibly poisonous, nobody came into contact with them whilst we were there. But I wondered, if ever there was a casualty, what would they do? There were quite a few of them too, they looked impressive and I wouldn't mess with them, the spines on their dorsal fins were very obvious.

But I fully intended to get into the water and swim over this gorgeous coral, wishing that when I'd had a go at scuba diving it had been here. I was ready with my rubber shoes, to avoid slipping and standing on anything horrible, the snorkel and mask then my float. All I needed was a big rubber ring to complete the picture, but I am still freaked with swimming … more so in the sea, still haunted by mental images of when I threw myself into the water off the boat and nearly drowned.

But I was helped off this jetty into the sea and it took me a little while to settle, to get the floating and breathing synchronised, but I am glad that I did this because it was amazing.

To see clown fish for real, the coral itself was a palette of colour and texture, there were so many different species of marine life to look at it was transfixing. In this mode I had scraped my shin against some coral and had to get out, in panic I had imagined sharks from miles away sniffing me out, blood was pouring down my leg … the water made it look much worse than it was … but it was still bleeding a lot! I was blinded, my eyes were on fire, the sea was really salty and my mask had leaked, then my mum insisted and escorted me off the pier to the first aid hatch.

The young chap had over reacted, beyond the call of duty, he had covered all of the lower leg with bright orange iodine.

Then masked all of that colour with a massive white dressing, it could have been an incontinence pad, it looked as silly as you imagine. The rest of me was brown and tanned, so this had to come off … and it did.

People stare at me anyway whatever I do, I imagine that this looked a lot funnier than it was, so Scoutman was holding the video camera and I was instructing him to follow me walking. I wanted to see what I looked like.

They were all playing volleyball, because in my mind I used to play and was quite good, I stood in place. The first time the ball came to me I wasn't sure what to do with myself, then the sun got in my eyes, I panicked and I waved my arms in the general direction … of where I thought the ball might be.

Not sure how but it was returned over the net and I picked myself up, it didn't go over the second time and I fell heavily again.
Then I gave up, volleyball hurt, I'm not bouncy enough.

I did swim in the pool, but not as much as I could or should have done, my young nephew was really funny … he was just jumping in then getting out and jumping in again. He wouldn't be put off his chosen activity, they live by the sea at home and thankfully he is not afraid of the water, at all.

Off the resort again, the whole group went to drive buggies through the desert, Scoutman and I shared a car and I drove. We had to follow the chap, leading the gang, on a designated trail. I was told off for overtaking and speeding (in a desert), Scoutman also kept telling me.

"Slow down", he laughed with me nervously. Honestly I was behaving like a child.

It was great and we stopped to watch a sunset, but I've seen better and wanted to get back behind the wheel.

We all got the provided transport to the nearest town, there were lots of other cars on the road, the numerous vehicles were zipping about, some were dirty and crammed with people, a few cars were big and clean, taxi drivers were scouring for custom, other hotel transport was trying to find stopping space and nearly everybody was sounding their horns.

The hassle continues when you are on foot, at nearly every shop you are greeted with smiles and then invited inside to look at their selection of dusty ornaments, if we had succumbed to every stall owner we would still be there.

We bought bottles of coloured sand … with it they drew a picture behind the glass, they were very clever.

A gaudy glass bong, because it was cheap and somehow we had persuaded ourselves that it would be a feature in the flat. Mm … it would certainly go with the mess?

It wasn't that long ago that the touristy Spanish doll, the dancing senorita in full regalia holding her flowing skirt, was a status symbol of privileged decadence. Now you can tell where people have been on holiday by looking in the charity shops, there will be a glut of unwanted gifts or stupid buys. That don't sell and then are all sent to Goole, there must be loads of junk in poor Goole.

But really how often do you get a present, from well meaning tanned friends, that you a) like or b) can use?

The gorgeous hand stitched table runner that you bought … looks silly on its own here and will never get used. It will be kept for a little while then more stuff will need the space it's claiming, that's when the charities are happy.

Truffle won't remember what was given to her and I have no idea, I might ask her.
Aren't modern things brilliant? I have just twiddled my thumbs to question her, she replied immediately!
"Sorry, what use am I?".
So, it was a memorable and useful gift then.

Back in the real world I had been given quite shocking news, the pottery class was to be no more as from now on really. We were the last class. The college was expanding, with the appropriate and politically correct toilets, into a three storey block, which appeared suddenly with a lift.

The courses offered are more vocation and career oriented than they were, my old high school is a performing college now. They have to teach a multitude of obscure languages here, I'm beginning to feel like a visitor on holiday and you dare not say anything to anybody. About anything. Somebody will scream and accuse you of being racist, or ageist, or sexist, or homophobic, blah blah ... What?

It has been raining for days, ironically, it's just awful, what a mess. When watching the news it saddens me to despair, they should only show good reports of countries that are happy and prosperous (if there are any).
Really, how many civilisations are at war or fighting? Who is getting killed or is affected by this?

Not the politicians ... as the news tells us they are all in the game for themselves. 'You can use public transport ... I'm gonna drive my jaguar to my meeting, cos I can'. 'As a thief I will get out of prison, where I wrote another book, and will still have all my privileges so will get more money ... guaranteed'. 'I will buy lots of property, then cry on television when caught taking the Michael.'. Or am I convincingly talkin' outa my bum again?

Who you know ... money ... nothing will change.

I was more unhappy about my pottery class though.

It was held in the long-standing part of the building, Scoutman's old primary school, it was deemed financially unsuitable for renovation and was due for demolition. They had not allocated room for the kiln in the new construction, it was now surplus to requirements and wasn't making money or boosting the achievement figures ... something like that.

But anyway pottery was going to end, I was gutted along with all of the others and our lovely tutor cried, so the whole class was rushing to get things done.

Bro wanted me to make him some Easter Island heads for him, brilliant, I got busy with this project and made him two that were as big as the college kiln would allow. They were pretty good, small but true to the originals, he liked them. But they are displayed inside his house, I thought he meant them for the garden.

Reminds me of a funny film, Spinal Tap, it's a spoof documentary about a pretentious rock band. They give a drawing of Stone Henge, to be copied, wanting a monument on stage. But the drawing is copied literally so what they get is tiny, a model of the historic site is lowered onto the stage.

These heads are small and would get lost in their garden, maybe this isn't quite what he envisaged ...

My final piece was completed just in time, it was a crocodile for mum's garden, it was brilliant and I felt like I had found my niche. The reptile was made in three pieces: the head baring teeth, a circle with scales for the midriff then the third part was a long and curved tail. It was glazed green, to copy the living creature, so when placed on her garden looks like it's swimming in the grass. It has raised comments and if the class was still going I would have made another, or something similar.

I missed it and felt unchallenged with no productive release. The writing, although creative, wasn't enough anymore.

Scoutman's attempts at pacification were repetitive, echoing my mum, "Look at how well you've done already".
Yeah … done.

One of my bad points is impatience, I know that, now team this with my feelings for people that dither and have no initiative! Especially when they have no excuse, there is no physical reason why a decision or action cannot be made. Scoutman did not possess this gene in his make-up, but it had taken me all these years to realise this and admit that I was actually making no difference.

My need for progression and improvement was not mutual.
As he'd explained, by shouting at me, "I've got nothing and I want nothing". Continuing, "I'm never going to be a brain surgeon".
Bless, I had to laugh, listen to him talking himself up, he might manage to get a job in the hospital kitchens?

Things were getting a bit boring, metaphorically speaking I wanted to fly again, interest shown and chats about Gillian Mk 2 were becoming old hat now. Although still taken and fascinated by reader's comments

I'd, generally, heard it all before. I felt that it had run it's course, the book had mental implications and had changed me, it had started something and now I wanted more.

The allotment kept me occupied, for the hours that I was there, it still held the sense of achievement and it still posed new challenges. Pottery, unfortunately, only covered two hours and that wasn't every week with school holidays.

All my art stuff was uninspired and I couldn't be bothered to tidy the flat or do anything else constructive. Except writing.

I was often sitting at my keyboard with coffee and a smoke, but I didn't know what to do, tapping the letters into a big pile of emotions was a good thing … going nowhere.
The second novel was eating me, being read aloud too often, I was chuffed that people were mentally cringing with my words, power to the author.
But what I didn't realise, being an egotist … Darlink, was that it was genuinely disturbing and upsetting people.
A friend asked if she could read the next novel, I had warned her it wasn't like Gillian Mk 2 and sent it, then with no given reason my proof-reader just cut me out of her life … completely.
Blimey.

I was completely hooked now and wasn't sure what was happening, it was taking up a lot of my time and energy, Scoutman was sitting on the bedroom floor distracting me and demanding attention.

It was bad timing because I was on a role with words and would not be interrupted, at first, he was reading the Trivial Pursuit questions out loud to himself and slurping red wine.

This carried on and in my annoyance I offered a compromise, "Let me finish this paragraph then I'll play with you", but no, he was determined to stop me.

To cut the sad sequence of events to an acceptable minimum, it was a nightmare, I don't want to dwell or dissect actions with possible reasoning. Everybody does it, alters words or actions in their head to theoretically change the scenario and therefore the outcome, so I will sum up and be brief.

Selfishly I carried on typing, or tried to, but was annoyed because I had now forgotten what I was going to write. He kept telling me, "I'm drunk", then in the next breath, "I'm not drunk", he denied this categorically. His behaviour was just stupid, Scoutman had my attention but was confusing me, he was being really out of character and was slurring his words now.

The wine I threw didn't work, I missed, so I slapped him thinking that this would.

I regret this now, with a hollow stomach, and wish that I'd tried harder to ignore him.

Or done something else, sickening behaviour that it was.

We were squabbling in the front room, the bad feelings had travelled, Scoutman was standing above me then the coward slapped me across the face as hard as he could. I was stunned and was wide eyed when he screamed at me, "Is that what you want me to do ... hit you?". Then was shocked when he got all excited and hit me again, but harder!

I shook my head to clear it, then stood up, "Well, no ... actually".

As this was said I had started walking away, I was afraid to be with him.

That was it, I was pushed off my feet, he rushed up to me and frog marched me down the corridor then threw me onto the bed.

I got straight up to sit by the phone and have a cigarette, he was sitting on the bed and leaning against the wall. With his arms folded and a big grin on his face, it was menacing with it's mockery and creepy in my vulnerability. I was frightened and that's when I called the Domestic Violence Help Line, because I didn't know what else to do.

The first time he hit me it was largely ignored and I had laughed, when I told him, "Don't do that again Bun". He was sorry and I wasn't that cross, probably because I didn't help matters.

The second time in my shock I'd warned, "Seriously, if this ever happens again … it's over. Basically". He was sorry and I was annoyed, this time he had chipped my tooth!

The third time was an outrage, I was shaking in confusion as I spoke to the woman on the phone.

"Yes, he said he was drunk. Yes, he has done this before". She told me not to blame myself and asked, "Where is he now?". He was still on the bed and laughing at me. What a sad mess.
As nobody could drive she told me, "Ban him to sleep in the car". I crumbled, "He'll be freezing", she was strong for me, "It's got a heater", pointing out my weakness
"If he won't go … call the police".
I told him what the woman had said and I felt sick when he grinned, then asked him to leave.
Almost folding again as I watched him getting into the back of his car, but I'd done it now and was questioning myself as I got into a warm bed alone.

Weeks of unpleasantness and days of tears followed, with blame and solutions being bandied around, big black circles were etched and scored as we went round and round and round again

The manageress at the charity shop had asked me, "What's going on?"
When she saw that he kept coming in to find me, all nice as pie with no hint of a problem, I answered her, "Erm … no idea".
Of course I missed him, being on my own for the first time in years, it's natural to cope badly, I was feeling sorry for myself and remembering the good bits.

But eventually the memory of rubbish episodes, in the relationship, remind you why this is a good thing. You must get yourself on your feet, literally, and get back out there.
There will still be occasions were you are sitting with coffee on your own, minds do wander, that's inevitable, but on memory lane be real and remember that you were bored with him.
Both of you had done your time, unfortunately that wasn't the way to end it and I feel quite justified with my writer's privilege of renaming him. Pathetic Two … is no longer a hero … is a middle child weirdo wuss of a mummy's boy.

Just realised: Only two men have ever hit me, both incidents were in my disabled life and both of them had black belts in martial arts. The two of them are Pathetic, for that reason alone and should be cringing with embarrassment.

Anyway.
I launched myself into helping at the charity shop for longer, I was having a great stretch sorting and ordering other people's junk, it

killed time successfully and I was being thanked whilst being fed coffee with biscuits.

I have got a fixation with cake at the moment, I am not pregnant, Music Man started this with a Victoria sponge. It was that simple, then with an adult head I suddenly realised that I don't have to eat a little piece.
Music Man just cuts it in half now, "You'll start beeping!", then takes his baby slice. Girl.

Thinking about children, although I don't regret not having any (look around), occasionally I do wonder how a copy of me would have evolved. I can think of one person who should have fathered my offspring … but as I said look around.

On a night out with Truffle we had gone off our usual, walking distance, route and into a drinking house off our pub crawl.
I turned around and saw Pathetic Two looking grungy and sheepish, I looked fresh and good (ha), he was with the Angry Young Man. Around the corner, trying to be small and out of sight, was the fat Turnip. I had introduced them and felt nauseous.

She looked shocked and didn't speak to me, I was numb but noticed that her shirt was cheap and dowdy, he mumbled some rubbish and offered me one of his cigarettes.
So she'd changed him already.

I just felt sick and the rest of my night was ruined, with discovery of the final betrayal.
I was furious with rejection and positively poisonous about Turnip, trawling over her bad points and general shabbiness, had they been in my shed?

She was married and he lived with Sourpuss and a skimpy bed. Yow … enough … putting images in my head that I don't want there.

I got silly (ier).
They were together in a shop and she was handing out some papers to one of the staff, Oh my, I reacted with uncanny speed and snatched the article. For some reason I thought that it had something to do with me, it hadn't and it was none of my business but I kept it anyway. I'd followed her and was livid, not because of the stupid Turnip anymore, because I was walking like a noodle and I couldn't keep up with her.

Eventually she stopped, now I could say my piece!
But I was crying when looking at the make-up, then blurted, "I've never felt so disabled".
She didn't hear the next bit.

It took a little while but I got back into my own space and was glad that he wasn't here, I found all the proofs for the professional photos taken in Turkey. Many happy minutes were spent cutting Scoutman, turned Pathetic Two, out of the picture … he spoilt the images anyway.
I felt nothing.

I actually missed the car more than Pathetic Two, there you go … sooo over him, but I'm pretty good on public transport now. Planning time, making sure I build in the last coffee and smoke, then making lists for long journeys and checking the essentials (passes and money) continually. So I know I've got them.
It's time consuming but rewarding, when at the other end of the trek, meeting friends unscathed.
I nearly always have a pen and paper, but will probably get distracted by talking or looking out of the window. Gardens and window

dressings absorb me, so do trees in any season, my simple imagination wanders down leafy lanes.

The allotment was suffering from lack of attention too, it had been the last thought on my mind, but one sunny day I trundled down there with my flask to reacquaint myself and do something?

The gate was unlocked, Pathetic Two was there with Turnip, I just stood and looked at them helping themselves to something green. She had that awful shirt on again, I don't remember saying anything but if I did I hope that it was mean and thoughtless. Pathetic Two mumbled something and took her away. Good, good.

The pumpkins had been harvested and had been designated to the children, but with a scorned woman's attitude, I had demanded the keys back for my allotment then … locked Pathetic Two's large fruit in the shed. It was a petty thing to do and I smile now, but I'm sure that he really couldn't have cared less.
I really wasn't bothered until the decaying mass had to be removed.

His Down's Syndrome nephew missed out, because his uncle was a disgusting coward with absolutely no excuse.
I wasn't omitting the details, any of them … including my input, when people asked. The general consensus was that he was a low-life, "You don't hit women, especially if they are disabled", I didn't argue the fact.

Posh Boy knew what had happened and calmed my shattered ego, by telling me, "The man is a loser". I didn't disagree with this either. People are entitled to their opinions, Posh Boy had one. As consolation he sent a surprise,it arrived via special delivery. I opened a big box of delicious smelling chocolates, each bar was individually wrapped and they all had slogans, telling you why they were better than sex.

For example: Q: Why is chocolate better than sex?
A: Save water you don't need to shower after chocolate A: No need to hide pictures of chocolate under your mattress A: Have chocolate by yourself … without fear of going blind.

That's a few of them, there were twenty seven small bars, but they lasted for ages they were so rich you can't eat loads. Hotel Chocolat was English not Belgian, they were rather special, what a lovely thing to do. He was on a mission to cheer me up and he did, he also made me laugh on the phone and I was getting used to his speech, Gillian Mk 2 had by all accounts made a difference to his way of thinking.

He gave me a pen, "I've bought you loads of nice pens", mum made comment, but this one had my name engraved on the metal barrel. "Never had that before!", I grinned, "My book signing pen".
It was given to me, "For signing books", and I loved it. A sturdy pen that was smooth and tactile with its weight. But it broke and couldn't be used. When told he was mortified and sent me a replacement, the same type of pen that was also engraved, he didn't have to do this and I didn't ask, but I was pleased that he had.

The brain is an amazing thing, even when damaged, if the blow to your head was on the left side the right side of your being will be affected and vice versa. Truffle and Posh Boy have not only learnt to write again, but with their unnatural left hand, both amazing and legible.
I have still got my first attempts at this skill, the first book, tried with both hands. Even though it was my right side that was affected and weak, my brain injury was mainly on the left, I am still right handed. The weird thing is occasionally, to complete any task, I will automatically attempt to use my left hand. My left hand is first to get involved, then before I make a huge uncoordinated mess and drop/

knock or break something, I will physically remind myself that I'm right-handed. I forget, it's easily done.

The nights out with Truffle, painting yon town pinkish, became a regular thing around this time.

She tells people all the time about Gillian Mk 2, if the book hadn't been written, if I hadn't marched off to the local paper all determined to spread the news, if not for the book we most probably wouldn't have met or spoken to each other.

Music Man has a local and invited us both to join him, it is an old drinking house with regulars, he too recommends the book to all and last night a new reader hugged then kissed me. "It was perfect holiday reading". He's going to pass it on, his whole family are going to be subjected. It made him laugh and think, there by the grace of medical science go I, he had his eyes opened to another pit fall of life. That can and does happen to anybody, at any time.
He is going to forward it to his English graduate son, he'll have fun with his red marker pen, but the book spells out my situation at that time. I should get him to read this, to see if there is any comparison, there should be improvement. But, then again, maybe I'm better off not knowing.

Still looking for other things, to occupy my mind, I became a resident panel member for the housing association. Meeting with a group of like minded people every three months. The venue covering my area is at the end of the road, because I could get myself there I joined the committee, gradually I became aware that the trappings (buffet and unlimited coffee) thinly disguised the politically correct twaddle. With all the paperwork and best possible intentions, another example of meddling with and bettering conditions with competition being so fierce. Tenant's rights are high on the agenda, as are the staff's conditions (they supply hand cream in the toilets at their offices), everything is correctly covered and documented. But what they are doing works and the staff look happy, the voluntary panel of residents are on my Xmas card list too.

It's like children have got rights and should never be hit, well that's worked hasn't it?
There's a distinct difference between a disciplinary slap on the bottom and a broken nose, I agree that children shouldn't be beaten but some kids need corrective input from their guardians.
When we have youngsters threatening to report their parents, for striking them, then we have children committing murder or hitting teachers … something is wrong.

Respect and discipline … bring it back.

I vividly remember my mum slapping my leg in a supermarket, at the time I was mortified, but then behaved myself and stopped whatever I was doing, so it worked.
Creating more grey areas, or exploitable loop-holes, is rubbish and is effectively making things worse. Some people, know what to say and do to take advantage then clean-up the system and claim all sorts of things. When I tidy up, it does happen, then drop something or knock it over to make things worse … then have to spend extra time clearing up the mess I've just made. Same same.

But anyway the housing thing … I liked the people (sandwiches), I was made to feel that my input was valuable, so I kept going. They are always pleased to see me, it's been a while now, a few of them own copies of Gillian Mk 2 as well.

To this day there is a lot of paperwork involved, they send me bound and copied stuff all the time, must cost them a fortune to keep us all informed about everything.

I feel duty bound to keep it all, but probably will not get round to reading it before they send me some more, though I don't really care about who's left and been replaced within the workforce.

Not sure I will ever read the finance reports either, somebody is having great fun and possibly fulfils a ridiculous title, they mess with numbers and put together graphs of achievement with colourful pie charts then tell us how brilliant they are.

It's all good stuff, really it is, but they would be saving loads of money if they hadn't fallen for and taken this route. My usefulness is limited, if I'm honest, but they have to have people there to eat all the food and I can do that (nay problemo), I don't really know why I am there or if I'm making any difference.

They have sent me a nomination form to select members for chairman, deputy chair and treasurer.

One of the gang died!

An untimely death as in he was quite young, the news was a shocking surprise, he was about my dad's age, so they need others to fill the gap forthwith.

I get invited to meetings about all sorts of things, one that did hold my interest was an editorial regarding their newsletter publication. But they have a team that are paid to make sure that this looks good, so I felt that any ideas of mine were pointless but of course they would deny this .

The Donkey Pageant in York, with Princess Royal, was this year! But hey … it's worth another mention and I wonder if she read the book?

Bandit read the book and identifies with disability, he only has the use of one arm, but taught me something. To open the main door to get into my building you need two hands, there are two catches that you must operate simultaneously, he showed me how to get around this by using his chin to open the top latch. Brilliant! I have lived here for years and never thought of that, this nugget of information was passed on, Truffle can open the door on her own now. If I have something in my hand it doesn't get put down whilst I open the door anymore. I have to take my own rubbish outside, but still cannot do the wheely bin.

I dug out Pathetic Two's passport, that is: separated it from mine.

I arranged to take it to the Angry Young Man, but can't remember if I did or not … well I haven't seen the document so I must have.

I tend to delete memories that mean nothing to me, that don't bother my fragile ego, which is good. But what isn't beneficial is that my unpredictable brain stores unpleasant memories, those that have scarred my brain cells when I have been upset or insulted, then lets them resurface at any time. Usually in moments of calm, I am often caught unawares by memories associated with bad feelings, when I have just woken up is a prime time. I am instantly freaked, but this gets better and lessens with impact, it is my start to the day if an unresolved issue is bothering me and ongoing.

But it doesn't last long … I put the kettle on and chill out with caffeine.

Move onto the next dilemma, Pathetic Two had found his genitals now I must find mine.

This was a particularly good night, one of the best.

Truffle had gone to the toilet, I didn't know she wanted to go home, so I had got another drink.

She was ready to go and left me, I sat alone to finish the gin and tonic.

A fit young man sat at my table with his drink, he kept looking at me, then an Elton John song was playing and I laughed with the memory of a concert I'd been to.

The man smiled at me and I told this handsome chap why I was chuckling, then he started to chatting to me, "I was sitting and wondering how to talk to you … to introduce himself".

He was a graduate and was visiting friends, we chatted for a while then he left me … to tell his mates he was walking me home. He was gorgeous and I was very happy with my escort, he held my hand and chatted easily, "I had been watching you for a while and did somersaults when you were sitting alone".

He was sat in my front room when he told me, "You are the most beautiful and interesting woman I've ever met", I kissed him. Blimey. How good is that? Eh. It doesn't get any better.

He was twenty three and crashed here with me, it got better! But nothing naughty happened and he left the next morning, with a book, never to be seen again … I probably wouldn't recognise him anyway though I do remember his name. Well this doesn't happen every day. So Dean if you are reading this … X … happy days, nice one.

I saw the epilepsy nurse, who has been a contact for years, she had a baby girl and is a happy older mother … apparently I still have time. Yeah yeah … but no, I'll just cope with the monthly curse—which is normal now by the way—with occasional visits to my niece and nephew.

I do like her though, she spoke to her superiors regarding the book … ?
I still see the head doctor every so often too, to monitor progress
I presume or to predict problems, though I don't like him much
anymore I find him condescending.

This is my new philosophy, I can and do cope on my own now, but
I love this:

THERAPY … IS EXPENSIVE popping bubble wrap is cheaper. You
choose.

Wish I'd known this collection of words before … I got drunk and
was watching television.
I was watching the late night quiz slot, the word game, you know …
the one that offers you half a word and you fill in the rest. Easy money!

Black —.
I thought of answers that weren't being said, then found the redial
button on my phone.
You can probably guess the rest, even when the recorded message told
me how many calls I'd made, I was always convinced that the next
sucker would be me.
My phone company noticed what was happening and cut me off!
Stop this right NOW. Stupido! Thankfully my mobile phone was
pay as you go, but the credit available was used on this quest for free
money too
Sadder thing is: there were hundreds of people pressing their redial
buttons at the same time, thinking the same thing. Surely it will be
me next?

At the time I was livid, how dare they choose the course of action for
me and take control!

It was sorted out and I was furious with myself, when I realised how much this compulsion was going to cost. I told mum what I'd done and felt really stupid. "How many times did you get through?", she shook her head with horror when I told her, "Not once".

Music Man offers, he doesn't get phased, "There's nowt spoilin". That's a good attitude to have and it sorts most things.

I must mention my immediate neighbours, because they are brilliant, they will help me out if I ask them and we all live together in harmony. Respect is the key word, with a civil understanding of living in a shared house, none of us are selfish or intrusive, this is a nice place to be.

It's raining again and there are no birds around. Do they shelter from the downpour? If they do they will be starving, because it rains all the time now. Global WARMING! What's that all about?

I joined a Stop Smoking group, deciding that help to quit this disgusting habit was needed, it was about time. The first week I got a taxi there but was given a lift home … by one of the men at the meeting.
The lady running it had smoked herself, she had decided that cigarettes were not good and started smoking cigars, but that was no better and she had stopped all that too. The group was a good bunch of people and we all had to speak about ourselves, well what else could I say? Of course I told them about the book, rather than letting them know that I'd just been dumped for a Turnip.

There was a lovely mixture of characters which made it better, the feeling of togetherness was strange as we were all fighting the same daemon, the meetings were informative too. We were given a list of all the chemicals that are used to make a cigarette, it was a long list, there were a few poisons too.

We all gave our reasons for being at the meeting, cost and health were the main culprits, one I remember was a lady who was pregnant with her first child. You have to find things to occupy your craving mind and she commented: "My house has never been so clean".

I stopped and couldn't believe the difference, when carbon monoxide presence was measured on my breath, then I had my teeth cleaned. The variation from the first week was quite astounding.

But it is an addictive habit and I missed it when I was sat, in front of the computer, being a Darlink. Feeling that they were needed to get creative juices flowing and was stuck without them.

At a standstill thinking about them more like.

Posh Boy made use of Hotel Chocolat again, even the presentation was yummy … I licked the box, this time it was champagne truffles and they didn't last as long, Well I had just stopped smoking and they were rather nice!

The phone conversations were quite frequent and the texts were regular, this friendship was due to the first book and he said, "I'm driven by you", I was getting to know him quite well and looked forward to contact.

I had a web site now and it was a brilliant idea, it cost me but they had done a good job and it looked professional, discovery and recognition were my prime goals and I told Posh Boy about this and the BBC one too.

www.gillianfirth.co.uk and www.bbc.co.uk/tellinglives (Humberside Region: Gillian Mk 2)

If you haven't looked! Now you want to eh?

Well Posh Boy did.

The book theoretically could be bought on the www.gillian site, the order would come through my email inbox, for weeks I waited for the flood of response from curious browsers.
Nothing.

I wondered if it worked and went to speak to Fat Cat, somebody who knows more than me (my niece and nephew know more than me and they're not in high school yet) about computers.
He sent an order through and didn't see a problem, he knew the chap who had done the site too, it was received by my PC so there was nothing wrong with it …

I was emailing randomly, within the sphere of head injury, thinking that if I let people know then a result would be imminent.
That didn't work either and it was a boring chore, that I soon got fed up of doing when there were no results. Back to the drawing board, Oh there wasn't one, I really didn't know what else to do and so did nothing.

"Try publishers again" my mum suggested, I did some research at the library and approached four, what a good idea I was all enthused and buzzing with anticipation once more.

In a café drinking coffee and sitting on a big leather sofa, in the smoking section talking to other outcasts forced into the same area, you meet some interesting people … sometimes.
One sunny day there was a lady there, older than me, she lived in a local village and was an amazing person. She had travelled and been on cruises, her stories were interesting and she'd been around, I was surprised she had crammed so much in, she did not look her age.

With a copy of Gillian Mk 2 in her bag she gave me her telephone number, to arrange another coffee meet.

In this spot I met a man who did charity work, he'd been in the fire brigade but had been retired through ill health, he spoke a lot about his disability and identified with the frustration (wouldn't have guessed). I spoke to him a few times over caffeine and discovered that he too finds solace in writing, he carries it around with him and let me see, it works for him and he is constantly inspired.

Met the lady and she enthused widely and bought me a cake, the next time I saw her she had slotted me in between appointments and came to the flat. She gave me a spare umbrella from her car, which I used for ages but eventually lost. Shame, it was a good brolley.

In town one day I chatted to SHe, we had a mutual friend in Samba, the leather sofa was utilised again. SHe was going to be a brief spell in my life, as was Samba.
The meetings and chats were revealing, the book was discussed in detail, Gillian Mk 2 had hit somebody who was literally living through a personal trauma. Something to do with sex and kids or money, with pointless confrontations, both sides seemed to be creating barriers to conclusion.
Supplied with coffee I am a good listener, being curious and downright nosey helps, the disabling issue was real. Although I didn't really understand, I was there … to change the subject. I bought SHe flowers, they were gladioli so tall stemmed, then I got rid of a spare Vase.

In my front room the main light had gone, having somebody tall around for coffee can be a good thing, SHe offered to help and balanced easily with the spare bulb.

Then tore the paper lampshade, whilst fiddling about, with big hands.

How annoying, I could have done that myself, but how can you be cross when somebody has tried to assist?

It is only a lampshade after all … and the light works now, I convinced myself, the hanging paper only looks bad if you actually look up at it.

She had dealt the tarot cards when I took the phone call, I had shuffled the deck, it was a publisher, "I love your work and want to offer you a contract".

I wrote the word 'publisher' on a notepad and shook my head, did that really just happen?

She smiled at me and turned the first card over then gasped, it was a man holding something, "It's the publisher!".

We both shook our heads now, in wonder, I didn't know for certain if that was totally coincidental … or not?

The rest of the reading had to be believed, blimey, it spoke of fame and recognition with a bit of money thrown in. I could be converted.

I told EVERYBODY about the publisher and made sure that a few more knew too. Going straight down the road to see my friend Ed, at the local news, he smiled, "What have you done now?".

"I've only got a publisher", I was grinning and nodding positively, "Well done you and of course we want to know more".

He despatched a reporter and a photographer, to take a new picture of me … holding Gillian Mk 2 again.

He went one better and is a star, who you know, the story appeared in their Extra Coverage publication. It was featured as the News of the Week … another article for my collection.

She pointed this out to me, it was a printing error, "They've told untruths here!".

The paper was quoted, "The second book will be out at the end of the year. The cards said, do some bloody work! Stop messin about".

There was talk of her becoming my paid help, it was my brainchild and I thought it was benefiting us both, but that idea fizzled out in reality when it got too complicated … with rules and paperwork. This camaraderie also petered out.

It was at a dinner party, held by Samba and her new man at their smart house. Other than stairs to the toilet, a minor detail, that became a pain as the evening wore on with alcohol … when my legs went stupido. Their pad was lovely and the praise continued over dinner, as the food was served, the wine I had brought was opened too. Samba continued to fuss, "It would be better if all the ingredients were authentic", throughout the meal, but you can only say 'it's the best thing you've ever eaten' a few times.

But the pasta was good, so was the wine.

Posh Boy called me on my mobile phone, he finished the call saying, "I love you". Ah.

Then we retired to the sitting room and the tarot cards came out, I joined in the conversation and listened to most of it, but I was sitting on a big squishy sofa that was too comfortable and I fell asleep.

They woke me up when the taxi came to take me away, feeling stupid I got up apologising, then I looked stupid as my legs were in a drunken haze and had gone to sleep.

I hadn't thought and had to borrow some money, for the fare, maybe that's why they stopped talking to me?

I really don't know why but they both decided they didn't like me anymore, I've seen them since, SHe is courteous and Samba avoids eye contact. Strange but true and I wasn't bothered … they had made me fall asleep.

Mum saw the lampshade and shrugged, "It looks stupid", then she marched off and came back with my stepladder. Armed with sticky clear tape she set to work, then tutted and growled, "This is uselessness, it won't stick!". Undeterred she tried again with something else, the shade is now held together with masking tape, it looks quite good … at a quick glance, well it is better than it was.

An all day bingo outing was arranged, brilliant mum and I went, all the women were waiting and standing outside the coach having their last nicotine fix.
Once seated and comfortable we all play a warm up game of bingo, on the journey to another bingo hall, it's funny some of the staff are either manning the proceedings or actually on the trip.

The other clubs make a commendable effort, mum and I collected all the discarded hats at the Xmas do … they were good ones, entertainment is sometimes laid on too.
It's generally a fun day out and on the way back we play a wind down game … of bingo.

Then we are back at our club in time, for the evening session, we have to be the staff are sitting on the coach with us.
So … we go in to play again, the passengers have a fix then file inside for the next bout.
It's only rubbish when you don't win, at all, on the coach or otherwise.
But you were at least five numbers off on each game, (that's when an unexpected shout makes you jump) all day … and night.

But you have to in it to win it! As they say, yeah that's what I keep thinking with the lottery! In all these years I've had a couple of wins … of ten pounds.

I am quite pleased to match with ONE number … unreal.

But I had high hopes and paid to have the contract looked over by a lawyer, it was strongly advised by my writer friends. We know one of the gang paid a lot of money to be published, then lost it all when the company went bankrupt, there are a lot of sharks out there who want something for nothing and don't care what it takes or who is affected. Anyway a few changes were made and it was signed, friends in the know had gasped at the rarity of a publisher … telling me, "They are like goldfish teeth".

I was just happy because the reader's had been right, my confidence was boosted.

It was arranged that I would meet my publisher at a football club, he was launching another writer's work at a book signing, my mum and I were early and it was exciting to meet the man that had changed my outlook. A.Man was tall and was busy setting up the table, he was talking to the man whose book was for sale, I was just entertaining myself and talking to anybody.

I had a few copies of Gillian Mk 2 and my mum with me.

A.Man seemed like a nice man, he chatted with me briefly and I swapped books with the other chap. The other three books went to the people I'd been talking to.

My new publisher, who had just been met, told me off for doing this, "You're being distracting".

Oops … but it has been self-published, I am my own agent, for a while and I can't help it now.

It's probably the only reliably automatic thing in my life!

Now somebody was going to do this for me, he would have the contacts needed and would know what to do.

I rang to find out if anything was happening, he was busy apparently, "I'm on the phone drumming up interest". I knew he'd have connections, also his PC credentials hint at a clever man, I was still excited. He was supplied with reader's comments and they looked even more impressive on screen. (for the whole world to see!)

A site paperbacks: Gillian Mk 2 Yipee!

In a swish of time I covered a discovery period in my life, in the learning curve you sometimes discover what you thought you knew, is true and you were right. Men are generally unreliable and think with the contents of their pants. Or is it me?

The man was watching me then had approached me, on a night out with Truffle, Angler walked with us to the next pub and we used him as a crutch grabbing an arm each.

With a drink he talked to me, we were stood by the dance floor, then he held my face gently and kissed me.

Then Angler pulled me closer, with one hand on the small of my back and the other caressing my hair. I was there for a while and have no idea what Truffle was up to.

Angler had to walk me home, hold me up, then he came in but had coffee and didn't stay.

During talks I learnt a lot about him and didn't see any problem, immediate or otherwise, he made me laugh and his visits were better than none.

I started to get girly and drank a bottle of wine before he came, excellent idea, I'd hid the keys on my person in a coy (ratted) attempt to make him stay. He jumped out of the window, the reclining and alluring position on the bed didn't work either ... I was asleep.

So that was the end of that.

A male friend demanded my attention on another night out, Positive was a bit too confident in my company, but he was funny and stayed in my sight for the rest of the evening. He too was thwarted and disappeared before I woke up. But it was the first time that I got up in panic, eventually remembering that he had to go to feed farmyard animals and he had told me.

I still see him round town and we always spend time chatting, to catch up.

Posh Boy was on the phone and I invited him to visit, he reminded me, "I don't drive". I knew that and shrugged, then I advised him in my flippant manner, "Catch the train".

Here responded, "I can't".

"Why not?", I asked the question but didn't wait for any answers, I now knew a bit about him and couldn't think of a physical reason why this might not happen, "You can walk can't you?".

I'm better at travelling now and offered my experience, "Well don't carry more than you have to, then make loads of lists ... about times and any changes, then ask everybody where you should be if you're unsure". Then I laughed, "Easy!", I do sound very clever or bossy, "Well that's what I do anyway, you'll be alright", this was my encouragement.

His mobile phone was to be busy and I was confident with the feedback, until I got the message:

'Next stop Brough'.

'Get off the train'. Was my reply. 'You are going the wrong way'

It was going far too good, but an hour later I met the man, it was obviously him standing on the platform. He was beckoned into the café to join me and it was the first time I had seen his disabled person. His mobility looked clumsy and his difficulties were more pronounced than mine, which made it more amazing that he got here with his incredibly heavy and cumbersome bag.

This is when he gave me the inscribed pen … ignore what I said earlier.

It was a good weekend and he stayed longer than he was supposed to, his mum had something to say about that. I didn't ask what was said, but could imagine, the tone sounded a bit cross.

Thankfully a lot of shops sell mobile phones, so contact was maintained, he had bought another having forgotten his charger.

The first night I had offered to pull out the sofa bed, we had looked at each other and sniggered at the thought of even attempting it.

Perhaps the wine made this an easy choice, but it did, maybe my next place should have two bedrooms.

That was nice, I'm glad that we met, he was a soul mate.

Nothing rude happened, there was no need.

In town I had bumped into a man, who hadn't been seen for ages, landlord of the pub I held the euthanasia meeting in, he invited us to his birthday celebration that night … but his birthday was on the same day as mine.

Just remembered a chap, I met him through a dating agency, it was a daytime meeting at the train station café and of course I took a book. He was alright and he now has a copy of Gillian Mk 2, but was remembered because his birthday was the same date as mine too.

My second and last date from this site was in Leeds, at an arranged café near the train station, I didn't know there were two of them … with the same name! He too was alright and ended up driving me home, I was meeting Truffle and Magico for dinner that evening, when we had talked too much and were pushing it to get me to the train on time. He joined us all to eat and it was fun.

But I stopped doing it, it was fascinating at first, there were a lot of men winking at me and typing messages, it's all very flattering and a bit of an ego trip. Chaps from down the road to overseas in Jersey, blokes aged eighteen to sixty, the world is your oyster … if you like shellfish.

Angler, who set this up for me, was having a marvellous time … he was meeting accommodating women all over the place. I got a bit sick of him telling me and didn't bother to warn him, to watch his tackle in case it goes green and falls off.

I would have done … if I'd really cared.

So … Posh Boy and I arrived at this pub, it's on the edge of town and a bit of a walk, where I was greeted by a few familiar faces some of whom have read Gillian Mk 2.

One lady came over a few times to clasp my hands and smile at me, telling me and those around, "I've read your book and your marvellous you are, she marvellous she is!", we all had too much to drink and it was brilliant.

We should have got a taxi home. I was in a dreadful state and Posh Boy had been drinking too, we had been served a 'killer' punch and it was fab … it tasted like pop.

I was alright, to the end to the end of the road, but when I got around the corner …

Out of sight, very independent and very very stupid on this occasion, my legs did not work and I had no sense of balance at all. None.

When I was trying to walk it was like my legs wanted to swap places, my fuddled brain was just throwing them in the general direction, then expecting me to correct this obvious mistake. But the rest of my brain is also muddled and thinking about it: 'Mmmm … no … we don't do that … stop it now … honestly we don't do the legs bit …'.

Now I am arguing with myself and getting nowhere … 'well, who does the balance and coordination part then? Come on, this hurts … just stop throwing me on the floor!'.

But harmony is not happening.

I am moving like an alcoholic and I can't cope, so I kept falling over onto concrete. About five times in all, but worse than that (as if this isn't rubbish enough) I dragged poor defenceless Posh Boy down too. Love him for trying to save me, but he could do nothing about it. Horrors, I think he was being a hero, when he shook his head and laughed, "Don't worry, I'm alright".

So we wind up to Xmas again and Posh Boy sent me a down filled duvet (I LOVE it!).

Bro and mum would not allow a repeat of last year, they were horrified it had gone unnoticed (lucky escape I'd say), so we packed off to his place by the sea.

It was Xmas Eve … the parents ran around and made last minute preparations, but grandma didn't have to do this anymore so was sat on the sofa drinking lager and watching them happily.

Aunty Gillian had no responsibilities either and joined in with the adult entertainment.

Five … FIVE … o'clock the next morning my nephew woke up to the sacks of presents, that had been left in the bedroom they were sharing. Like an excited kid he screamed his sister's name, that was the alarm call, then she woke up and started squealing too.

Grandma and Aunty Gillian were wide awake now, so we both got up, the parents sadly avoided this spectacle, they were still in bed, the kids were opening presents until eight o'clock. Three hours of tearing paper and shrieking, that's three loud hours, there were still sacks of presents downstairs from the guests too. I had started smoking again. My reason, excuse, was that I felt sorry for myself and was coping badly. I had spent weeks selecting, purchasing and wrapping gifts for my brother and his family. As usual getting carried away and then forgetting what I'd already bought. So they got loads, there were bags of used wrapping paper to get rid of, and my gift was (I forgot to take them home) three blank canvases.

She doesn't cook and so lunch was left to Bro, he's getting better and there were eight of us to cater for, the other set of grandparents had arrived … so more presents. They were on the Egypt trip too, so we did know each other.
There was nothing wrong with the effort made and it was nice, don't get me wrong Bro x, but Oh so boring. The best bit about it was the party hats, that we had nicked from the bingo trip.

No … the sausages wrapped in bacon were nice.
There wasn't even Xmas pudding.

"There was one!", according to the defensive cook, but I didn't see it!
No sighting of dried fruit and cherries wrapped in a stodgy mass of
spiced cake … bloody 'ell.
It will be better next time, I'm sure, he 's not silly and with a couple
of years in practice?

Mm. I did enjoy it but there's nothing wrong with eating toast, in your
own space, whilst watching the Queen's speech.

Maybe I'll wait … until the kids are drinking age … for a repeat
performance.
Told you … I'm the best Aunty.

CHAPTER IX

Mobility 2007

I have just washed my hair and you can't help but notice the grey now, the speckle of age is all over the place … nearly.

The adverts on television are right! Grey hairs are permanently curly and static with a life of their own, use product I reasoned, even with glue cementing the hair to your head … they escape.

But I won't dye it, to look the same as everyone else, yet. It's not that bad … yet.

Anyway the start to this year was brilliant.

When the publishers had been approached I had also spoken to the editor of a mobility magazine, she loved the book and it was going around the office, but it was the wrong format and they couldn't help me. Failing that … "Would you consider being a guest columnist, for the January issue?

How flattering? It was a writing challenge and I got busy immediately.

The article that I did came quite easily, only a few alterations were made by me and the editor (Nicky is fab) removed my ex husband's name. Drat … foiled.

As promised copies of the magazine were sent to me, more were delivered as requested, I was pleased and the column looked rather good.

It was inside the back cover, reading my work in print is different and the photograph was a good one. It had been supplied by Ed, my friend at the local news.

I checked the front, curious to see how my article had been listed, to notice that my name appeared again? A book review? That was a surprise, I turned to the page expecting a paragraph or so.

A whole page!

This woman had a lot to say, the book review started with:

"You know how sometimes a film or a documentary you have seen moves you so much it keeps coming back into your thoughts? Well here is a book that I guarantee will do the same ... probably for the rest of your life". Nicky Rogers Mobilise Magazine January 2007.

I'm sure that this document, my bit—coming up, was copied and saved. Surely then it can be cut and pasted (or something) onto this page, but it looks like I'm going to have to type it again, it would indeed save time and I wish I knew how to do it!

Anyway this is it, I've been given kind permission to do this from the editor ... who I haven't met yet but she sounds brilliant.

ONE MORE THING

Every month a guest columnist tackles the key issues facing the disabled community, this month, author (ooer) Gillian Firth writes about her bucket of frogs.

I put the phone down, I have just been asked to write for a magazine, be a guest columnist. How brilliant is that?

I whooped and clapped to my bemused house visitor. (Posh Boy)

Then I fell silent, what shall I write about? Issues that make me cross concerning disability?

He grinned and commented, Life is like a bucket of frogs.

Odd?? I smiled, bless, but he is right and has a better perspective than most.

We don't know what bucket we are destined to end up with. Be it the golden bucket wriggling with potential princes or the rusty pail full of squirming toads, you just never know.

What if you are happy kissing all your frogs and polishing the interior when your bucket is kicked back down the stairs of life

You end up holding a damaged vessel and all the frogs are now limping around trying top find a new home, disabled frogs avoiding the knives and forks of life.

Careless and unfortunate frogs get eaten don't they?

Anyway my bucket was the last car that I drove, I was found unconscious and taken off to intensive care, the resultant big sleep/coma was the easy bit.

Six weeks later the confusing and frustrating journey of a new life started. With my mum and brother in tow, the wheelchair and I went home.

Back inside my parent's comfortable bucket I was safe but could do little for myself. This frog no longer hopped—I was back to the learning baby stage of my life. You can only imagine what a pain in the bum this is: when bits of your brain remember that you were a married teacher once and you had control of your life. Your bruised and recovering grey matter is still struggling with the daily routines. Walking, talking and breathing.

So, many years of rehabilitation later I have risen from the wheeled chariot and graduated through various walking aids to end up living alone (yippee), alas—along with this came a divorce (when the going got tough—he got somebody else. Better or worse? Rubbish!)

I wrote a book to kill desperately sad and lonely time, Gillian Mk 2, this amphibian has mutated and is made of rubber.
Through the book I have been privileged to meet other survivors who recognise and live with the frustrations of disability.

They identify and agree with the principles of the autobiography: you just have to get on with it.
I imagine that most hurtful comments are said with malice, but try to ignore them. Try and look through the gawps and sniggers, even though there are still times when this is hard.

Imagine how these stupid and narrow minded people would cope … they wouldn't.
Me?
I'm looking for the right frog in my new pond. Look at <u>www.</u> <u>gillianfirth.co.uk</u> I'm trying.

I know … the magazine was forwarded to my publisher, look at me getting about!
"I'm still calling people", well that's what he told me, but had nothing to report.
It's early yet, so I wasn't worried, but I was disenchanted that they hadn't sold one book.
No … one's definitely gone, Posh Boy ordered it.
But none came to me, I still have the box of self-published work.

A.Man wanted me to give these books to him. Why? They cost me loads and they're the last print … so they are important to me.

He told me, "You need exposure", I thought the publisher with contacts arranged all that, "But your story was too long ago".

Go figure, I am still disabled and my life is still affected by this day in day out?
Should I be a little disillusioned and totally disappointed? But something will happen—hopefully before I am dead.

It was about here that I had a phone call, the man said, "It's Pathetic". I know a few men called Pathetic and answered, "Pathetic who?". "Pathetic Dufus".
My ex husband was in contact after thirteen years, I was shocked and commented, "You took your time … what do you want?"
By all accounts it took him thirteen years to pluck up courage, to speak to me … told you he was feeble, he must have been curious, the last time he had seen me I couldn't stand or walk. Without the use of two heavy and clumsy walking sticks, coupled with heavy and clumsy legs, it was not fun and I sat for hours alone in his pokey flat watching CNN.
Playing scrabble on my own, spilling coffee everywhere (he had to clean this up), cutting myself out of the wedding photograph he had displayed (too much time to think and embellish the truth to be sadder than it was) and then being punched. Good memories.

He wanted to visit and my mum laughed, "Well tell him to piss off!". She had a point, "He wasn't there when you needed him and he wasn't pushing the wheelchair! He didn't even pay your dad", she had looked at me and scowled, "Bet his third marriage has failed"

He did visit and didn't bring me flowers, they would have been nice though, he explained to me, "I was really selfish and only thought about himself".

What a selfish and boring revelation, "Oh, did you?". (It didn't take me thirteen years to suss that one)

"My third marriage was a big mistake, which I regret", I didn't really care … boo hoo Pathetic Dufus, but he had twins now. I shook my head at the man I was married to, "Poor Pathetic Dufus, you will be paying child maintenance for the rest of your life".

So he's got four kids now and his third marriage had gone pear-shaped … my mum was right, again.

Brilliant, I'm so glad she's on my side, I am crying now … at the thought of being without her.

He took a book with him, that wasn't a gift … by the way, so was due to experience the trauma all over again with my eyes and thoughts.

He must have loads of people bugging him for money, his phone does not accept in coming phone calls now … adding insult to injury one more time, but am I bothered?

As noted in Gillian Mk 2: "A lucky escape". But I enjoyed our stretch together … a lifetime ago.

At the end of the day I am writing a second book, he's got four kids and is Pathetic Dufus, so he will not be mistaken that I have any respect for him. I was curious too.

To see if I remembered him and to look at what I married, but right now was secretly glad that he knew what I thought. Other people were reading this and he was having a hard time.

But he will be alright, he always is, I had to smile with some new material for this book and it gave me the opportunity nay privilege to rename him. Pathetic Dufus … do you like that?

Chapter endeth.

The staff member talking to me used to be a helper in the days when I was a resident in the rehabilitation unit, she has been promoted a few times. She knew and remembered me well, she laughed and there was nothing I could say. I doubted that she remembered anything that well, it was a long time ago, but Gillian Mk 2 had been devoured. She was obviously impressed and sang the song of praise, that I wanted to hear, then invited me to an open day at the unit.

I told her about my publisher, as usual the website address was spelt out, she gasped, "Wow", then told me to bring some books when I came to see them.

Mum was with me when we stood at the door, it has intercom entry now, it was answered by a woman we have seen before. She was rude again, to me only, my mum noticed this attitude and attempted to interject. I vaguely remembered this woman, but was offended and annoyed. Unbeknown to anyone I was collecting stories and interruptions, if remembered for Typically Gillian, I'm sorry but you are in the book. How do people like this keep jobs here?

But I saw a face that I recognised and dragged my mum away from this horror, she too was shaking her head in wonder and she has seen a lot of shit.

Sitting with food we looked around, only the shell of the building remained, it has almost changed beyond recognition and it had been extended.

So there were even more Headbangers here now, bet meal times were a riot!

They were often rowdy whilst I was there and there were fewer clients, maybe they have sittings or more staff are on dinner duty with big sticks. (JOKING)

It was the staff that I spoke to in animation, to thereby spread the word, mum marvelled my progress in the background. It was strange to be back at the beginning … of what was another journey. Maybe it was a reminder of very different times, I have come a long way and there's no denying … but it's not hand stand good yet.

Anyway a lot of people said positive things and enthused wildly, it is nice to hear from staff that worked with the victims of TBI.

They spoke of helping me publicise my work and vowed to look at the websites, this of course would be better if people did what they said they would. Then there was a flood of orders, to a site or me, with renewed interest.

If I was inundated with feedback and there was an explosion … I didn't notice, missed it.

I felt alone, like I was the only person that was bothered about Gillian Mk 2.

Grrr …

The manageress at the charity shop retired, she was lovely but had had enough and was looking forward to finishing, a breath of fresh air came in with a new face.

Dingle is brilliant, one of my fab people, she had new ideas and eventually would laugh at me and then tap the badge that said she was, The Manageress.

The shop looks good and all the volunteers are happy, naughty people always enjoy doing their community service here and go home with a new wardrobe, Dingle has worked hard and is luverly.

You can't help but buy stuff when you volunteer in these places … one man's meat is another man's poison n'all. I haven't seen anybody wearing any of my donations yet, they're probably amongst the culled rejects sent to Goole. But would you say: "Yeah yeah … that's why I got rid of it!". Or, "Blimey, it looks pretty good on her! Damn".

Dingle's children are a credit and her grandson is SO cute … even I recognise this.
I see another side of her on a Saturday night, Dingle is funny and makes me giggle, I am glad that she knows me and Truffle.

I don't look after myself very well, I don't know if my cooker still works … ha ha … I do know the door is sprained (it was open and I fell straight onto it then sat down) and the markings have rubbed off the dials.
The only way to be sure you haven't left anything on is to turn it off, all together, at the wall.

I have broken the freezer compartment door, in my small fridge, so it now produces icebergs. Which my mum blasts with the hairdryer.
I will forget the mass is there, and a problem, because it cannot be seen. When the ice creeps into the fridge … I might notice it then.
When she melted some of the ice she found the end of a wooden spoon? Yoyo had tried to help, with big drunk hands he had prodded the ice to no effect, not only had he broken the spoon but the freezer itself was damaged. More so … nice.

I should get rid of the lime scale in my kettle too, Pathetic Two used to do this … so it can't be that difficult.
The white goods in my kitchen are getting old, suffering with wear and tear, my fridge is filled with things in pots that are out of date or evolving, we are all going down hill together.

My computer is slow now but will get this book out no sweat (mm), surely then my bank account will have funds enough for a super duper laptop, I'll of course need new gear for the next instalment.

The keyboard has been abused, if you shook it there would be enough tobacco for at least one roll-up, so the c key plays up, the space bar is temperamental and the m has joined the rebellion.

Eventually this will have to be written using the grammar and spell check facilities.
Actually, I wonder if that would work? (Oh yeah, the question mark sticks too)

It would be a bit bland perhaps? There must be loads of mistakes in this, done on purpose obviously, I am aware of that but ... I don't care. Hopefully neither will you, my audience.

It was coming up to Brain Injury Awareness week and I had another plan, to gain recognition, to flog some of these bloody books. York hospital were setting up tables, partly for this event, I spoke to a lot of people, "You can have a table at a cost, unless you have a sponsor". Brilliant my head doctor works here ... who you know.

I spoke to a lot of people again, secretaries and the like, to eventually get the message that my doctor not only refused but had said he wanted nothing more to do with it.

With what? The book you wouldn't pay for? Or was that a reference to me? I took this news badly, finding the refusal to help me without reason quite rude and hurtful, wait until I see him next is all I'm going to say. I am really confused and don't know help is not forthcoming, from anybody.

I was fed up about this and had already spoken to York radio station, about the possibility, they were keen and would speak to me when I had more information.

Blimey, what do you have to do? Naked handstands? (I will do this again)

But I was impressed, distracted like a goldfish, when it was discovered that Gillian Mk 2 could be found on a site, Amazon and Google. Music Man showed me the entry on the Richard and Judy Book Club. Not sure which site this was, but I found a message from Morris? If it's who I think it is, a blast from the past, hello there! Long time eh?

I was on the train, for a return visit to Posh Boy at his house in Gloucestershire, I love just flitting off and seeing new places ... my mum has got used to it again. He lives at home with his mum and sister.

It was on the edge of Tewksbury, which most of you will have heard of when it recently turned into a lake, it was very pretty where he lived but there was no public transport. He was totally reliant on his mother in this respect.

Posh Boy looked after me well and kept me busy, we had a meal at a nearby hotel which was rather nice, then we made a trip to a local theatre to see Mad Jocks and Englishmen playing live.

But I enjoyed the walks around beautiful and different spaces, looking in the charity shops, going to a tearoom and eating cake then just hanging around in Cheltenham.

He was totally in awe of my ability to live alone, my situation made him think about his own, he was ready for a change and it was my fault.

Reading the book, then getting on the train and meeting me, had spurred him into positive action, blimey it was my fault.

Living independently, nearly, is brilliant it must be said. I could only appreciate his need to feel normal, with choice. But it's not always that easy, there's a lot to consider, though with thought most problems have a solution, with a bit of determination a lot of challenges are met.

If you are seen trying to achieve, asking for assistance when you need to, not expecting people to complete tasks if you are able. Then the greater public will want to get involved and will appreciate the effort. That sounds good eh? It's not always true, unfortunately there are some shallow and ignorant bodies about, but it should be that easy really.

Anyway his guardian raised objections, "The doctor said you will never live alone again", quite rightly so if they were valid, but she quoted a doctor's diagnosis from nearly twenty years ago. That he was buggered basically … but he was physically at a disadvantage in comparison with my situation.

But he has swallowed Gillian Mk 2, I didn't need to say anything not that it was going to nor it was any of my business, he rose to the bait and muttered stubbornly, "You don't know until you try".

I was so proud and smiled, the response surprised me too, it pleased me that he was thinking like this.

His mum was going to move up north, soon, he had a lot of his stuff to sort out. "Great, I'll help!", I volunteered. We laughed, "Is'n it?", and talked whilst we pottered about.

Then he had brought up the fall(s), on my birthday weekend and my fault entirely, that had damaged his leg.

I just felt stupid with the reminder, but had tried suggesting remedial amends, I had encouraged him to use his clever rowing machine—to build up his leg strength and therefore control.

"It might work, well it will do no harm surely", I felt awful with responsibility and shrugged at a loss.

On the phone he was reporting, that the machine had been put to good use, then he was telling me about distances or something. But I was impressed that he rowed to France, not sure if he's kept it up … to come back, but they have all moved since so?

Holiday time!
Fabulous, mum and I went to Ibiza, the party capital was going to be home for two weeks. The hotel was allocated on arrival, I told you, the brochure had described our choices, one was deemed unsuitable for those with walking difficulty.
"That's were we'll be", I joked.

How true a word spoken, they were right, there were a lot of steps. There was a lift to the second and top floor, where we were of course, but you had to go up a flight of steps without a handrail to get to it. I was alright there was a wall to lean on.

There were bloody steps everywhere, to and from everything, to the pool, the dining area, to the bar, our room, to reception and the goddamn toilets! But I was alright here, either: sit near to the toilets or, set off ten minutes before you are desperate or, try to go whenever you are passing or … just get into the pool. The secret is not to make it obvious, but there will be others in the water doing the same thing, that's why there are chemicals in the water to calculate for such mishaps.

But, the view from our room was stunning and the panorama was not blocked by anything, there were no bars, noisy nightclubs or shops on the doorstep … it was just great.

The bar was really good and the staff were easy to talk to, there was one young chap there who flirted with me. His hazel flecked, chocolate sauce, eyes glinted in the moonlight and made me smile ... a lot. Not that I took much notice ...

It could have been even better though ... the inclusive bar closed and you had to pay for your drinks after eleven thirty. The staff serving were used to the rush, at precisely eleven fifteen, when tipsy tanned people were at the bar stocking up on cocktails ... well me and my mum were. I had discovered, and had a penchant for, gin fizzes or pineapple juice with coconut and white rum.

The entertainment in the evening was really good too, they were funny and spoke all the languages they needed to, my mum and I were the only English holiday makers there ... easily spotted as the whitest people in the resort. Still the palest people after two weeks. They had exercise classes, in the swimming pool, instigated by a young and fit body standing on the side.
The pool was full of women hoping that bouncing around for a bit under the cover of water, with your weight off your feet, would make a difference.

Well I joined a group hoping it would, but I couldn't stay upright! I was trying to jump with the others, but couldn't land or stay on my feet! Then not able to keep up with the group, at all, was hilarious and I was mortified at how rubbish I was. But just kept laughing. I looked drunk.

From thereon I was happy to watch mum splashing in the exercises and wished I was able to join the volleyball teams, but had to be content with my poolside seat in the sun and a frothy coffee
Writing about me.
Hard life.

Mum was cross with herself for not checking, for thinking that I was alright, believing me when I said, "Yes, I've packed my drugs".

I had … but only enough epilepsy drugs for one week … idiot. Don't ask me why, I was really put out too.

We had to use the hotel reception to get this problem sorted out. They were fully equipped for this eventuality, it must happen all the time, but could not get the 100mg dosage. Of course we had to pay for this service and a lot of holiday money had to be used … bugger.

Later my mum sat with her glasses on, messing about and fiddling, to take the 400mg tablets to bits, in an attempt to rectify this. Mm … I let her, she was absorbed in remedy.

I was annoyed with myself again, because I have been here before and should know better (stupid woman), because I am quite happy to slurp too much alcohol. I cannot judge …

Basically I cannot drink, to ridiculous excess anymore, it is just silly … but sometimes being a moron and forgetting is too easy.

It's like my limbs don't belong to my body, they become alien and don't speak the same language, trying frantically to keep up my overtaxed brain just gets confused. Then gives up … it just gives me free reign and lets me do what I want.

With no control of anything, loose legs and flapping arms, it surprises me that serious damage hasn't been done. To me anyway, Posh Boy might moan. One day I won't be so lucky, there might not be people around to make sure I am safe and I get home in one piece.

This time it was my, also drunk, mum. She should know better, or did, when we got to the room I wanted to talk about mother daughter stuff. (head up my bottom scenario)

Ignoring me she got into bed, "I want to go to sleep", but no!
I wanted to slur rubbish and drink some more, so I did and turned the television up to make sure she wasn't sleeping either, this went on for far too long.
There was a knock at the door and mum got up to answer, in her disgruntled night wear, it was hotel security with a complaint about the noise.

Mum nodded and then pointed back into the room, "It was her!".

Oops … I had a cigarette on the balcony and watched the calm black sea for a while, then went to bed.
Honestly.

Mum is a snorkelling junky now, since discovering the Red Sea, so encouraged me to join her. It was nice but the swimming and breathing bit spoilt it, there were a few little fish but I generally don't last very long, it scares me and I don't really like it, especially if there is not a lot to see.

What I do like is wandering around looking at things and talking to people, the day out at the huge market was exactly this, different sights and smells
One day we took a bus to the centre of Ibiza.
Here we were drawn to a café bar, on the main stretch, by a smartly made up couple. Although they were both stunning, he was grabbing the most attention. Walking and balancing on shoes that were so high, they were a Z shaped platform under his foot, I was in total admiration and felt quite sick just imagining.
Turning positively green when the bill came for two halves of lager, we had just paid for this chaps shoes!

We only stayed for one drink, cheeky monkeys, then explored the back streets where all the best bits are. It was a brilliant holiday and I wish that I hadn't tried to spoil it … for a change.

I didn't wear the gorgeous jewellery Posh Boy gave me, thank goodness, the stone fell out at home. I threw a complete wobbler when I noticed the empty setting! Dingle found it, if it had gone missing on the beach …

At home there was a letter waiting for my attention, the local council had written to tell me, "We have noticed that you haven't been to your allotment". Big bloody brother … how did they know?

It was a mess and they were telling! "We take this very seriously and if the site doesn't show improvement … we have people waiting". Yeah for a decent plot with a shed, there were a lot of wilderness patches that were empty.

I was really miffed, there were worse sites than mine!

My pleas of a deserted fantasy were unheard and I was given time to clear my plot, Bro took the contents of the shed … because he could. Not sure what he did with them, they're probably in his hut, but you never know when you'll need a spare fork, rake or spade. I gave the shed to a chap, who knew Yoyo and was talking about his new allotment, because I could.

But I drew the line at ripping all my fences up.

It was quite sad, somebody had dug my roses up and taken them too.

Only one fruit twig had blossomed and looked healthy, well it was definitely alive, Bro dug it up and took that too.

I asked him what happened to the tree and he laughed, "It was transferred from the bag to a planter, so it's not dead but it needs planting out". Then he can have an orchard with one fruit tree too!

Now I can introduce you to Yoyo, a local self-employed man who has peaked with his career. All on his own, clever chap.

It was getting late when he came over to me, at the bar, he was alone. Then he tried to talk but wanted to take me elsewhere, so I could be heard, that was fine by me and I was being too giddy with the rose tinted haze of Saturday night …

Wobbling to the next venue I linked his arm for support, he slid down my arm and held my hand, but I had to hold on … what a dreadful sight for the CCTV people.
We were at the bar of the next pub when a little, dumpy, woman came from nowhere and stood in front of Yoyo. Then she started screaming abuse at him, I knew her by sight from bingo and touched her arm to calm her down.
Oh Gillian! Stupido.

But she just grabbed my arm, to shake me off (phew), then continued yelling at him. He was just looking over her head, so I turned back to the bar and picked up my drink … nothing to do with me.

It was his girlfriend (CT)'s aunty. I had no idea what was going on, it was unpleasant, but could see that he had blanked her.

She followed me into the toilets and started shouting nonsense at me? Oh my God.
She was swearing with insults and threats, pointing with menace, but this show was all for somebody who wasn't in the least bit interested. I wasn't even curious as to why she was so upset and I would not

respond to this verbal attack. If she had told me what was wrong, I wasn't listening, I ignored her but wanted to leave the building immediately.

I told Yoyo, "I'm going", then we left to find Truffle. To tell her I was going home and why, during the trip (literally) back to my place I was answering a question.

Yoyo had asked about my disability … and I found this to be the perfect cue.

He came in to look at the book and talked a lot, he didn't seem to want to leave, but I didn't really notice the clock and the wine in my flat had been drunk. Then it was time for sleep, without question and he crashed here with me.

Now I'm not really thinking, at all, or capable of rational consideration. I want to lie down to get comfy and warm … then that's it.

But a few hours later I sat up with my eyes open, fully alert, then woke Yoyo.

I made him go home, this was out of order, she had been drinking out of town but would be worried as to his whereabouts.

I settled in bed and went back to sleep, but was woken by noises at my bedroom window?

Yoyo was standing outside, with a stripy shirt on, it was really really cold.

So I let him back in, writing this now I can pinpoint this as my exact moment of error, CT had refused him and the back windscreen of his car had been smashed.

So not happy then.

He seemed nice but was troubled by his past, the onslaught of unreasonable behaviour started here, beginning with the constant silly messaging, then came the abusive and lengthy phone calls in the small hours of the night. He wanted out, but she didn't, CT in her desperation came to the flat.

In my stupidity I LET HER IN?

CT was sitting in my front room, she kept fiddling with the foot hole of her jeans to subtly show that boots were being worn (would have been better had I not seen) and she would not shut up, it was tedious. She was stuck in a groove and she went on and on, until she wore him down, it was funny at first then it was painful and so so boring, but he would go back to her.

Yoyo wasn't bothered about anything, as long as he earned enough, as mum and Music Man pointed out, "It was a shame for him".

Me too.

Because I'm foolish: firstly, for thinking that I could make any difference to this nonsense. Secondly, for expecting the discourse to be on the same wavelength of normal decency. Then finally: I am guilty of believing words spoken, much too trusting and or simple. But I enjoyed sitting in the park and reading, it was the first time I have witnessed a flock of Starlings retire. It's amazing, I watched the show standing near their chosen trees, the group of birds got bigger and the last time that I saw them it took three drops to clear the sky. The whole flock of birds just dive into the branches, at the same time! They must be tasty if they go to all that effort, but they moved on, there were so many of them now they needed bigger trees.

Now I was really wrapped up with Yoyo, still thinking he needed my help and I was there being me, but it started to get sillier when CT would be demanding and quite horrible to him. It was awful but I was having fun, most of the time, mainly because I was drinking every day now.

It took me a while to realise, even though an ex of his (small town) confided, over a pint glass, "Yoyo drinks a lot". Wrong place to tell me, it was a Saturday night in a pub, I may have been just a little cynical and tipsy so had laughed. He didn't want help, he had no intention of changing his actions, Yoyo was alright and he was happy. I had already noticed that he likes his cheap cider and was starting to find his habits tiring, little things that you tend to disregard at first.

But with help they soon became big things, I was getting harassed by CT and her nasty family. Well known to be unpleasant when out drinking, but nobody told me! I didn't know.

I found out when CT shouted at me and called me, " … that retard", another time her half sister was mouthing off and referred to me as, "the cripple" and yet another day her fat cousin forced me back into the toilet. Then this woman told me: "You know who I am, I know you, what you do and where you live". I was shocked (ugh), she was sitting on and using the toilet, because I didn't know who this big woman was at all!

Well that's never happened before … it's taken a few weeks but … I have now heard every remark regarding my disability. From the thesaurus of stupid and offensive crap.

I was helping Yoyo to get back on track, until he got his own place, it was temporary believe me and I didn't know I had to tell the council about my personal life.

I told Music Man who shook his head and then sighed, "She's not going to let him go and he's not good for you anyway".

My mum had met him too, "He's a waste of time and he's going nowhere", she knew he was clumsy and rolled her eyes when I told her about the toilet. But groaned when told of his latest exploit.

When Nomad spoke he too was critical, though a little too bombastic for my liking, he said too much (as is his want … liking the sound of his own wisdom) and I couldn't decide which stance he was taking with me or why he was taking one at all?

CT and her offspring were on my doorstep, shouting at poor confused Yoyo, they were one and the same like sperm in a condom. The daughter had looked down her nose to stare at the ground, then she could tell me, "You look about fifty!". Then whined to Yoyo, "Yoyo! Tell er to stop looking at me".

But CT weaved her magic and he went back to her, again. I was annoyed with both of them, they were being really stupido and it was getting on my nerves now.

But he was still contacting me and had planted flowers, in tubs, outside the front door.

My neighbour went out in her pyjamas and with dishevelled hair asked them, "Can you keep the noise down, I'm trying to sleep". They both apologised, then CT started again the moment she could. No respect, I watched in horror from my front room, she hit him in the face and then kicked him in the groin. Quite sickening to see, she was training her daughter in the art of seduction and showing her how to control a relationship.
The police came, about three cars, then it was quiet again.

When he was messing me about Dingle had her say, another friend knew him and she too had words, this is not going well and I am becoming an Alco frolic! Bless though, I thought I could see something different, the intoxicating haze of cider painted a different picture. Using my new listening skills well, thanks Starfish, but I was short sighted and drunk.

When I discovered the obvious and thoughtless lies then realised that a) the house isn't left before any remaining booze is consumed b) there are pubs on his route c) he knows where they all are and calls the bar staff by name d) his friends have bets on a Saturday night as to whether CT will hit him or not e) he's really boring when drunk (unless you like reggae or store useless trivia about nothing) f) I was misplacing a lot of things? Too many things, that I'm usually good with.

He would get up in the night and potter about, he told me this when I made comment about something being moved, Yoyo would drink lots of milk and read apparently. (I can imagine) Now questioning myself and my motives, I just felt silly, but when he was drunk and trying to cook that was ridiculous.

He had images of master chef in his head, but looked like the Swedish chef from the Muppet show crossed with the fat cook in Southpark, it wasn't funny when he scarred all my work surfaces instead of using the chopping board and almost set my kitchen on fire.

The night he ruined a dinner party, Truffle and Magico were also agog at his absurd behaviour, we were all drinking so amounts weren't really noticed. But he must have stocked up in the kitchen, because he when he burst back he was suddenly loud and rude, which was annoying. He announced "You are all boring", then turned the music up. He accused me of flirting then turned on Magico, who was guilty of fancying me? Yoyo was being aggressive and drunk.
Then I offered desert, which nobody wanted and it did look horrible, before excuses were made to end the farce.
That won't happen again, in my lifetime. He would not leave.

"You won't change him and there's nothing you can do", friends were free with their advice, "Alcoholics and smokers are synonymous". It was then I stepped back and slapped myself hard to wake-up. Fool, it was an addictive and volatile ride, but I cannot drink and it was all his baggage not mine! He went somewhere on foot, with his carrier bag of possessions, but it is a small town and he still sees me.

The night.
Truffle had just gone and I spied Yoyo, because he was making silly smirks whilst mouthing something at me, he was demanding attention and looked a fool.
Blimey, I thought, what a state … now that's drunk.
But CT saw him and followed his eyes, to me. She walked over and spluttered, "Just fuck off Gillian!", then punched me in the face!
I saw Yoyo as he stepped back with both his hands in the air, he was nodding denial and she saw him again so hit me a second time. That was one way of stopping him, get rid of the competition, Yoyo had no control and I was on my own. Fat cowards.
Now a doorman was there, "Let go", he was trying to make me let go of her T-shirt, "No", I was holding the neckline and dragging it to her knees, but I didn't touch her. (it might be contagious) I did let go then was escorted out of the dump, but not before I did a childish impression of her doing a sumo wrestler. I was furious.
Note: Yoyo remembers the sumo incident and laughs.

I pressed charges with outrage, as Music Man said, "Go to the police! That's crap, you can't go out for a drink in fear of being twatted!" …

That's a good word and he was right, I'm too old for this kind of behaviour, my disability was also an issue.
Nothing happened, the video footage (in the pub!) was eyeing up the toilets and therefore useless to me but fortunate for her. I know … and CT knows that she hit me, twice.

But Yoyo is an alcoholic, I'm sure, he was told what happened so he knew what to say.

I will need police protection, but they will know the score, when Typically Gillian comes out.

But I'll have moved to my bungalow in the sun with a garden, where I'll get another Tom (seriously cute kitten), in my dreams.

I'm so sick, to my very being, of people getting rich enough to buy a few big houses etc … all from doing nothing!

Except being horrendous on television … where do they get the contestants for these shows?

Can't they find nice, pleasant or interesting volunteers? But can you imagine being stuck, day in and day out for weeks, with some of these plebeians?

Did I tell you the benefits people crashed me out, they stopped everything … with an immediate response, CT reported me, "Yoyo is living there". My mum and I had to go and sort it out.

What a mess, this whole episode left a bitter taste in my mouth and was ridiculous, I actually felt sorry for him but he didn't care. I try not to look at her now, CT is an ugly person and I have nothing to say to her. She may not understand anyway, "There is not one book in her house", Yoyo told me as he picked literature off my shelves.

There was an organised Goth event at Whitby and I planned to go, an excuse to get away for some organised fun and do fancy dress, Yoyo was caught up in my campaign and agreed it looked brilliant. Bought some new boots, that would complement the black dress, so my outfit was looking good and I was all set for the weekend. Complete with my black nails and dark red lipstick …

But booked the bed and breakfast in Scarborough? Because the owner had the same surname as me …

It was a thirty to forty pound taxi fare, to get to the party and where we needed to be, oops hadn't thought about that.

So it's not looking good, at this point Yoyo crumbled and wanted to stay here, but I was determined to go. Friday night was cancelled because I just didn't get it together, Saturday was beginning to look dubious too and I spoke to my pal.

I had arranged to meet my married friends for coffee in Scarborough, where I was meant to be, but told him about the situation.

"Pack your bag, we are coming to pick you up", No Messin was adamant.

So the weekend, that started in Whitby, then moved to Scarborough, ended up in Filey.

On the way we stopped at a big warehouse, that sold a variety of cheap and cheerful stuff, I bought some boots that were better than those in my bag.

Mrs No Messin bought her little dog a coat, it was pink with Princess written on it, I had laughed and said, "I won't be walking with her". It was a joke but it was true and he had sniggered too, oops, she crossly took offence and snapped, "I didn't ask you to! ".

"Of course I would walk with her! But not holding the lead", I just thought it was funny …

No Messin introduced me to his friends, a no frills bunch of fishermen who were fun to be with and talk to, for the first night there we were to all stay at one chap's flat.

I was annoyed that I had forgotten my black tights, but the boots still looked good, anyway I was managing quite nicely to forget this.

At the end of the night a strange text message came from Yoyo … 'Truffle has been in a fight'.

Blimey, I've been gone one night, what's she doing? But I was otherwise occupied and anyway was too far away.

My night was getting strange too, Mr and Mrs No Messin seemed to be unhappy and were niggling at each other in earshot … but this was normal and they bump along.

When the pub was closed we weaved to their mate's flat, then the dog had to be walked and they would stop for a Chinese.

They came back and we could hear them and looked at each other, something was wrong, the voices were raised and angry, the Chinese was put in the kitchen. Then the host and I were forcibly subjected to both sides of the argument.

An altercation had taken place at the take-away. He had got involved and felt it his duty to intervene, loud youths were responsible for the shabby and abusive behaviour to an elderly customer, but they were also drunk. Not good and I don't know what I'd have done.

But Mrs NM had stepped in, to stop the situation, fearing for her husband. He was quite able to look after himself, so was mortified that she was having a go at him? In front of them too.

Me and the host were nodding and picking at the displayed food, they could not agree about anything and it was getting silly, but in principle they were both right and just saw it differently.

A no win situation remained unsolved, neither of them were willing to give in.

No Messin was one of the first strangers that had made comment, regarding Gillian Mk 2, I knew that he was impressed by the book and had time for me. But, I put my hand over his mouth when he tried to kiss me, no.

Tomorrow was another day.

Yeah … but Mrs NM was still not speaking to him, or me, or the host. I escaped to walk down the hill on my own, good practice I reasoned, towards the sea. I found a small shop where I bought Posh Boy a postcard, depicting Filey in the sixties. There was a small arcade too, which I had to go in, here I got the message that they would pick me up for a day out in Scarborough, I was happy about this.

Mrs NM didn't speak in the car, to either of us, it was parked up and we rode a tram down to the sea front. Then she stropped off, with the Princess dog, miles ahead of us?

Poor No Messin was flitting between us, trying to make sure that everybody was having fun and was happy, I smiled but was uncomfortable and had no idea what was going on.

The day was disappointing and I was pleased when we went back, to get dressed up, for another night out drinking with the fishermen.

For the second night I was staying with another seaman, his tales of lobster pot fishing were intriguing and it sounds a bit dangerous. Another man, who I already knew, had travelled to arrive at the party. We sat in the front room and giggled, about everything, I was telling them both about my fun day out at the seaside. I sat alone when eating my fish and chips, just me and the seagulls.

Host two had given up and gone to bed, leaving me and this young man sniggering in the front room. Well, this was a surprise, he kissed me … a lot and it was very nice.

He had laughed, "Well that never 'appens wi our lass!".

That never happens to me either, he had to leave for work the next morning—before anybody was up, perfect it couldn't have worked out better.

I was glad that Yoyo wasn't with me.

Three of us had to get home, they must be squabbling with new material now surely … what kind of costume to buy the dog next or something, but it was more of the same.

I wasn't making things any better, so I shut up and stopped trying, but I'd had a brilliant weekend, regardless, and thanked them too much.

Now Truffle, what on earth had happened?

Basically Truffle had taken offence, at the disparaging looks of disgust she was receiving from one person, she had approached CT and asked, "What's the problem?".

Apparently CT had sneered her answer, "You know!".

Truffle had shaken her tipsy head, "Um … no idea? What are you talking about?". Then she lost all sober reasoning, wish I'd seen this, when Truffle grabbed a handful of thin hair and yanked. Nice one!

It was stopped and Truffle groaned, "I am so sorry and I started it!", but they know she's not a trouble maker and CT was thrown out onto the street.

The Xmas party at my local bingo hall fell on my birthday, how good is that? Yoyo came with me and my mum, it was brilliant, the girls with the new manager had excelled themselves and bubbly alcohol was being passed round. I insisted that we all wore our hats, it was the celebratory day of my birth so I could be bossy, then we pulled the crackers. Yoyo found the bar and won, so he had a good day, at this point he is funny but it gradually winds down.

There was live entertainment, the man was singing and he told a few jokes that were good … but because they were risqué of content.

But it was a joke.

Go to the bakers: Ginger People and the sweetshop: Rainbow Mice.
What's that all about?
It makes no difference to our existence!
Why are you wasting time, money, ink and paper, even talking about it? Who's bothered?

Anyway Yoyo was gone, he thinks it was his decision.
One evening he interrupted an ongoing bingo session, then crashed to sit with me and mum, no idea who let him in, he was being really giggly and loud so was drawing attention to us.
Sh!
Sh!
Sh! Mum was not laughing.

He got bored and went back to where he had started, away from us thank goodness, mum was on the verge of stabbing him in the eye with her bingo dabber and making a red mess.

So Xmas ambles onto the calendar and I have forgotten to tell you about another trip, made earlier in the year, to Amsterdam but this time it was with Posh Boy. My publisher might move this to just before Ibiza, that's just reminded me A.Man is on holiday again.

Posh Boy came up here to meet with me, then we went to Manchester airport together, it was an adventure and everything was go.
It was brilliant and so funny, you had to be there, we stumbled around lost, stoned and giggling all the hours that we were there.

Finding things by mistake all the time, I did spot a sign for the police something or other and said we should seek their assistance after coffee.

Never saw the sign again, we must have turned off somewhere or somebody took the sign down to confuse us a bit more? Funny. We always managed to find the hotel too.

A taxi took us back to the airport, that was a good move the onus was on the driver to get us there now, we even navigated the huge airport and had a final coffee. I hope he enjoyed this expedition as much as I did. We took a lot of photographs of interesting windows, an artistic notion had taken my little fancy. I had wild visions of window, eye and soul amalgamating on the same page.

Somehow, I did chop a few of the photos up and tried to put them in some type of order, but I think less random shots may be better next time.

His family moved and he's been kept busy since.

The firework display had escaped Yoyo and I was happy to stand with the local firemen, leaning on their big engine, having reminded myself that I cannot stand still on uneven ground and look up into the sky. I looked really drunk, overbalancing and stumbling all the time, families were pulling children away from me.

So Xmas.

Just me and mum, much easier, she would come to me on Xmas day. So Truffle and I hit the pink town on Xmas Eve, as you do, then drank too much … as we do.

I bounced about quite happy on Xmas morning and was surprised I didn't feel totally crap. I really should feel quite bad, considering.

But it is now, with hindsight, I know, I was still drunk from the night before.

Mum came and all was going well, until about four o'clock when my dehydrated brain caught up, then I was really ill with the DELAYED HANGOVER. My pounding and crystallised head would not let me keep my, bloodshot and aching, eyes open for too long. So I was lying still and suffering, on the sofa, the television was on but I wasn't watching it.

Mum woke me up, "Gillian … Gillian … GILLIAN!"
I moved my head slightly and opened one eye, she had her arms folded and she announced, "You're boring … I'm going home".

I whimpered, "Ah don't go … don't leave me!".

She pushed her boobs up and responded, "I can sit on my own at home!".
"I'll be alright in a minute", I groaned, well I hoped so anyway! But I was and we'll do something different next year.

CHAPTER X

The Year of Completion 2008

C aught up with myself!

I'm going to be organised and keep a diary, to complete the trilogy, well that's an idea eh?

I remember this sentiment from childhood. The new Xmas diary is religiously and neatly written for a few days, then you go back to school. The odd date is mentioned from thereon.

When I went to Paris, I was about ten, notes were written and the months in Israel were too briefly documented. What a good thing, they're funny reading now, I wish that I'd thought about this and done it for every trip I ever made. But I didn't know that I'd be so buggered at aged twenty seven and would end up writing a book (or two).

Over a quarter of my life has been disadvantaged so far … I'm getting used to it now.

But as I'm getting older, it's downhill again as it were, I am addicted to cake.

Truffle brought me a home-made Victoria sandwich last night, which she made, a whole cake for me … how lucky am I?

There are some big, curvy and voluptuous, rears around here and on display. I had joked to Music Man, "They beep when they are walking backwards!", then the idea for Porkies jeans was born.

The designer denims would display WIDE LOAD, in neon colours, on the backside and then they would have a beeping sensor for reverse movements.

Good eh?

"What ya wearin tonight?".

"Me new Porkies!". If you've got it flaunt it

(I blame Music Man entirely and Truffle (they are having a thing), for encouraging this habit. I'm going to start beeping ... then I will have to buy myself some Porkies!)

Truffle doesn't think we'd have met if I hadn't written Gillian Mk 2, she's probably right, there have been a lot of things that wouldn't have happened. I would probably have never seen Elvis again and I really wanted to see my old sixth form registration teacher, they both wrote the most encouraging and praising letters after reading Gillian Mk 2. BB told me, "Write another book", what a commendation and apparently ... even better, "Your readers need to know what happens next."

Well, all on my own, I am making a bit of a mess and starting to realise that I have a different agenda to most. But being me, I am still finding people that make me smile and are worthy of my time.

Yoyo is not one of them and he came to the flat for a chat, I let him in because I'm always ready for coffee, he sat down and smiled then asked me, "Do you still want another cockatiel?".

Strange question, I thought about it then answered him, "I did ... but nah, not anymore".

"Oh …", he shook his head, "I'll take it back then". I followed his gaze to a small and covered item on the floor, under the sheet was a baby bird! "Ah … ", that was it.

The old cage was rescued and cleaned, blimey getting her into it was a joke, she was only a few weeks old and so not trained, I had no idea what to do.

Pippa was tufted with growing adult feathers and softened with baby fluff, Yoyo made her his reason to "pop by", my mum had asked, "Why did he buy you a bird?".

When she was flapping about in the front room, I was beside myself, Pippa kept flying into my collection of bottles!

If one was knocked over and I tried to catch it, inevitably I would misjudge and punch it into other GLASS things! Mum was with me as we followed her around the room, from speaker to picture to curtain rail and back again, trying to get her back into the cage. Eventually throwing a T-towel over my baby bird, which did not make me or her happy. But, needs must.

This is when I noticed my breath was bad, Bro had scrunched his nose to comment, "Yeah it's rank".

I recognised the taste and it smelt like garlic, Yoyo ate garlic paste in an attempt to disguise the odour, second hand pungent bulb breath is quite sickening.

My dentist prescribed antibiotics for the gum infection and warned me, "Do not drink alcohol with these, it will make you very ill". The pharmacist had shaken her head and advised, "You don't want to be drinking with these!".

I had been invited to a party that weekend, at Nomad's, blimey wouldn't you just know it?

Now there was a dilemma—should I start the drugs before? or after? Easy decision, my breath is like rotting flesh and I don't want my teeth to fall out of my head yet, so I chose and didn't drink at the gathering.

I smoked a lot instead, there was an interesting bunch of people there, I watched the party in full swing, the dancing chap turned the music up.

Which may not have been a problem until the big lad, in his excitement, started jumping up and down on the same spot! Which was the ceiling of the flat downstairs.

Of course the signal, of banging, wasn't heard … so the police were called. Nomad, the host, dealt with it.

This was funny. I was returning from the bathroom and knew the police were talking at the door, "Turn the music down, the police are here", I directed. When this was repeated the smashed and bearded chap, J, pushed himself upright behind me.

"Gill, Gill … Gill … shurrup now … you're being boring".

That told me, I laughed then sat down, Nomad was busy handing out roast potatoes.

Teeny gave me the best Xmas present, a calendar that has Gillian written differently in a scene each month. Gillian is written with shells, flowers, as clouds in a blue sky … I will keep it forever!

She used to collect frogs and I remember her saying, "Don't buy me anymore frogs!", Oops. It was her birthday recently and I bought her a frog.

But it's a copper frog as a wind chime and as soon as I saw it Teeny came to mind, the amphibian has got googly glass eyes, I hope she likes it when she gets it. It's still in the front room.

Years ago I had quite long hair, with an idea for a different haircut. I wanted a ^ cutting from the middle of my neck, at the back of my head, to produce drastic and severe shards of length past my ears.
Me going into great detail must have flummoxed the first hairdresser, she snipped away happily, but just cut my hair.
The second hairdresser was "not really surprised", of course, but when I told her what I wanted she told me to sit still whilst she, "got the stylist". I stopped her, "You said you could do it, that you'd done this before?". She laughed and answered, "Once", then, "Yes, it was you". "Just cut it", I said with a laugh but was serious, "It will grow back", I was fed up of hairdressers that can't actually cut hair.
The fourth attempt at this impossible style was the nearest, each time I vowed that when my hair grew back this style would be accomplished!

The next time I did a drawing, of what I wanted, as usual the hairdresser did what she wanted.
I think a scream of irritation may have ensued, as I pointed out, "THIS is not right, it's not what I wanted!". She huffed and told me, "You should have described it better".

I had snatched up the paper and held it aloft, then pointed out sweetly with pursed lips, "I drew it for you!".
I paid half the money, although she was sulking and had said, "I don't want any".

My hair grew and I was ready, so went to see her, this woman stood up to tell me, "I don't want to cut your hair anymore". Then I was barred. Not good for my street credibility, being thrown out of a silly little salon. But that Posh Beckham woman had her hair cut, similar to my idea, now everybody has a variation of this style!
Even CT! How nauseating.

It's raining.
(I have just found and bought a copy of Spinal Tap (page 110) told Truffle).

I applied to be on Countdown, how exciting … will this be my owed eleven minutes? The last appearance, was timed, had been four. (fifteen minutes of fame)
Mum took me and she sat outside to wait. I went into another room, to play the game with the other applicants.

This chap kept getting seven and eight letter words, when the rest of us were getting six. With the numbers we were given … the woman just asked what we got, therefore how near we were to the target. I bent the truth a little here, I didn't want to be the only person who was miles off the answer.
I gave them a copy of Gillian Mk 2, but a letter told me I hadn't been successful and I heard nothing else, how disappointing.
I am going to apply again, for a day out.

Truffle and I were out and it was Saturday night, we were stopped by the new doorman and refused entry, "You can't go into the pub, because we'd had too much to drink". Imbecile, we were shocked into futile explanations. But should have said, open your eyes! Stop those that sound and look as though they've had a skin full, spot the trouble makers that will probably be spoken to by the police later.

A member of staff that knew us intervened, telling him, "You're mistaken … they're ok, let them in". Then we were given a drink, as an apology.

I decided that I wanted to have a party in the flat … and why not? Music Man was excited too and offered to be an accomplice, so we corroborated, on decoration, with food and drink.
My suggestion for a theme party was rejected, but my idea for a party punch needed exploration.

Armed with big bottles of cheap and colourful alcoholic pop, a bottle of vodka, some wine, mixers and other stuff we were ready to do some research.
"Let's try it with red stuff first", so a crimson cocktail was the first of many, "Do the green one next". A rainbow of mixtures later and a winner was selected, the pink mix was the killer invention, we called it 'Hindsight'.

Music Man had to literally carry me to bed, a fruitful evening, but I was not at all well the next day.
I had an evil hangover … ironically that I wouldn't have had without 'Hindsight'.
The next punch would be made with the green alcoholic pop, we already had a name, it would be called 'Slime'. As in you've been slimed

Music Man provided the disco lights and the front room was rearranged, nibbles were made available and the Hindsight creation was labelled with a warning. My immediate neighbours were informed and cordially invited.

It was better than I'd hoped it would be, Music Man flittered around as did Nomad making sure everybody was alright. Nomad had arrived, though he had warned me, "I might not be able to make it, plans and people …". But I was happy to let them be and just got caned, but I wasn't as bad as Bro … who was a giggling wreck on the sofa.

At one o'clock in the morning I turned everything off and we all went into town, Bro couldn't walk very well so we left him with the lights.

It was a good party, not wild and raucous but fun, people chatted and danced (well I did). We smoked and drank then finished the bowl of Hindsight. I did notice that one guest stayed next to this bowl all night, he was extremely happy.

The bedroom has curtains again and they're clean, my mum took the cream drapes and de tarred them, but the pole has come off the new wall so I can't close them now. I saw the builder on Saturday night and told him, "My curtain pole is coming off the wall". I'll have to remind him that my curtains are just hanging … barely!

Nomad came for the weekend, he seems to be around a lot at the moment, because he's a bit of a clever arse I like him, but I was more than pleased that he was going to complete the job that Bro started.

When I got my new shell of a flat it had to be furnished, with no money, because my finances were rubbish the furniture was donated and any extras were cheap. Like my shelves, in the alcoves, that were carrying my bottles on one side and books etc on the other.

The pretend wood did it's job for a long time … but eventually it buckled under the pressure. The shelf supporting the most weight, some of my photograph albums and scrapbooks, collapsed and threw all the said items on the floor. Brilliant, I had to pile them all under the table, I can't find anything anyway so why make my life easy?

Bro had got me some REAL wood and there were eight shelves that came from the same tree, they were cut so the edge you can see is the bark, when stained they looked even better. Shame they're covered with books really, but they are still super.

Nomad had previously taken the remaining four shelves and stained the wood, this weekend he had brought them back, he stood in the car park for hours sawing the timber to the right length.

I had to clean all the ornaments off the original shelves including the bottles, please imagine: Approximately seventy breakable bottles, of varying size, in shelf order, everywhere in the front room and on every surface amongst all my other shit in the kitchen.
Then remember that I am paranoid, about the seventy strong hoard of coloured glass items, and I am clumsy. On a good day.

But it was a good opportunity to thin them out, the collection was becoming vague and too varied, those that had cork stoppers rather than glass were ousted, Nomad took all the rejects.
Less is more they say and they did looked better. Some had been bought for me, I remembered these people with a smile, but they had to go.
I knew it would be worth the effort, hours of, this task took the whole weekend to complete.

It was, we were both happy and the shelves looked brilliant, they were complimentary to the other alcove and all the glass was clean.

Nomad had taken Pippa, with all the trappings, telling me his reasoning, "This will get rid of Yoyo, he will have no excuse to pop in". He was most certainly cross with me and did not approve, "Gillian what ya doin? You can't help him and he's got big fat issues! You know that …".
I did and he convinced me, Pippa was taken, on the understanding that she was coming back … fully house trained.

Yoyo was disappointed with me now, in a no win situation, but I didn't care and I knew Pippa was alright.

I have just seen the most amazing thing, after I firstly tried to spray the blue bottle fly and missed … good job the cake was covered. I then attempted to hit it with the T-towel, a few times and missed, well I knocked the annoyed fly onto the floor. Where it was caught in an unseen strand of spider's web, under the cupboard door, the job was there to be finished.
But I left it and watched. There was an inhabitant!
It was smaller than a money spider and the fly was huge, like an American portion to a starving beggar, it ran to the buzzing insect and wrestled a little then went back under the ledge. It looked like it was daunted by the prospect, but kept trying in excited greed, I was not there for that long before I noticed that the fly was moving upwards. When back in the kitchen a bit later I saw that the fly had gone, so down on my hands and knees I looked under the ledge, the tiny spider had dragged the protesting fly up into it's den, it was there wrapped in silk waiting for dinner.

In my bedroom the big wooden unit that came from a friend's garage, was really imposing and one of my favourite things … it was acting as a wardrobe. Mum was with me and I needed to get the box down from the top of this unit, the big strip of wood that fell off missed us and was met with a groan, the big side panel falling off and hitting the wall made us jump.

"You need a proper wardrobe, this is falling to bits", mum moved the chunk of wood, but I leaned the wood panel back against the unit and denied this, "Bro might be able to fix it?".

It was only a bit broken, but I still liked it.

Mum pointed at my hanging clothes, "They look rubbish too!", my dad had made me the rather large metal hanging rail, there were a lot of clothes all open to the elements but hidden behind a cane screen.

I say hidden … I mean masked off and difficult to get to.

I was opening the drinks cabinet section and the whole door came off, in my hand, now it was starting to look really shabby, holding the evidence of collapse there was no denial anymore.

Music Man came to my assistance with his chargeable drill, he started to dismantle the big piece of furniture, a handy friend indeed.

Bro finished the task with a friend and they took it away, he knew somebody who would be able to use it. It was a good time to cull the wardrobe, I was amazed at how much stuff was taken to the charity shop, I haven't missed any of it … quickly forgotten. Then the search for new bedroom furniture started.

It was decided that this would be an ideal opportunity, to decorate and spruce up the bedroom, we loaded the car with paint and relevant extras, so mum and I got ready to tackle the big space.

Beginning on the wall that would be behind a new wardrobe, how exciting we were going from peach to trendy off-magnolia. The woodchip wall paper, that had been stuck on this surface, was coming off the wall and wrapping itself around the roller?

The wall was damp, the back of the wallpaper was black, we had used half a tin of paint already then had to stop. The housing association would have to be called, to inspect this, because it was more than one wall and it was definitely not healthy.

In the meantime the new flat-pack wardrobe was damaged in transit, Bro had travelled specifically to erect the furniture, we were told to "mark and label the damage" ... for replacement purposes.

It was piled in order ready for collection, now I am bored with this, I'm fed up of sleeping on the sofa and have forgotten what all the boxes and bags contain. So I have no idea, at all, where my clean underwear or T-shirts are and I keep losing my purse.

The builder came with the maintenance chap, they agreed a plan of work, three of my walls needed covering and it was quite a big job.

Mum and I had been instructed to strip the room of wood chip paper in preparation. I did as high as I could reach and made coffee, mum balanced on the ladder and did the rest ... she just did it and is brilliant.

It looked awful, cold and damp, it was very messy and dirty.

The wardrobe arrived!

They took all the bits of the first wardrobe, every nut and screw, then told me that the whole package would be binned, blimey, so we did all that sorting for nothing.

Bro came and built the shell, I was his assistant, he had asked me, "Hold the (big and heavy) side panel upright, whilst I attach this!. I'm really helpful, "Hold it still". Bro barked the instruction. "I am", or I thought I was.

"Gillian stop leaning!", he shook his head at me, "I'm not!", I laughed because I was trying to hold it still and straight.

Bro sighed, "Focus on something … and concentrate! Stop laughing you nightmare", that method didn't work either and though it was funny I was being an unwitting hindrance.

He didn't put the mirrored doors on so it would be easier to move, when the builders came to make my bedroom smaller. A waterproof membrane was first on the old bricks, then blocks of wood that held the new plaster-board wall in place, anyway my bedroom was now lesser.

Odd, without the big old furniture and minus the hanging rail, the room looked bigger.

The builders answered my incessant questions and managed to get round everything, they used my dustpan and brush to sweep up plaster so I had to buy a new one, but they agreed to decorate the room for me. They like me … I do constant coffee in clean cups. One of them was telling me they had only ever refused once, because the house was disgusting, they had declined but nominated their colleague. But he wasn't bothered and drank it. I was happy too, with half a wardrobe and plastered walls, it was starting to be right at last.

When it had been decorated Yoyo called by to see the bedroom, I let him in to see it because it was starting to look good and I was chuffed, he saw the mirrored wardrobe doors leaning against the wall and asked, "Have you got a screwdriver?".

I had looked at him to question, "Can you do them?". He had snorted and shook his head, "Of course!", I was only asking.

Music Man's drill was still here so I let him mess with the doors, they didn't shut right but my wardrobe was now complete, I can see myself (if I turn sideways … the bedrooms not that big) sitting being a Darlink. How good is that? Eh?

Music Man asked, "Who did this?", when he looked. Then sighed and shrugged shaking his head, when I told him, getting his drill (that was still there) he twiddled until the doors shut in a whisper.

So, nearly there, the matching drawers were next and I wondered which of them would help me this time.

Now I'd gone and got myself roped up with something else, feeling slightly obligated, this time I had volunteered to join the Editorial team at the housing association. Blimey more sandwiches!

The newsletter that comes to us is actually quite good already, they don't really need us, they did a feature on me once and used a photo taken for something else.

It was an awful photograph. If I'd known it was going to be large and on the front cover! I would not have worn that shirt, which I never wore again, I tried to give to Yoyo before it went to the charity shop. Then I would have put loads of make-up on, loads, well at least I would have bothered to comb my hair.

I show people other things.

In a phone call I was invited to speak on Radio York, as part of the Brain Injury Awareness week, my friend from rehab days was going to be there too. I hadn't seen him for a long time and was looking forward to saying hi again.

On the train, to the appointment, I had my writing implements with me and was taking notes for this.

I was reading something I'd written and laughed out loud, then looked up and smiled at the bemused young chap. When I laughed again he had a quizzical look on his face.

So I told him what I was doing, then ended up reading the piece to a sniggering audience.

He grinned at me, "I like it, where are you going?". He smiled and asked, "Do you know it is?"

Then he told me he was going the same way and so he'd show me where to go.

As I linked his arm to walk, he was telling that he would look at a site, he was lovely and he stopped when we were standing outside the radio station.

Ah … the gallant young man had taken me all the way to the door.

In the waiting area was my smiling friend, we had been given coffee and sat chatting, we get on well in short doses.

The disc jockey came and took us both to the recording studio. It was really funny as we knew each other and the banter was natural.

He didn't talk as much as me, quelle surprise, but the disc jockey had asked him questions so he did say something.

I had told the DJ, "Tell the listeners that I looked good", divulging my obvious error "I have made a big effort and this isn't television".

The book was mentioned and the interview was to be aired the next day, when the recording was over my friend and I wandered around York for a while.

Yoyo was there when I was tuning the radio in … to the wrong station!

Yoyo found the programme when he recognised my voice, we heard the end of the interview but it was the best bit. The DJ announced that I had told him to point out my appearance, then added, "She did look good though … and I approve". I was able to listen later on tintonet, my voice is noticeable, even when it had been edited I did most of the talking.

Bro text me, 'You could have let him get a word in!'

I can't help it, if I was more interesting … and spoke a lot, there are things that need to be said.

I'd love to do that again.

There is often a pile of dirty dishes by the sink, they will get done when all my cups have been used, my mum visits to scowl at me and accuse me of laziness then she washes them. Method in madness? No, I am saving water … 'if it's yellow let it mellow if it's brown flush it down'. The toilet isn't emptied until it has to be, Truffle grimaced with a look of disgust as she told me, "I couldn't do it!".

I still don't bathe everyday, I would if my being was crispy or smelly, nor is the bath filled. I put in enough water to do bathroom things … then simply do what I has to be done and get out.

The Wee Lassie bought me a desk top calendar, brilliant idea bet she's got one, which reminded me that I was due at the library for a book signing appointment.

I wore a pale grey trouser suit and did mascara, Darlink, then was armed with a few books and a clip board done for me by Yoyo. He had helped me to get everything to the library and was still there when the photographer from the paper came.

It wasn't until I took the jacket off that I noticed it was covered with stains, it had been hanging in my den for a long time, then I looked down and the trousers were the same. Mum turned up and shook her head and sucked in air, the kind of where did I go wrong breath, "You look filthy!".

There is a charity shop next door and mum found a complete replacement outfit, a dark grey trouser suit with a black top and a black bra, all my size too. I tried them all and kept the clothes on to pay the bill.

The staff in the library did a retake, on me, when I went back in the new attire. It was an awfully disappointing day, when I had the dirty kit on one lady spoke to me, nobody else wanted to talk to me about anything.

Dingle asked me to do a book signing in the charity shop, I got this date in the paper, she found a space and set up the table for me, Yoyo had his advertising board outside again.

What a brilliant day, lots of people walked by me and a few stopped to talk, Gillian Mk 2 encouraged lively chatter and again it amazed me how many people were affected by some sort of disability.

What surprised me was that so many knew somebody, who had suffered a TBI, a lot of them took the book for that reason.

One lady comes to chat with Dingle regularly, she is lovely and talks a lot, when I am there she enthuses about Gillian Mk 2 but insisted on calling me, " Alison". Which she changed to, "Fergie, because you sound posh".

She's got it now, but I will answer to any of the above 'cos I like her.

I'm very untidy and disastrously disorganised (dissing again), I hope that A.Man … who I cannot get hold of and who doesn't bother returning my calls … sorts this jumble of words out. I wonder how much of this he will edit and cut …

Let's try this, my favourite joke at the moment.

Young man joins the army and is telling his mate about his first parachute jump.

Yeah yeah we climbed to thirty thousand feet and they all started jumping, one by one, then he got to 1 me and I said *** that. My captain got his *** out of his trousers and said if you don't jump now you **** **** I'm gonna shove this right up your ****.

Mate gasps, did you jump?

Mm … just a little bit … when it first went in.

A.Man may make publisher power notes in my text, that would be quite cool, rise to the challenge Sir.

Anyway, that's all coming I hope.

Back to real life.

The theatre was showing something I wanted to see, Truffle and Nomad were told and maybe they would come, my friends wanted to see the act too and Nomad asked me to get an extra ticket for his visiting ally Clotted Cream.

Truffle and I were going to a wedding reception before the theatre, the married couple already had photographs developed that had been taken an hour earlier. Their alternative wedding made fabulous pictures … she looked slinky in black and he was her dashing escort. But I had to leave to meet Nomad and Clotted Cream.

I stood by the theatre to wait for them, he walked towards me and it was the first time I'd met his married friend Clotted Cream. Both of them plucked strings and the show tonight was a musical performance, I had thought they would be staying over but they didn't, it wasn't as good as the write up claimed and I was entertained but disappointed. Nomad and Clotted Cream stayed for one drink afterwards and we bumped into Yoyo, how embarrassing, the man was not sober and made himself look like a fool. He was moaning about shoes or something …

Truffle and I carried on, in a happy vein, we'd had a good day.

The drawers were on order and due in a few weeks, I had to have them, the wardrobe is smaller and has less space to hide things … extra storage is a must.

Nomad had told me about a music festival he was involved with, Springboard in Hull, it sound like fun and he was very enthusiastic. He went on, "Loads of people would be playing live music and Clotted Cream will be one of them".

Truffle was invited too and she drove, Nomad gave us the details of the hotel he'd booked for us … because, "My flat is already full of bodies". I was acting as co driver and holding the map.

We are a pretty good team and had already experimented with this liaison, on a trip to Whitby, to see my brother and his family. So it was a good start, I had been here before, my brother was on his mobile when I had a blip and didn't recognise anything. I was in fear of getting us lost, on the moors.

It was a good weekend but Truffle wouldn't drive to go and see Posh Boy … "He's your friend and anyway I want to get home". But I still thought we should go and see him, then she threw her toys out of the pram, but she held the car keys, touche pussycat.

We had directions to meet up with Nomad, this is where neither of us really know where we are. but the man was standing in the street and waving. We went to his flat for coffee, I was pleased to see him but I wanted to look at Pippa.

She was not in her cage, which had been mutilated, she was perched in the front room and as free as herself. Nomad demonstrated his control with a stick, Pippa didn't stay on it long but took seed from his hand, she looked alright but the cage looked stupid.

Nomad was curt with me, this attitude was uncalled for, when he was explaining how I should hold the stick!

Then he started to point out my flaws, "You don't listen and you're not doing it right …". I know! Should have told him to belt up and suck his ego in, but I didn't take any notice … that skill apparently was one of my failings.

Clotted Cream was there, grinning in admiration for his school chum, but he didn't really say much.

We had followed Nomad to the hotel, that provided breakfast, where Truffle and I collected keys then dumped the car to go PARTAY!.

Nomad opened the proceedings, an energetic and eager interpretation of notes strung together on a ukulele, he wasn't brilliant and I think it might have been a clever ploy by the organisers. Everybody after him looked and sounded better, actually some of the acts were really good and we saw Clotted Cream also brandishing a ukulele.

He sang a song that I knew, Dream a Little Dream by the Beautiful South, but he changed the words and was looking at me when he crooned, "soft, furry and bouncy little dreams".

In another song he had stopped playing and I clapped alone, it was a musical break? He stopped again, I applauded on my own again. I was starting to look silly now.
When he stopped for the third time?
He looked at me and grinned, over his blue tinted glasses, "You can clap now".

Looking back the weekend was getting strange, but I didn't think about it at the time, Nomad seemed to be really uptight with me and it was just weird and irritating.
Nothing really clicked in the moment, it would have been pointless saying anything anyway, Nomad was as high as a satellite dish and was taking the impromptu comparing very seriously. The confident exhibitionist was having a marvellous time.
I was talking to Clotted Cream a lot and went to see him play at another bar, Truffle and I came in late then walked in front of the stage area, he saw me and made a mistake then quickly looked at his hands. But I heard it, how flattering!

Later I was sat with Clotted Cream, on a big leather sofa, we just giggled too much, it felt like nobody else was there, eventually we moved but then he kept finding me and monopolised my time.

Truffle and I were eating fish and chips, sitting outside near some greenery on a bench, when Clotted Cream sought us out. He smiled at me then sat between us, we both offered him some food but I knew he would turn to me. He ate my chips!

Then I linked his arm, as we wandered around, he was easy to talk to and I liked him, we seemed to be alone a lot.

Truffle had seen a necklace she liked, but the shop was closed. Then the day was over and we all dispersed.

Truffle and I had no problems sharing the room and were ready for breakfast the next morning, I was looking forward to bacon and eggs, but everything was covered in cellophane or in sachets and boxes.

Time to carry on, but we weren't booked into the hotel for tonight, the car was taken to and parked near one of the main venues. Suddenly it was boiling!

It had been positively cold when we'd set off and I had two coats with me (day and evening), now it was scorchio and I was just too hot.

Next to this pub was a Peacocks store and it was open so I bought a T-shirt, then rolled my cotton trousers up to my knees. It looked alright too ... saved.

We found out that there had been a gathering at Nomad's last night, I was a bit peeved that Truffle and I weren't invited, but hey.

I was pleased to see J again, I recognised him too though I had only met him once before. That was a good bit and he hugged me.

What happened next wasn't so pleasant.

I was behind the cubicle door and Truffle was messing with lipstick, I overheard Long Hair, "You and your friend can come and stay at my place tonight".

Truffle replied, "Thanks ... I'll tell her".

I wanted to stay and persuaded Truffle, "Go on ... it'll be a good thing!.".

Then we went to find Long Hair, to accept her idea with thanks.

Nomad stepped into the foray with a grin and looked at me, he told Long Hair, "Take no notice of her! She's just creeping for somewhere to stay. She'll just go on, until it's a done thing".

I shook my head in awe to explain his blundering mistake, but he was adamant with his insults, I was surprised by this outburst and alarmed by the childish ferocity.

Long Hair erupted and crossly corrected him, "I invited her to stay with me!", but she carried on. She petulantly called him a few choice names, she was pouting, beautifully.

Truffle and I were silenced, this was getting interesting.

We watched with wide eyes as she flounced her hair and told us, "I've seen Nomad in a new light, I want nothing more to do with him!". Blimey, that was good.

Nomad was with the sound enhancer again, being a one man show host, it was when his Man Skirt fell off (oops?) to reveal he wasn't wearing any pants. I groaned. Exhibitionist.

But it worked for Long Hair and later, when they were sat on the bench, I couldn't resist and smiled at Truffle before I stumbled over to them. They were all made up and giggly again, but went quiet as I approached. "I am not happy with you, your earlier tirade was out of order and it was nothing to do with you!", he made excuses for his behaviour and blamed his manic involvement with the music festival. He just went on and on, with the sound of his voice, all he needed was the microphone, but I wasn't listening anymore. I thanked Long Hair again, before I went to tell Truffle that they were alright now.

Clotted Cream was near or with me the whole day, we linked arms again to go around the village and explore, Truffle was busy entertaining a chap with Lycra cycling shorts on.

I found myself looking for the goofy man, then grinned when he was standing next to me.

Long Hair had a few people round and some of us were stopping over, Truffle noticed this I didn't, we were the only women in this group. Strange enough but then she got her collection of drums out, some where quite big, for all her guests to play. I asked about her neighbours, but they were very understanding and she does this all the time. So they're as mad as her then.

Actually it was a good evening and I was chatting to an interesting guy. in the kitchen, Long Hair clutched the biggest drum between her legs and everybody was happy.

The toilet was upstairs and I was concerned that Truffle had been gone for too long, one of the men laughed and told me not to worry, if anything had happened somebody would have seen. True ... so I had another drink. I checked on her when I needed to go upstairs, she had sparked out in the allocated bedroom.

The next day she had explained: "I sat down to think about what I should do next, then I laid down to way up the options".

I went back downstairs, being afraid to miss anything, but by now only a small group remained and some were still banging drums. Mm. When I knocked an ornament off the shelf, then couldn't keep my eyes open, I gave up and joined Truffle.

In the morning we traipsed downstairs with the bags and got a coffee, I sat next to Clotted Cream on the sofa he was fully dressed but still under the duvet. We talked about nothing and smiled a lot, it was sunny again, when we topped up with coffee everybody ended up outside. Long Hair was up and stood by the kettle to announce herself, as being there, she was wearing the Man Skirt and Nomad followed shortly with trousers on.

Truffle noticed too, she raised her eyebrows and grinned at me.

We went back to the car but had a last coffee, at the pub, with Clotted Cream and Nomad. They had to go to the train station, Nomad seemed a little sheepish as he hugged me goodbye and I turned to hug Clotted Cream too.

He wrapped me tightly in his arms and bent to breath in at my neck, Chanel No 5 doncha know, but then he pulled me closer and held me a bit too tight for a bit too long. It was nice but I pulled away and laughed, that was a little awkward. He looked down into my eyes and he was still holding me.

He walked away but turned back to look at me, as he disappeared.

Then the strange thing happened: roughly from thereon in I couldn't stop talking about the man.

He was just on my mind and I was vocalising my thoughts, about dreamy songs with chips on benches.

Eventually Truffle threatened to crash the car, if I didn't shut up.

A few hours later, I'd been home a while now, Clotted Cream called me from Exeter, "I haven't spoken to my wife yet … I had to call you, I've been thinking about you the whole journey. I couldn't stop thinking about you. You have filled my head".

Blimey, I felt like a teenager.

Then he was calling me so much, that when the phone rang … I was disappointed if it wasn't him. In a collision the whirlwind of emotion was idyllic, in theory. He left his wife, this had nothing to do with me, so was at his parents. I had no idea what was going on, but the phone conversations became intense, I felt like an adolescent stuck in the pages of a romantic novel.

Truffle went back for that necklace and we went to another music festival, well we would have done, but we parked the car and couldn't find anything. We stopped at the pub for coffee and Clotted Cream called me. The calls and text messages were more than daily now.

When I had seen him playing, at the first festival, he did a stint with a battery operated fan. This item arrived in my post, why? The text message explained: Keep it—use it to cool you down when you think of me.
Well, I was floating with the unexpected silliness.

The four hour stint on the phone, he had to keep calling me back so we had coffee and toilet breaks, this was evidence of besotted teenage behaviour.

The chats about hot sand between your toes, feeling the hot sun on exposed flesh, was adult behaviour. He spoke with imaginative prose and I wanted him to groan at my neck, he told me, "I love you and I have to see you again".
Oh my God!
I fell for it completely, with no doubt in my simple mind, Music Man and Truffle were amused with my ability to just sit and grin with thought.

He was reading Gillian Mk 2 and had seen the websites, when I answered and told him that my fingers were on fire with the heated typing, he told me to decelerate he was a slow reader.

He sent an alarming message about A.Man, he'd try to call the publishing house and only got the answer phone, he joked that maybe the man was on holiday. Which was, in fact, probably the case.

Music Man advised, "Just go for it girl … eh … this doesn't happen often". Truffle too was smiling for me, but I would have understood if she'd whispered, "Bitch!", under her breath. I felt smug and shuddered like a cocooned butterfly … I trembled with readiness to erupt and explore this further.

I saved the texts because they were good, stupido, in reality I was wobbling at the top of a gilded staircase. With stupid and impractical shoes on. I had just gone into the shop to see the much neglected friend, Mr Arty Farty, but the visit was postponed as I went back outside to answer my phone. It was Clotted Cream! So he was monopolising my mobile too, but it made me happy.

He arranged to visit and a poem arrived in the post.

Gillian,
Everything has changed—Everything
The same air moves with a new consistency
I breath it deeply and it tastes sweeter
The whole world is now a different colour
The earth has shifted on its axis but
Few have noticed
I sense it keenly

It has sent a wave crashing towards me
I exist for the moment of diving in
As it envelopes me
I feel the stirring as it rumbles on towards me
And I will it on impatiently
I will swim through the miles of ocean and come to you
I will not tire
I will come to you as freely and openly as you beckon me
And I will not blink as I smile into your eyes
And embrace you
And draw you into me
And breath the same new air as you.

8 days … Clotted Cream xxx

The messages on my phone were messing with me, he was speaking to me on his work's line too, he wouldn't get out of my space but I didn't want him to.
"I wish I was there 2—music sunshine & your smile—unbeatable … spent all pm gardening hated it couldn't get you out of my head u & your black lacy soft (clean) knickers 0898 eat your heart out! … hope your day was better than mine private uke performance on your phone only, for your ears only tomorrow, 1.30pm (I'll ring you) take care, hugs, Clotted CreamXXX … my head is spinning, my heart is pounding, I feel high. I'm in a mess over you & in a mess without you XXX … I'll do a lullaby—live performance for U only—soon …".

Well? I ask you. Would you have ignored this unadulterated flattery, these hot and heavy strokes to your needy little ego? No, if you could go with the flow … go on you would have fallen too.

Well I did … then went into manic overdrive with cleaning materials, I found them under my sink. Mainly to stop myself from thinking too much, but I wanted the flat to look pretty damned good too.

Music Man shook his head, "He's a lucky man", then laughed at me when I saw bits on the carpet and went for my dust buster to remove them. "What you like? Sounds like he's in the same state as you!", he'd read the messages, above is a selection of, I didn't save them all.

He didn't tell Nomad, I was now part of this conspiracy but not by choice, it was nothing to do with me, I did not advise him to leave his wife or lie to his buddy.

June 2008 I was inspired to write poetry myself and speared into thought by his words:

AN ENIGMA
She's leaning casually, waiting calmly.
I hope it's her.
A vision of cream, a bubble of laughter
Expressive eyes of changeability
Cool greys flashing blue with greens
The woman.
My head is spinning, my heart is pounding
She incites a swell of emotion
I am weakened with surprise

The sparks fly at a chance meet
More time to explore this exotic planet
The loud social mix is not distraction enough
A butterfly perches in admiration: she waits
The music, her smile, the stolen images disturbing in secret

Time is over, in a blur of pictures.
But she remains. Draped in black lace.
She burns my waking thoughts
—like an ache of desperate hunger.

He gushed appropriately but I reread the poem, it's an ego trip for me
through his mouth, so I wrote another.

CLOTTED CREAM (the title has been amended)
It's you.
Sorry, I've forgotten your name.
I know who he is, a nice chap.
In our gang of fun
The music starts, people are alive with sound
Moving and swaying
Faces smile but I scan for him
The tall blond with blue eyes: he's funny

Hogging the sofa, the crowd is distant
Like silly children, we are in the moment
Now chatting and mingling, amongst the voices
Where is he?
Concentrating on his instrument, he sees me
The sound stops: I clap
He stops again: I applaud alone
Third time he nods at me: you can clap now.

I choose his proffered arm, it's good
Dormant memories are stored.
I seek him out, then lean into him easily.
I like him, we will meet again I'm sure.

The melding farewell hug lingered with travelling hands
Too long

I broke away, then laughed, feeling silly
He grinned.
Constant babble flooded the journey
His name was tattoed on my moving tongue
Giggling softly with recall.
He called me first, on home turf. I believed him.

That was it.
The moment.

A madness of tumbling cats, they bounce high.
Vivacious colour streaks cloudy skies as he talks huskily then laughs
Then the line is dead—he has gone.
But he hasn't something is wrong
Too much time to think
Must keep busy
I have to stop these thoughts disturb me
Final clinches stick like a hot brand to flesh
His hands splay my back, the pull was noticed.
How he haunts my days, slips into foreground.

I gasp: I cannot shake him back.
But the miles stretch power to the word
My ribcage pulses at the thought
Of the tall blond with blue eyes.

We will meet again.
In champagne with strawberries.

"Blimey ... you've got it bad!", Music Man cut the cake and gave me my half, that's when we hatched the plan. I had tidied the flat to death and there was nothing left to clean, now it was ready for dressing to set the stage, Music Man suggested a visit to the shops for fluffy bits. He found the bed sheets I was looking for, a luxurious cream satin ensemble, how exciting! I gathered a complimentary candle holding lamp thing, two new glasses and I had to get the strawberries. Clotted Cream was bringing the champagne, it had been discussed ... in detail.

A week before he was to arrive he told me, "I'm going back to my wife", being in your forties and living back with your parents must be a pain though.
So, he wasn't coming here now ... blimey.

I was stunned, wondering if I had dreamt all this, then angry because I'd bought bloody shiny sheets!

I jest in bravado, I was up here miles away feeling numb and was not bothered about his wife. I had no idea who she was and I had nothing to do with his chosen action, to leave her, but I was confused.

The next day I was writing in the car, on the way to my grandmother's funeral, my mum and brother were sitting at the front. They only knew what I'd been like for weeks, in a dream world, behaving like a love sick and emotional adolescent.

CHI 2 (written in the car)

Sun beams radiantly regardless,
Nobody knows.
Clouds rumble with menace, out on the horizon

Smiles are obvious but
Storms are brewing.

Electric skies are waiting
They gather momentum with charged emotions
Rainbows hang in suspense—aching with colour
Will it be forked or sheet … lighting the way

Time will tell, but it will be spectacular,
All tempests are unpredictable in beauty.

Waiting is hard, tiring with intensity
Nervous thoughts of outcomes.
The weather may pass—all that for nothing.

Words were wasted, be shamed by clumsy cowardice,
Be a storm chaser—follow that promise!
Beckon that tumultuous falling ride,

Into the unknown.
Be guided, instinct is powerful
Have faith in yourself.

Well it's shorter than the last one!

I overheard my mum talking to my aunts and uncles, they were
asking after me, she was talking about the new chap and laughed, "I
haven't seen her like this before".

I'm sure she has though, but not for a long time, it was that long ago
I can't remember it either.

The week to follow was a blur of time-filling, waiting for a phone to sound.

Truffle and Music Man were privy to my innermost thoughts, I had to burst with perfumed anticipation occasionally and I didn't know what was going on, both of them knew the sequence of boat rocking events. Music Man gave me a male perspective and Truffle had met him as many times as I had, she nodded, "He'll come".

I think I knew he would too, we are not children after all and life is short, then remembered that Nomad does this. When you are invited to something and you edge your bets, "I will come, if I can make it", just in case something better turns up. But it doesn't, so you do make it, hopefully the host will be impressed that your busy schedule was interrupted to be here!

(Maybe it's just me. But I was happy to see Nomad at my 40th birthday celebration).

The trains let Clotted down or he messed up, but the tension was building as he was late. In waiting I was just stumbling around, drinking coffee and sweeping the carpet.

Then there he was standing outside and grinning.

He stepped up and pulled me close then kissed me, well, he had two bottles of champagne so I let him in. I did get the strawberries.

He grinned, "I was going to end it all", I had laughed and then shrugged to question, "All what?".

Clotted had no intention of terminating anything and kept kissing me, don't get me wrong I joined in … rude not to. There was talk and laughter too as we set up the den, on the floor in the front room, a complete picture with champagne and strawberries. This is where the run up had taken us, to romantic silky sheets, he was unfaithful to his partner.

She probably had no idea and thought he was getting trashed with Nomad, but I was determined to have a good weekend … so didn't really think about it.

There was a lot of snogging going on, kids, as I showed him round the town. We stopped by the pond and he held me, what he was saying was interesting a SWift or SWallow was pointed out from the sound it was making, he kissed me and he loved me for being so cute. Getting it wrong, but I was so near!

The second bottle of champers was shared in the bath, scented … candles … music, nothing was left to chance not even me knocking over one of the (new!) glasses onto the tiled floor would deter the moment.

Because my friends were doing a drum roll and waiting in suspense, to meet the man, I had told him to pretend to like me. He groaned at my neck and whispered huskily, "I don't have to pretend".
Oh my goodness … I AM LOVING THIS!

Poor Truffle was shunned in the threesome, Clotted and I could have been on the sofa again we were so oblivious to the surroundings, but we met up with Music Man later at our new local … that we have to get a taxi to.
Here Clotted became a man possessed, when I was outside with Truffle he was watching me, inside he held me tight to the music and brushed my lips a lot with his. We left early and my new friends had watched the show, Clotted told me that one of the men had pulled

him aside and told him, "You'd better not hurt her!". Ah … I didn't know who the man was.

It all started so well: Was it nerves,? Was it me? Was it guilt ? Was it old age? Was it hard to live up to expectations? Well no it wasn't really, not hard at all, his wife had called to remind him about when she had tried to kill herself … which didn't help matters I'm sure. It was a bit below the belt though eh? Well it worked, below the buckle, but good intentions get tiresome after a while and sleep calls. He was a good hot water bottle at least.

The sexy sheets are a nightmare! You slip and slide in them, the duvet will not stay on the bed, then you wake up in the morning with a stiff neck. Because the pillows are on the other side of the room.
Music Man got some too, no one cotton sheet doesn't work either, he got fed up of them and put them away only to be used on special occasions. Maybe.

Nomad had called, he was abrupt and rude, he demanded to know, "Have you got anybody there with you?".
Clotted's wife had been on the phone, so did she think her husband was there with him?
Nomad thought of me immediately?
It's getting weird now and Nomad told me to put Clotted on the line, I weakly denied that he was here … I was only fibbing a little bit as in sitting right here and now technically wasn't that man he knew. Eventually I got fed up of the nasty abuse, I should have just put the receiver down … bloody hindsight, so just passed the phone over and have no idea what was being said.

He managed to be unfaithful again, but hey, it wasn't worth the wait and wasn't at all how I'd imagined it would be. Blimey I've got a creative mind … leaving myself open to disappointment. Damn.

But he did meddle with my drawers and I have a complete bedroom now, with wonky curtains, so it takes four men not three to finish a flat-pack. I was his number three on the word game, by the way, on page 94-5ish, he kissed me.

When we stood at the train station, after a full on weekend, it was sad and strange that he was now just going home.
You would think.

If you were travelling half the country, to a suicidal (all's fair …) wife and a job commitment, you would know what time the train you have to be on leaves. So you can meet up with all the connections etc …
But no! He was an hour out?

The woman looked across the tracks and told him. "You want that one". His train was already standing at the platform.
He kissed me with gabbled goodbyes then disappeared at the stairwell. Brilliant timing as it happens, I watched the train leave and Nomad drove past the station, again timing par excellence!

"You've just missed him", I shrugged like I was bothered, he drove off to park the car. I turned around and Clot was standing there, with his shoulders hunched, looking like a silly boy . He was muttering and shaking his head, "It's Freudian", I was shaking my head with disbelief and thinking 'idiot'.

At the meeting on the pavement Nomad told me, in all seriousness, "I have to talk with Clot alone, there are things I need to discuss". It's getting weird again, why and how is this any of his concern?

This is when I started to disrespect my friend Nomad, I was effectively dismissed from the proceedings, in no uncertain terms he told me that I was superfluous to requirements. It was none of my business … I told them I'd be at the café down the road, waiting for them.

But the café was shut, so I wandered back to the train station, I saw Nomad's car so knew they were still here, I sat on a nearby wall in the sunshine then got my pen and paper out.

When I looked up the car had gone, they must have seen me and laughed so hard at their sneakiness, I was devastated and shaken by such childish behaviour.
I sat for a little while and shook my head, what was going on? How does one respond to this? I was annoyed, Clot wouldn't answer his phone, and now I'm numb because I don't know what to do with myself … how did I get it so wrong again?

Music Man shook his head, "Ah man … you just don't do that! Bet his wife doesn't know, he probably told her he was seeing Nomad … bet they're gay and having a thing! What a Knob … told you he was a Wuss".

They had shaken hands on meeting and Music Man had noted it to be a girly, "Fairy liquid hands", then observed his behaviour with me at the pub. "Clot was obsessed with you man … he couldn't keep his eyes off you! What a loser. You have to tune your bullshit detector in Gillian!"
Mmm …

Truffle had met Clot before … as many times as me, she too shook her head in disbelief, "He came up here? You didn't make him do anything! Tosser".

I told mum and showed her the photo of him … on my phone, she blinked and shook her head, "He looks a bit geeky to me!"

I am lucky and have some good friends, my mum is just brilliant too.

In our love den Clot had been telling me about where he lived, "My house is down the road from work and they are building a supermarket across the road!". So, I observed, he would have the perfect triangle and would never need to go anywhere … ever again, I had laughed at his good fortune.

He was serious and told me, " … come down …", looking at him I had questioned, "Are you sure?".

He nodded, "Yes I'm certain, that's what I want to happen".

How exciting … I was going to see the triangle!

Nothing is that simple.

He called me the night before and whined, "I don't want to see you", the holiday was booked and paid for I told him this. "But I can't stop you", CC was kicking me again.

Even though the advice was, generally, "Don't go, you will be wasting your time and money" and "You will feel crap".

Even though the advice was, well meaning and for my benefit, "Clot is a spineless geek and he's a coward so you won't see him".

I still went.

Because I could and I didn't want to stay here, feeling sorry for myself and wondering what the triangle was like, so I had already reserved the caravan for a slot in my diary.

I needed and wanted to get away, to lick my wounds as it were … I'd been to Dawlish before but many years ago with my family. I had spoken to my aunt and uncle, who live in Newton Abbot … another town nearby, fully intending to go and see them.

There was one change at a central station, that I had to be alert for, then the main line took me down to the southern regions. It took hours and I was reading a print-out of this, people don't talk to each other, nearly everybody was either fiddling with their mobiles or talking loudly on them.
The others were reading or staring out of the windows, with wires coming out of their ears.

A pretty station by the sea, a taxi ride to the caravan park, it was all very twee and I was beginning to regret my being me.
My headstrong independence and my fluffy idealistic dream world, Typically Gillian, were not looking so good and it was raining.

Clot's workplace was in the industrial park next door to the holiday site, I recognised the address, so the taxi dropped in for me. The man told me Clot wasn't there? Grr

The site was nice and the mobile home was alright, there was a bar and a restaurant on camp but the pool was empty, I was given all the literature about caravan etiquette and the scheduled entertainment.

The site shop was open, so coffee was happening at least, back inside my cubby hole I made the bed up and hung a few things then made myself a smoke.
I definitely had no intention of moping around and driving myself crazier, so I got dressed up and did make up then went out. It was better than I'd hoped, a lot of men spoke to me that night some to ask

me if I was ok? When my legs were full of gin mostly, I was escorted to the taxi.

The first night I washed, did my teeth, then put my pyjamas on and got into bed.

In the morning I sat in my pyjamas happily eating toast and drinking coffee, the television was on chattering in the background, it was sunny now but it was getting cloudy. I was happy at my new writing station, next to the ashtray and kettle.
It was now raining.

I did some work before I set off to explore, but it was still wet and I advise everybody right now: sell the house and buy a boat.
The wander was interesting and I saw the shop, where Clot must have bought the necklace he gave me. If it was payment … I wasn't worth very much, though I do like the said trinket.

Charity shops are always worth investigating and one that was tucked away, was the most interesting, looked like the set of Steptoe and Son. The owner was busy trying to tidy things up, but kept stopping to talk to people and was being approached by shoppers. I made a flippant comment and she laughed with me, then stopped again with an armful of books, I was more than happy to talk to her and she was like a magic potion. She had set up the trust after her brother had died, it had all snow balled into this, then smiled and asked if I wanted any books. Well … that's a cue if ever I made one up or heard one …

"You wrote this", she exclaimed with wide eyes, I nodded and laughed, "Yeah unbelievable eh?".
"I have to have it", she clutched the book possessively, "You are brilliant". I liked her too and she had given me an idea, on my walks

I had noticed other people with mobility difficulties, she thought other people would want to or should know about the book. Round the corner was an office for the local Gazette, she pointed me in the right direction.

I had taken four books with me and the receptionist was holding one, she was impressed but couldn't do anything, she gave me a contact and suggested that I wrote a piece for the paper.

So I started collecting stories from obviously disabled people, it was interesting and I will do this again, young, old, male and female were all approached. The only real gripe, that was a common factor, was thoughtless drivers who parked in front of ramps in the pavement … making it inaccessible to anybody in a wheelchair or pushing a pram. The taxi driver was young and had a debilitating disease, that he knew was getting worse but had an attitude for survival, he smiled with a shrug.

I wrote my notes up before I went out, this time I went to the site bar and ate whilst watching the show.

Can't remember what the act was, lots of singing, but the kids (God I'm getting old) were good and probably hoping there was a talent scout in the audience. Eventually I went back to the caravan to smoke and write.

That night I went to bed but didn't bother getting undressed this time, I was disappointed that Clot turned out to be a stupid shit but was getting a lot of work done.

The shower was tackled the next day, all clean and dressed I had just wrapped a towel round my wet hair. The door was knocked and my senses jumped with anticipation, as I answered, but it was Nomad?

I smiled with surprise, "Oh hello".

I put the kettle on and asked if he wanted one, that's when he started ... by growling, "I haven't come for coffee".

He was standing in the kitchen area and he let me know what he thought, about me, first of all I was shocked by the aggressive verbal assault. He was calling me names and the accusations were offensive and insulting. He excused Clot, for being a bit sheltered and out of touch with life, then blamed the wife for being a "manipulative cunt". He went on, "What are you doing here?" then, "You lied to me!". So ... oh my God, this is all my fault? Oh yeah and I was, "manipulative too".

That was enough, Nomad's friend was indeed a geek. I felt stupid and was too old for this crap, plus I was stuck in a box with windows ... on my own ... in a field ... in the rain.

I was now upset, with myself too, because I am rubbish in quick fire situations especially if they are unpleasant. How dare he? Who did he think he was? AND AGAIN ... What business was is it of his???

I couldn't believe this was happening and my attempts to speak were quashed, as if this wasn't quite hurtful or bad enough. So with frustration and in shock, I cried. For more abuse.

Then I just had to ignore him and had lost any respect or feeling I ever had, he told me, "You have been used. Clot used being unfaithful with you as an excuse to leave his wife".

Charming I'm sure. Bloody men ... it was still raining.

The young people on reception, at the caravan park, had all clubbed together to get Gillian Mk 2.

But I stopped talking to my friends, I didn't want to tell them how foolish I had been or how cheap I felt now. I was not happy … at all. I sat and smoked, then looked at the pen, with my head on I finished my report for the Gazette, not willing to dwell on the events that were upsetting me.

I was still stunned by the intrusion into my space, the nasty eruption had slated my very being and negated any nice thoughts I had for myself … I'm horrible. But was devastated as I realised that Clot really couldn't care less about me, but he must have been bricking it whilst I was down there (Music Man pointed this out). This was the ultimate let down and insult … when you send your friend to do your dirty work.
We are all in our forties.

Anyway. I dried my hair then went to talk to some chaps, with a car, in a neighbouring caravan.

They would give me a lift, they were going the same way, I found the tiny library and typed up my work.
Then I went to see my new friend, Pixie, at the best charity shop in Dawlish … it's interesting.

I have just spoken to Pixie to ask her permission, "That's super Honey!", she responded immediately and gave me a website address to look up the details.
www.myspace.com/thesnookytrust
Then I had to go and Pixie told me, "Take care Darlin!"

I took a bus to Teignmouth and thought I might recognise something, but stumbled around in the rain finding things by chance, I sheltered briefly in a music shop? Where I momentarily forgot that Clot was a jerk and bought him a plectrum holder, he'd said he needed one and I remembered that, idiot. It was posted to his work, why not? It would have been churlish of me to throw it away and I had, after all, bought it with him in mind.

The bus back took ages and the visibility was rubbish, but when we stopped and the door opened I still didn't know where I was. Where I originally caught the bus was a stop near to the train station so, to get my bearings, I turned to ask the bus driver where the train station was?

She laughed and shook her head, "You're in Exeter".
I groaned, that's why it had seemed so long! Because it was! What a pain in the arse.

The driver was still laughing then told me, "Hang around, I will get you back", the bus was about to change drivers and it was the end of her shift. The replacement driver was waiting in the shuttle bus and we all swapped places, this lady took me right to the caravan and was lovely. We chatted all the way and she was telling me about a pub that I should go to, "It's a friendly joint and you should mention my name".

So with somewhere to go, knowing a friendly name, I got dressed up again, this is turning out to be quite good now.

The venue was small and I stumbled, then grabbed the door frame at the stepped entrance.

The barmaid obviously saw me, the two men at the bar were also looking at me, I held my purse and ordered a drink. The woman behind the counter refused to serve me, "You've had too much already".

I blinked, that was a surprise.

I wasn't annoyed or upset by this final slap, I was still raw and smarting from the earlier assault, I got the card out of my purse that explained. It says: I am the victim of a head injury. Asking the reader to be patient. I have only felt the need to use it a few times and this embarrassed barmaid looked at me, shook her head, then apologised.

"You should see me when I am drunk, I'm a danger to myself", I laughed but it's not funny.

I mentioned the bus driver's name and I looked around, "I wonder why she sent me here? Is it the riveting company, do you think?".

They all laughed, thankfully they appreciated the clumsy sarcasm, then felt able to talk to me.

A few more people turned up and they all heard why I was here, they all laughed with me and chatted freely. After two drinks I wanted to go and asked them, "Where should I be next?", one of the chaps gave me his arm and walked with me up the hill to the next pub. I think he was hoping that I'd ask him to join me, mmm … no, I thanked him and released his arm.

There was a high stool by the bar which I claimed, I climbed onto it trying to look like a lady, then spoke to the man sitting next to me. He was funny and encouraged me to talk about my disability (cue … I am dreadful), he was shown the book I had with me, like Pixie he wanted to read my story now.

He left to go and eat so I sat alone watching the karaoke, then had to tackle the toilets … thereby making myself as discreet as a panty liner under leggings … which were upstairs. I would put my name down to sing whilst I was up.

I was already getting myself noticed as I blocked the stairwell, by holding both of the banisters, trying to get myself to the top as quickly as possible. I still had to find the toilet, if anybody had asked me to I would have paused to step aside, there was a roof terrace and I would stop here for a smoke after my bladder had been emptied.

I sang my usual number, the only song I really know, which considering, wasn't as bad as it could have been. Well they clapped anyway!

Flower came back and smiled, "You're still here …".

He was visiting from Brighton, we talked about nothing easily and the time flew, I gave him my telephone number and he made sure I got into the taxi safely.

My last day in the soggy caravan park, I would be near the station HOURS before my train departed, I was ready to go … understatement … but was annoyed that I hadn't made time to go and see my relatives.

My last commitment: I got a taxi to a converted stately home, with the giveaway ramps and no smoking (anywhere near here) signs, for my appointment with a photographer from the Gazette.

The image he showed me was a good one and I gave him the last book, because I could.

The cream tea had to be done and I bought my mum a present, from my jollydays, my last few minutes were spent drinking free coffee in an arcade … I say free but of course it wasn't.

Before I knew it I was in my bedroom, looking at the crumpled satin sheets, the bed was stripped (final closure). I hate doing this and it takes me ages but it could be put off no longer.

I had an idea, as the women scorned, I got my scissors out and cut the bottom shiny sheet up. The ragged snipping produced a triangular apron, with my black marker pen, I wrote in each corner. HOME, WORK, SUPERMARKET, then was really mean and highlighted the DNA sample.

Music Man snorted at my handy work, "He'd love that! But you can't send it … that's on the verge of bunny boiler and stalking. He'll think you're bothered too   so stop being mad".
He had bought a battery operated fan, I have never seen anything like it, you could programme the spinning blades to spell out a message. They appeared in red lights and Music Man got it to say, ' CC Soft Knob', it was funny but maybe I should have been a little more discreet and not told him about those episodes. The letters span and flashed it was brilliant. "He'd like this!", I chuckled, so it was sent to him at work. The apron was not sent, it looked silly, the cut was rubbish and he couldn't have used it anyway.

GRANDMA'S FUNERAL

I did write a big fat poem, expressing my thoughts, detailing the build up and then describing the fall down. But I don't like it anymore. Actually the last line is quite good.
"Now he is a folic ally challenged geek".

You get the drift? This was much easier to type too …
Cruel but true.

Flower called me and began with, "Hello gorgeous", for this he deserved a mention and I had asked him what he likes? Clues for a code name. "I like flowers", I had asked him if there was any type in particular?
Warning him that Orchid had gone. "Any", he replied so   Flower.
He got a friend to do an astrological star chart for me, he took the date and time of my birth   which surprisingly I know, I also know my blood group. Pathetic Two didn't know what his was, after me grumbling disbelief for a bit, he found out and went one better. He started giving blood, I'd told him how I knew what my blood group is and encouraged him to do this because I can't.

Anyway this star chart was complicated and very involved, there are a lot of symbols and numbers under strange headings, I don't understand most of it. Neither did Flower and he told that the lady responsible would give me a reading over the phone, then he added, "If you can afford the phone bill".
"Is it going to be a long phone call?", I'd laughed and Flower came back, "She likes talking".
So it has been agreed that I will see her, to talk, when I visit.

Talking of friends—Betty Boop has just passed a load of exams, she has qualified in a nursing career, so has got letters after her name now. Betty Boop CLEVER CLOGS!
She told me, "Yeah … all my other friends have sent cards", well I give you a line in a book.

My walking is laboured anyway and I was experiencing pain, enough to stop me and it would literally make me have to sit down, I was convinced that I'd got a stone in my shoe because that's exactly what it felt like. A reactionary lump of hard skin was forming in the middle of the ball, on my left foot, then the digit next to my little toe started screaming abuse and also formed a callous. My hobbling was getting worse and I was worried, my mum told me to make an appointment with my doctor.

My chiropodist brother had looked at it, when I'd first complained of discomfort, he'd diagnosed a fallen arch. Great. The way I move and balance has encouraged this apparently, fabulous, what's next I wonder?

Anyway my phone number was checked so the doctor could call me back, to ascertain whether I needed to see him or not, he is fully aware of my difficulties and made me an appointment to go to the local hospital. I presumed for a referral … to a chiropodist.

The taxi delivered me to the outpatient's department, I seem to encourage people and the driver was telling about his general unhappiness with this country, but of course I wasn't at the right reception.

The physiotherapist took me around the corner was being questioned, I was asking him what I should do to improve my outlook. With a view to throwing myself onto my hands again, on purpose!

"A referral and practice", was his advice.

The next receptionist told me, "You're honoured … the doctor's slipped you in at the end". I was extra and was surprised to see my GP there?

I love him he's brilliant, he smiled as he shaved shards of skin off my foot with a scalpel. Not in his job description, but he knew I was in pain. My toe was trimmed of excess layers too, when I stood an immediate difference was felt and all was silent. Nothing was screeching, in agony, at me anymore. He'd removed a quarter of an inch of hardness, there was no stone in my shoe now.

My brother was at my mum's when she called me, to make sure I had been to the appointment and hadn't managed to ignore the reminding notes … that she'd placed strategically round the flat. There were two memos by the kettle …
"Quarter of an inch!", I could hear her shaming my visiting brother and he was asked, "Did you know anything about this?". Then she screeched at him again, when I blabbed and confirmed that he did.

"I'll get a good blade and do it myself, easy", I was confident as to the ease of this task.
Mum reminded me that my coordination is rubbish and that I'd end up slicing my toes off, that's a good point actually. Later, when Bro looked at the mess I'd already made, the chiropodist told me, "Don't pick at them again".

They're alright at the moment, so I don't have to wear my slippers with the outfit on Saturday night. I have got a protective sleeve, lump, of pink plastic around the said toe that was troubling me … you can see it if sandals are worn, it's very becoming.

Bro fixed my curtain rail!
The window dressing is straight now and can be opened then closed … yippee!

He also hung the picture, that I've been kicking for weeks, the bedroom trellis is back on the wall and then he started washing my backlog of dishes. There's a postcard in this room, it says: Make yourself at home! Clean my kitchen. (May leave it there, it works!)

Music Man bought me the collection and the first card is: You say I'm a bitch like it's a bad thing!
He smiled, "It made me think of you", marvellous, that's nice.

Bro finished off the doctor's efforts and my feet are all soft and pampered—at the moment.
He's my favourite brother.

I was persuaded, not that I needed much, to go to the housing association's AGM. It was being held at Leeds football ground and the guided tour was optional.

There were familiar faces and the meeting was as you'd expect, nothing short of impressive, they spoke of their brilliance and plans for improvement.

The chap that took us all around the building was an ex footballer, Ian McLellan, he pointed out all the trophies and spoke about his career on then off the pitch. Which we couldn't go out and see, we had all watched the car park filling with rainfall and flooding. People were nipping out to move their cars, our tour was over and I was chatting to Ian. He had noticed me, by waiting for me to catch up and watching out for me as I was tackling the stairs. I showed him Gillian Mk 2 and gave him the site address, then got him to sign it. I wish I'd given it to him now, but he'd signed it.
I had got my book, signed, to me, by an ex footballer!

I wonder if players from yesteryear are gutted they are not playing now, it must be sickening to read of the second houses (Mansions) abroad and the naughty (legal and otherwise) behaviour of the new crowd. Looking back makes me sick anyway.

I would change our laws and bring back the draconian code of conduct, all this namby pamby stuff has been tried … but it doesn't work, the system is so blocked up with bullshit there is nowhere else to go.

Get rid of the nutters who think that they're invincible, they can be rehabilitated? Am I hearing you right? Who cares? Use the money for something useful, there are more worthy people who will not get the attention they deserve because they simply haven't killed anybody!

Leave prisons open to punish those who get caught for violent offences or for being greedy. When I've finished this I might make up a list of crimes then draw up appropriate penalties. Then …

Changing the subject … I am on lots of sites now: Tesco net (every little does help), Richard and Judy (shouldn't have let them speak to Pathetic Two), Amazon, Google and a site. Yoyo showed me his phone, I was on there too!

I'm getting to the end of this now and hope that I've made you chuckle, but not enough to forget that disability is a very serious issue! Those of you that are not totally enthralled with my words, what can I say? I don't lie … though my mind does harbour grudges, (don't mess with me) that unfortunately and literally fill pages of my life. There is no need to make things up, to please my audience, real life has more of an impact.

I couldn't make these things up anyway … I'm not that clever.

I have made a note to tell you about Bridlington further up (page 54), but now seems a good place because this could not be fabricated.

It was a day trip to the coast with Pathetic Two, in the good old days, before he mutated into a pile of garbage and stank. We were walking on the pavement and had to get round the scaffolding that was blocking the walkway. I sidestepped and fell off the kerb and into the main road, in front of the on-coming traffic.
I saw the car hurtling towards me, I hit the ground and was sprawled on the road directly in front of the quickly approaching car, in the next second I was waiting for the moving vehicle to make impact. But it swerved and missed me … then kept going.

I was stunned and couldn't believe that it had managed to avoid me, how did it miss this woman who had just appeared from nowhere and was now in the middle of the road!

Pathetic Two was amazed, he too was expecting blood and was stunned that the car had managed not to hit me. We were both in a state of shock and blood drained with pale faces. Blimey.

Otherwise an uneventful day that wouldn't have been mentioned.

I am sitting in the sun and drinking coffee outside the pub, as Truffle and I walked into this place on Saturday night a young man had walked past us. He cleverly made a snide comment over his glasses,

"Don't you think you've had enough already?", then nodded his brilliance to his silly friends.
Now one side of my brain still says: follow him, tackle his ignorance, whilst making him look and feel like the dweeb he unfortunately is, point this plank in the right direction and suggest that he keeps his crap comments to himself in future.

But the other side now says: Just ignore the Nerd, don't go there you are wasting your time.

I take the second option, by the way … it's much easier, I am so sick of explaining myself to morons.

I have noticed that Truffle doesn't bother trying to explain to rude strangers anymore, she makes comment to me now. Is this the best thing to do though?

But at the moment I am watching and listening to the locals, it's funny but not worthy of repetition. Yoyo has just arrived, but he won't be drinking coffee, he is about to be a grandfather and has reacted accordingly.

Dyed his shaved hair, sports an earring and had his eyebrow pierced, a trendy young grand daddy. Somebody should tell him to stop now, he's starting to look silly … another reason for you to look and stare at him? (shaking of head optional)

But hey, he and CT look good together and that makes me smile.

One of the women has just asked me, "What are you writing?". Then she told me, "I'm next in line for Gillian Mk 2". Apparently the book's doing the rounds, eventually everybody here will know that I am Dippy in Bed and I'm honoured.

They are joking that they should be careful what they say, because I'll write it down, I overheard one chap saying I'll tell everybody what he said, "I'm a big knob". Sorted.

The woman went to the bar for me, to carry the next coffee.

I'm going to Turkey in two weeks, my mum was going with her friends and one lady had to drop out. Mum asked, "Can I tell Gillian?", not find out if I wanted to go. They all said yes and I'm going to start making lists … sun cream has been ticked off already (ha … it's going to be cold here).

Mum felt it her duty to prepare her friends and warned, "Gillian can be a bit awkward". Mmm … no idea what she meant by this …
But the woman responded, "Can't we all?". I like her already.
She went on, "We'll just leave Gillian at the nightclub, she'll be alright", it's getting better.
Two weeks in the sun at a private villa with a pool … I fully intend to get my swimming sorted. That is, of course, if the pool is actually big enough to swim in.
I bought my nephew an inflatable guitar, I might borrow it … then again maybe not it is a child sized float and I'd flatten it then drown.

People always seem to be asking me when this is going be finished! They all know me by name, which can be awkward sometimes … to this day, a lot of them are quick to tell me, "You should be on the next book by now".

The group that supply my nicotine habit are worthy, one lady was a recipient of the first batch of self-published work. I tell her all my latest jokes, she laughs then forgets them and tells me, "I'll forget it … I always do!", but she will. If I tell her the same joke every time I see her, it's alright, neither of us know.

At the other place I talk as much and am getting to know them too, the polite chap always greets me by name and smiles. So I noticed and was disturbed when he blanked me, he was positively scowling his disapproval in my direction, Yoyo was around then and was gathering his quota in the background.

He's like a big brother and is back to brilliant, with me now, he may have sold the champagne to CC.

One of them here did this massive walk, she did a lot of training o'er hills and d'ant vales, it was not easy obviously and apparently people were falling out of the competition with heat stroke. But she completed the trek and raised money for charity.

The other lady volunteered to read Typically Gillian, should my publisher do this? Anyway the last chapter she had upset her, "You made me cry", it was 2002 Daddy Dearest.

I told her, "It makes me cry too".

The bingo ladies, they are seriously funny, one makes yummy cake (the coffee cake is my favourite … hint), the new mom smiles all the time and jokes with all the customers. They are a rare breed and moan, outside in the rain, with the rest of the smokers.

The managers keep changing but these gals do not, there is a good attitude.

Everybody grumbled about one woman, she was loud and interruptive, but eventually she was ejected never to return. They should do that with a few more, bit of bingo rage, especially if they are horrible and seem to win a lot. You know what really annoys me though? Those that shout, "EEEYAR!" or those that have a nice win and squeak, "e …", then are in danger of being missed. Grr.

Orchid and Kebab should win, I smile when they do. Kebab had a nice spell recently and so her son started coming, but he hasn't won yet … close but no banana.

A lot of my characters have been given code-names, that are generally met with nodding approval, only one person has disagreed with me. The lady who arrived at the flat on business and thought I was drunk, she had spoken to me on the phone to ask directions, then she saw me … and still thought I was ratted.

She was the first person to hear my BBC Telling Lives script, impressed enough by the proposed voice-over to take a copy of Gillian Mk 2, the ensuing contact of a personal nature means that she is still in my life.

So a book-name, because she takes care to look good and is one of those people that makes it all look so effortless (I should hate her), my first thought was a bit risqué and eventually I settled on Glam. But she reacted, "I don't want that … call me Fag Ash Lill", mm ok … Lill it is.

Lill was visiting one weekend and she streaked the town cerise, on the evening out, with Truffle and I … the hardened duo, but we paled in comparison.

Walking back to the table, after a visit to the powder room, I had to blink and glanced at Truffle who was looking on wide-eyed.

Lill was leaning over the table, she was holding a man's chin firmly and talking into his inebriated (obnoxious) face, she was annoyed. He is a well known turnip and deserves more, but the little bouncers with radios came, Lill was stopped from ripping his stupid head off. She continued the evening with as much gusto, we all had lots of fun and drank lashings of pop.

Lill had a friend that I had spoken to on the phone, his smooth and silky voice wafted down the line into my head, the Man of Steel had the smoothest and huskiest of tones. I went all soft and gooey, like wet clay.

We did meet at Lill's and I wasn't disappointed, though he wasn't quite what was imagined, the Man of Steel was a harmless and funny flirt. He goes on my list of favourite people with Lill.

At a Rotary Club event, he had arranged, he auctioned Gillian Mk 2 for charity and pointed out, "The author is sitting in the room".

Clever that … so don't you dare bid fifty pence!

The charity shop continues to hold my fascination and I wander on down there when the mood takes me, I love Dingle because she is happy with that and makes me laugh. Her son is a diamond too, he's a ripple of humour, he recently tried a loud and flowery coat on then flounced in front of the mirror. It was too big for him or, love 'im, he would have bought it.

I now have habits that are borne of adaptation and necessity, with TG thrown in, I am still getting used to my limitations and trying to put my trousers on without sitting down.

I occasionally wonder about driving again, Truffle and Rigid do! I'm not sure how to set the wheels in motion to get my driving licence back, I really don't know if I suffer petit mals anymore, then it's forgotten along with the notion of a return to teaching. (Yeah right … stupido)

Recently I saw Pathetic Two's sister-in-law, her girls have gone now so they got a convertible sports car … nice one. She laughed as we parted and thanked me," … for leaving me with Sourpuss". I know she loves her really and smiled back, "No problem".

Me, mum and Truffle went on a coach, with our new gang from the pub, on a day trip to Bridlington.

It was sunny and it didn't rain, a few of them went to the pub and were happy, we just roamed around looking at things and stopping to eat and drink.

At one café we sat outside, next to a couple who came back from Benidorm the night before. I started talking to them and exchanged a few jokes with the man. They were both in their seventies and looked well, he used a stick and had had a few new knees, they were nice but he did talk a lot.

But he gave me the finishing line of wisdom, for which I cannot take any credit at all, he folded his arms to tell me what his attitude to longevity was: "You must think, I'm IT … you're shit".

I shrieked, "It rhymes! You're a poet Sir".

Blimey, I'll talk to anybody, but he's just got into these pages because I'm going now. When I write again it will start in Turkey …

The editor of the local paper is waiting for me, they will cover my progress and I will add the clipping to my collection.

Oh yeah … Clot, the pen's unusable …

Sorted.

PS.

Nomad called me and spoke quietly, maybe he thought I'd want to speak to him, "Do you want Pippa back?".

The scrawny little bird, with the unusable cage, "Ahh … erm … no".

I think he was telling me something … but we'll never know. Shame.

PPS.

Epilepsy Action did a book review in their magazine, it was brilliant, thanks.

PPPS. (This is the last one …)

A.Man asked if I had really parted with so many copies of GM2? How insulting … so, with thought and after rereading TG, I hope I've managed to cover you all : Thanks, for your belief and support:

To my family, friends, staff at DYH, my partner, Fallons—the local book shop, the local papers, Daily Express, the sun worshippers on holidays and cruises, Yorkshire Television, recommendations, my dentist, my doctor, the nurses, acupuncture and epilepsy staff, Art Circus gang, as presents, Scribe, scout leaders and families, the catering, counselling and English tutors, Landlords and public in local pubs, shop assistants: at the bakers, the tobacconists, the off-licence, the jewellers, the frozen food place, the Post Office, my bingo ladies, the AGM of the head injury charity, the teachers at my old school, mates from school, my Cornish Doctor with his own sales pitch, landlady and family in London, staff and chums at the housing association, the footballer Ian McLelland, Radio York and OAR … Olivia, Annie and Rupert the BBC Telling Lives team.

Just about anybody who talks tome long enough …

That's it … nay you get no more from me, for I am done and I am glad …

Glossary

GM2 = Gillian Mk 2, first book

TG = Typically Gillian, second book (!)

CCTV= Close Circuit Television

TBI= Traumatic Brain Injury

AGM = Annual General Meeting

Darlink = me

Client = term for inhabitants of rehabilitation

XCL = Xmas Card List

WI = Women's Institute

Characters
in order of appearance.

FRUITCAKE—he introduced me to Scoutman and is gaining notoriety through his UFO encounters.

SPRUCE GIRL—starts in GM2 and ends her reign in TG, she was my favourite support worker.

SCOUTMAN—we were happily together for long enough, then he became PATHETIC TWO.

LANDLADY—from student days, she's brilliant!

DIVVY—an ass-istant scout leader

NOMAD—a pal from my previous life, one of us wishes he'd stayed there, a disappointing friendship.

BETTY BOOP—my dearest friend who has been around for most of my life. Love her but she's very bossy.

OLIVER TOBIAS—the actor who stroked my leg.

TRUFFLE—a survivor of TBI who I probably would never have met, if not for GM2, we literally bump along together nicely. We may be friends for a while.

OAR—the BBC Telling Lives team, their names provide the perfect acronym for their art, steering us to complete a successful project. LINK: bbc.co.uk/telling lives

LILL—I chose a different name, Glam, but she wanted Fag Ash Lill. Because I like her ... Man of Steel came into my life here, a good chap to know. Both on my XCL. LINK: Rotary Club

CHRIS—a really yummy tour guide in Cyprus, if Scoutman hadn't been there ... would definitely be on the XCL.

FAT BADGE—was just that. I found her unpleasant, unprofessional and unkind. She did the talk but not the walk. Not even near my XCL ... Oh no.

WEE LASSIE—(No 1 and 2 fans)—she is a survivor and meeting the couple was a highlight. Without doubt on my XCL.

MR THINGY MP—I have little or no respect for this man, he is rude and boring.

MR ARTY FARTY—we chat easily and he had a lot of questions for me, after reading GM2, he makes nice coffee and gets on the XCL with Mrs AF.

ROUTINE—a TBI survivor, with his own coping mechanism, he differs to me.

STICKY VICKY—has to be seen if you go to Benidorm.

OLGA—another chap another holiday ... wonder if he got the book

ELVIS + BB—teachers at my old high school, the letters they both sent after reading GM2 were just brilliant. Mentally on my XCL.

PAULOS—a TBI survivor who is brilliant, glad we met.

MUSIC MAN—has a brilliant attitude and appreciated GM2, eh, a XCL contender forever.

GADGET BOY—from GM2 days, I think of him and owe him thanks.

TOM—the cutest kitten, that I could not keep.

TURNIP—a boring nonentity that needs make-up, ugh, she's not on my XCL unless I can find one that says something horrible about weight and thin hair then wishes a shit time.

KEBAB + ORCHID—bingo chums that make me laugh, on my XCL.

BANDIT—with the use of one arm he showed me how to open the front door, another person with a good attitude. XCL.

ANGRY YOUNG MAN—he always seems to be annoyed with something or somebody.

DEAN—a chance encounter which was rather nice, x. Would be on the XCL.

FAT CAT—a local business man who keeps rescuing me with the computer. XCL.

SHe—was a brief spell along with SAMBA they both have issues which affected my birthday, the silly excuses mean that I now have no time for either of them.

A.MAN—my publisher, who has turned out to be a disappointment and I fear a con man.

ANGLER—he approached me and is worth a few paragraphs.

POSITIVE—he predicted we would have relations but we always talk and I like him, on the XCL.

NICKY—sounds brilliant and gave GM2 the best review. LINK: Mobility Magazine

PATHETIC DUFUS—my ex husband, he looked old but gave me the opportunity to rename him. What a disappointment, he will never be on my XCL ... ever.

DINGLE—the charity shop manageress who is fab, definitely a XCL.

YOYO—not the most stable of people and was not good for me, I can't do stupid all the time. I don't do violence either, intro' CT, a regrettable and nasty intrusion into my space.

NO MESSIN' + MRS N M—a lovely couple, their wedding was a good day, the weekend away was a bit awkward and didn't go to plan. He's a mate though and they're still on the XCL.

MAGICO—a hypnotist who was pleasant enough but he did speak about his work a lot, maybe that's why Yoyo got so trollied.

PIPPA—the baby bird, a gift from Yoyo, that was taken by Nomad ... who wrecked her cage and got her to stand on a stick.

J—I like him and am sure we will meet again.

TEENY—I love her, she's brill, still around from GM2 and she liked the frog wind chime! Definitely on the XCL.

CLOTTED CREAM, CLOTTED, CLOT, CC—one and the same. As Truffle said, "Tosser".

LONG HAIR—had long hair.

PIXIE—super lady who brightened up a wet weekend. LINK: Snooky Trust

FLOWER—a lovely chap who also made this weekend bearable, a worthwhile contender for the XCL.

ED—pal spreading the news, should be on the XCL.

www.ingramcontent.com/pod-product-compliance
Lightning Source LLC
Chambersburg PA
CBHW020916140626
46545CB00015B/69